From the Ballroom to Hell

Elizabeth Aldrich

From the Ballroom to Hell:

GRACE AND FOLLY IN NINETEENTH-CENTURY DANCE

Northwestern University Press Evanston, Illinois 1991

Northwestern University Press
Evanston, Illinois 60208-4210

Second paperback printing 2000

Printed in the United States of America

ISBN 0-8101-0913-1

Library of Congress Cataloging-in-Publication Data

Aldrich, Elizabeth, 1947–
From the ballroom to hell : grace and folly in nineteenth-century dance / Elizabeth Aldrich.
p. cm.
Includes bibliographical references and index.
ISBN 0-8101-0913-1 (pbk.)
1. Dancing—History—19th century. 2. Social history—19th century. 3. Etiquette. I. Title.
GV1619.A43 1991
792.8—dc20 91-3225
CIP

The paper used in this publication meets the minimum requirements of the American National Standard for Information Sciences—Permanence of Paper for Printed Library Materials, ANSI Z39.48-1984.

Design: Hayward Blake and Company

To Charles—husband, critic, and best friend

Contents

Illustrations

Musical Examples

Foreword

When, a few years ago, I saw the American Ballroom Theater perform the elegant "Salon Waltzes" staged by Elizabeth Aldrich, I did not suspect that I would one day have the pleasure of writing this foreword. And pleasure it is, for in this book Ms. Aldrich, a noted authority on nineteenth-century dance, has recreated, this time for the mind's eye, not just the era's dances but the whole society they reflected—its manners and morals, its amusements and fashions and intellectual yearnings. That world may seem to us to have vanished without trace, but in the etiquette, fashion, beauty, and dance manuals excerpted here, it speaks to us with irresistible appeal.

That appeal is not just to the dance scholars and sociologists for whom the work may initially have been intended. For them, and for theater and dance professionals, *From the Ballroom to Hell* does indeed provide a wealth of information nowhere else so available or so knowledgeably presented. But this work should also interest many other readers, for it lights up a terrain that has been familiar to us since childhood.

Remember *Little Women,* and Jo and Laurie dancing the polka in an empty hall at a New Year's Eve party because Jo did not want the other guests to see her scorched and mended dress? or to notice that she was wearing only one clean glove, her proper sister Meg's ("Gloves are more important than anything else; you can't dance without them!"), and carrying a stained one of her own?

Marmee's girls were well aware of the rules of etiquette so indefatigably preached by the manuals included in this collection—and of something more as well. Meg's visit to the fashionable Moffat household is a look at the new rich of the time, a class spawned by the country's rapidly expanding industrial economy. "Meg felt, without understanding why, that [the Moffats] were not particularly cultivated or intelligent people . . . all their gilding could not quite conceal the ordinary material of which they were made." The Moffats and their ilk were ideal matériel for the manufacture of silk purses—a growth industry that nineteenth-century social advisers of all kinds made haste to exploit.

As for nineteenth-century social dances, the polka that Jo and Laurie romped merrily through in *Little Women* was a comparatively new dance, having become popular only some twenty years before the Civil War period in which the novel takes place. Other, older dances—the cotillion, the quadrille, the (scandalous!) waltz—weave like a bright ribbon through the whole of the century's fiction, from Jane Austen to Edith Wharton.

One of the charms of this book lies in reading descriptions of the quadrille by dancing masters of the time while reflecting that this was the very dance in which the haughty Mr. Darcy and the spirited Miss Elizabeth Bennet first took each other's measure in *Pride and Prejudice.* What's more, the plot of Jane Austen's classic revolves around a class system based on a hereditary aristocracy; it was the absence of such a system in America that gave rise to the immense appetite, chronicled in these pages, for books that claimed to teach the reader the rules of proper behavior in every sphere of life, from kitchen to ballroom.

As time went on these rules became more and more elaborate, and Ms. Aldrich's book treats us to the instructive spectacle of how, as successive groups rose to the top, they endeavored to create an increasingly exclusive class system of their own—a notion incompatible with that freedom of social opportunity which, by definition, etiquette manuals are designed to produce. In *Rudeness and Civility,* an extensive analysis of the code of manners established by these nineteenth-century manuals, historian John Kasson emphasizes that "the experience of the city and social life generally in this formative period cannot be understood without an appreciation of the cultural demands such codes involved. They built the inequities as well as the opportunities of life in a democratic capitalist society into the minute structures of everyday conduct, presenting oneself at home and in the street; mingling with strangers and greeting acquaintances; expressing pleasure and affection, anger and conflict; dining with family or guests; attending a concert or theatrical performance." All these minute structures are on view in the wide selection of primary sources Elizabeth Aldrich has included in this book. As she says, "Ballroom etiquette is shown to be a microcosm of etiquette in the society at large."

In *Vanity Fair,* at the great ball in Brussels before the Battle of Waterloo, the parvenue Becky Sharp carries off George Osborne to dance the quadrille before his neglected wife's very eyes, adding insult to injury by leaving her shawl and bouquet for poor Emmy to guard. In that very bouquet (bouquets and fans were favorite ballroom accessories as illustrations in *From the Ballroom to Hell* show), the philandering George later hides a love note for Becky.

Decorous as the quadrille was (a group of eight dancers performing a series of figures at a caller's bidding), it did have social hazards. In *The Pickwick Papers,* Mr. Tracy Tupman's ill-advised disregard of the niceties of etiquette in joining in a quadrille with a rich widow to whom he had not been properly introduced almost embroils him in a duel with her fiery suitor. And the aging hero of William Dean Howells's *Indian Summer,* Theodore Colville, makes a fool of himself ("his progress was attended by rending noises from the trains over which he found his path") when he rashly tries to dance the Lancers quadrille to impress a young woman.

What reader with memories of these and other novels in which ballroom dancing plays so pivotal a part can fail to be fascinated by the details this book provides concerning the elaborate code of manners, dress, and toilette with which etiquette manuals endeavored to arm real-life guests at the ball? These same manuals also provided help for the many other exigencies of social intercourse so forbidding to those from humble backgrounds. The eponymous hero of Howells's *The Rise of Silas Lapham,* for example, suffers agonies of indecision about whether or not to wear gloves to dinner with the proper Bostonian Coreys. Unfortunately, in this instance, that burning question was not answered in the etiquette manuals which the equally anxious Lapham ladies consulted in preparation for the event.

The *première danse* of the nineteenth century was the waltz—ah, the waltz! No dance of our own sensation-filled century, not the Charleston, not the Lindy, not even the lambada, has aroused the passionate moral disapproval once generated by this dance, which seems so chaste to us. At its first introduction in England in the early years of the nineteenth century, the waltz was considered vulgar and "indelicate" because, for the first time in the ballroom, the man and the woman were in close physical contact. Even the mad, bad, and dangerous-to-know Lord Byron disapproved. Condemnation reached its peak in the tirade by one T. A. Faulkner, "Ex Dancing Master" (see pages 155–56), that provides the provocative title for this book.

But a society that was capable of progressing from regarding eating with a knife as appropriate social behavior to coping with the proper use of a whole battery of specialized forks, knives, and spoons was also equal to the challenge of the waltz. The dance's unseemly intimacy was tamed by the emotional control polite society demanded, a control so absolute that in some circles even kissing a baby in public was deemed vulgar. The band played on, fortified by the intoxicating melodies that flowed from the pens of the Johann Strausses, *père* and *fils,* and the waltz swirled unrestrained to the end of the era.

What has all this to do with our own fast-receding century? The quadrille, the "German," the mazurka, are, save in the historical recreations in which the present author is so expert, as obsolete as the minuet. And although the waltz is still taught at Arthur Murray's and in de rigueur dancing classes for upper-middle-class children, and is occasionally seen on the dance floor, its main survival is among members of ballroom dancers' associations. Numerous as these enthusiasts are (their numbers doubled in the last decade), they are "out of the loop" of current dance styles. The young crowd favors the hustle (an oldie from the 1970s), along with the newer "voguing" and rap dancing.

A whole book could be written about the social revolutions that have intervened between nineteenth-century dance and that of today. The women's movement, of course, is one of them, and perhaps it is not fanciful to see a connection. Certainly, conservative critics have not hesitated to read sexual politics into dance. In a 1988 essay in *Commentary* championing partnered dancing, Peter Shaw approvingly comments: "Each partner accepts the constraints and enjoys the prerogatives of a frankly sex-stereotyped role. The woman accepts that she must follow . . . but she has the more desirable steps and a degree of freedom from care. . . . [The man's] is a role of responsibility, as it was once universally believed to be his sexual role in life."

It could be Ibsen's Torvald Helmer speaking. But if Nora Helmer has run out of the doll's house and slammed the door—and if in today's dances the man does not lead nor the woman follow but both do their own thing—where does that leave the concern with etiquette which played so important a role in nineteenth-century dancing? Right where it always was, perhaps, even though it has suffered a change of venue. The desires to be accepted by one's peers and to aspire to what is perceived as a higher social sphere are timeless human impulses.

Popular American magazines, particularly women's magazines—among them *McCall's, Ladies' Home Journal,* and *Good Housekeeping*—bear witness to the continuing appeal of the subject. One of the best-read columns in the current *Good Housekeeping* (founded in 1885, "in the higher interests of the household") is "Etiquette for Every Day," written by Elizabeth Post, daughter-in-law of Emily. In recent years *McCall's* and the *Journal* have carried etiquette advice from Charlotte Ford, Letitia Baldridge, and "Miss Manners"; the latter's syndicated newspaper column appears in the *Washington Post* and three hundred other papers. And etiquette books, including fourteen on children's manners listed in the *New York Times Book Review* in May 1990, are still staples of publishers' backlists.

Society has changed enormously since 1900, but one effect has been to broaden etiquette's base even as its more esoteric reaches have been cut back. What sociologists call the "consumer culture" has endowed all but the poorest classes with products and services once available only to the well-to-do. Along with these has also come the doubtful middle-class luxury of worrying about the "proper" thing to do in all kinds of social situations, including some so new (how to introduce an unmarried couple, for example) that the rules have had to be reinvented.

Then again, some rules never change. In an 1880s issue of *Harper's Bazar (sic),* one Maude How advised social aspirants to "Give liberally to charity, go on committees and meet there the educated and well bred. Keep your eyes open to the way they do things, and soon you will be able to play the game." It sounds remarkably like the strategy of today's "Nouvelle Society" ladies, as the fashion journal *W* calls them, who work for the "arts and diseases" to gain a place on the big-screen social scene.

Yes, etiquette is alive and well. *From the Ballroom to Hell* is an instructive glimpse at its ancestry.

Mina Mulvey
Executive Editor, Good Housekeeping
September 1990

Preface

What place is so proper as the assembly-room to see the fashions and manners of the times, to study men and characters, to become accustomed to receive flattery without regarding it, to learn good breeding and politeness without affectation, to see grace without wantonness, gaiety without riot, dignity without haughtiness, and freedom without levity?[1]

The nineteenth-century ballroom was the perfect setting in which ladies and gentlemen, attired in the latest fashions, could exercise their considerable dancing abilities and, more importantly, demonstrate their mastery of polite behavior, which was required for acceptance into genteel society. Proper organization of and successful attendance at balls demanded the strictest attention to numerous rules and regulations, including the protocol of invitations, proper introductions, choice of dances, and appropriate music. Ladies and gentlemen needed to know the fashionable dances; how to make and to accept an invitation to dance; how to converse agreeably on topics appropriate for the ballroom; even how to handle one's fork in the supper room. In addition, at small private parties, ladies and gentlemen might be expected to sing or play the piano for each other. These activities were also governed by specific protocols. In fact, explicit written rules and regulations seemed to dominate the age.

Nineteenth-century men and women were preoccupied with learning the proper way of conducting themselves not only in the ballroom but in all social interactions. But it was precisely in the ballroom that ladies and gentlemen best demonstrated their mastery of these rules of etiquette and social intercourse. The ballroom was a microcosm of the society at large; in these arenas of Terpsichore, general, everyday social behavior was distilled and focused more intensely than normally occurred elsewhere.

In a rapidly expanding, highly structured, class-oriented society, Americans were hungry for knowledge through which to better themselves. And how did one learn the accepted, the proper, the au courant rules? One learned primarily with the aid of the dance and etiquette manuals published in great numbers throughout the nineteenth century. As the push for self-improvement flowed from east to west, book publishers rushed in to satisfy the growing needs of the expanding population.

This volume is a collection of over a hundred excerpts from nineteenth-century etiquette, dance, beauty, and fashion manuals. Additional illustrations and musical examples from a variety of North and South American and European sources are included to complement the text. Non–North American sources were chosen to demonstrate that many aspects of nineteenth-century life were universal. For example, the fashion periodicals published in Valparaíso, Chile, were based on the same contemporary French ideals as were fashions in New York City. All the excerpts emphasize, explain, reinforce, and teach behavior appropriate for balls and the ballroom. Of special interest are the changing attitudes regarding the place of men and women—especially women—in society. Just as dances went in and out of fashion throughout the century, and just as dance technique developed new movements and lost old ones, so style, demeanor, dance attire, and the place of dance in society changed. Included here are instructions for dance technique, comments on the utility of learning to dance, proper attire, proper deportment, bows and curtseys, and how to organize balls. Forming an important portion of this collection are those readings that offer hints on how to enhance one's beauty and fashion prowess, as well as those concerned with music, musicians, and instruments for an evening's entertainment. The Introduction discusses general trends in ballroom fashion, types and contents of manuals and their intended audience, and brief descriptions of the most popular ballroom dances.

Following the Introduction and Conclusion are seven chapters of quotations. These quotations are chronological and are presented with original spellings, punctuation, and headings. Following each quotation is a short bibliographic entry identifying the author, title of the manual, place and date of publication, and page number. Full bibliographic entries, many of which are annotated, can be found beginning on page 193. Each bibliographic entry is listed chronologically within the categories of Etiquette Manuals, Dance Manuals, Fashion and Beauty Manuals, Criticism and Satire, Mystical Arts, Exercise, Domestic Concerns, and Periodicals.

The real focus of this collection is ballroom dance in the United States during the 1800s, with an emphasis on the Northern states. Although most of the sources were published in America, a number of British manuals have been included because American social behavior was based on the British code. Other British manuals have been incorporated when they provide information not available elsewhere. Also, many British manuals were revised or amended with the American audience in mind; some were simply pirated and distributed by American publishers.

As no book can be all things to all people, this collection is designed for the general reader; it serves to illustrate only a small sample of readings relating to the nineteenth-century ballroom. As such, conclusions should not be drawn based on the limited number of quotations that reflect each heading. Also, as informative as these readings can be, they do not tell us anything about actual practices. For example, not reflected in any of the dance manuals are the certain influences on social dance exerted by European immigration or the African-American population of the South. Likewise, as in the twentieth century, few women dressed exactly like the models in the popular fashion magazines but merely used them as a guide. The readings in this volume are meant simply to introduce the reader to the wonderful manuals that frequently lie neglected in the dusty corners of our nation's libraries, museums, and historical societies.

Most of the quoted materials in this study are drawn from etiquette and dance manuals; being saved for another study are the numerous and important letters, diaries, journals, and ladies' magazines that so illuminate the focus of the century's search for self-improvement.

To twentieth-century observers, many of the selections in this collection may appear humorous, and, indeed, some are. However, when reading, it is best to remember the wise words of writer Arthur M. Schlesinger: "The account has its mirthful moments, but the reader who smiles should smile with compassion, for he is witnessing one aspect of the common man's struggle to achieve a larger degree of human dignity and self respect."[2]

Elizabeth Aldrich
The Historical Dance Foundation, Inc.
May 1990

Acknowledgments

This project began as a loosely organized collection of quotations and illustrations that were put together as a syllabus for the participants of the International Early Dance Institute. I am grateful to my many friends and colleagues who have attended the Institute and urged me to further develop the syllabus.

Much of this volume is based on the collections found in the Library of Congress, the New-York Historical Society, and The New York Public Library, Astor, Lenox, and Tilden Foundations. I appreciate the invaluable assistance and patience shown by the librarians in these institutions. My thanks also to Jonathan Brent of Northwestern University Press and to my editor, Lee Yost, who aided enormously in the organization of the material.

Many years ago, as a student at the New England Conservatory of Music, I was encouraged to pursue my interests in early music and dance by three outstanding professors, and my continued success in the field is owed in great part to Julia Sutton, Daniel Pinkham, and Grace Feldman. It was, in fact, a Conservatory colleague, my dear friend Richard Robbins, who first suggested—with prodding from Ismail Merchant—that I look at nineteenth-century dance. My gratitude goes also to James Ivory and Merchant Ivory Productions for providing my first opportunity to reconstruct some of the marvelous dances from the nineteenth century in their film, *The Europeans*.

Finally, I wish to acknowledge the help, support, and friendship of two very special people, George Alan and Carla T. Smith. This book would not have been possible without their assistance.

On the Thursday evening [of the party], Belle shut herself up with her maid, and between them they turned Meg into a fine lady. They crimped and curled her hair, they polished her neck and arms with some fragrant powder, touched her lips with coralline salve to make them redder, and Hortense would have added "a soupçon *of rouge" if Meg had not rebelled. They laced her into a sky-blue dress which was so tight she could hardly breathe and so low in the neck that modest Meg blushed at herself in the mirror. A set of silver filagree was added—bracelets, necklace, brooch, and even earrings, for Hortense tied them on with a bit of pink silk which did not show. A cluster of tea rosebuds at the bosom, and a* ruche, *reconciled Meg to the display of her pretty white shoulders, and a pair of high-heeled blue silk boots satisfied the last wish of her heart. A laced handkerchief, a plumy fan, and a bouquet in a silver holder finished her off; and Miss Belle surveyed her with the satisfaction of a little girl with a newly dressed doll. . . . [Meg] very soon discovered that there is a charm about fine clothes which attracts a certain class of people and secures their respect. . . . She was flirting her fan and laughing at the feeble jokes of a young gentleman who tried to be witty, when . . . she saw Laurie. . . . [H]e said, with his very best bow and his hand out, "Please forgive my rudeness, and come and dance with me." . . . Away they went, fleetly and gracefully; for having practiced at home, they were well matched, and the blithe young couple were a pleasant sight to see as they twirled merrily round and round, feeling more friendly than ever after their small tiff.*

Louisa May Alcott, *Little Women*

Figure 1

Introduction: The Ballroom as Mirror of a Changing Society in Nineteenth-Century America

Upward Mobility

The colonies of the northern United States were settled for the most part by lower- and middle-class people who were not necessarily familiar with the best "society" of their European homelands. Many had left to seek new lives because of religious persecution; others, because they were unable to improve their status through the only way open to them—the purchase of land.[1] In the New World, land was available for the taking. However, unlike in Europe, there was no established, native aristocratic class to arbitrate and set the standards for good behavior. This lack continued to be a frequently discussed subject throughout the century, and in 1880 Mrs. John Sherwood remarked, "The newness of our country is perpetually renewed by the sudden making of fortunes, and by the absence of a hereditary, reigning set. There is no aristocracy here which has the right and title to set the fashions."[2]

Classes arose which, in turn, looked down on yet lower classes for their instances of bad or vulgar behavior. Laws discriminating against the lowest, poorest classes were not uncommon in colonial America. Public retribution, such as tarring and feathering an offender or putting him in stocks, was frequently utilized as punishment for the accused. Important also was the effect made by such methods on the onlooker. Public humiliation demonstrated the consequences of bad behavior—which could include most any offense, including that of owing money.

During the early nineteenth century, while many Americans pushed westward, eastern urban centers were expanding, and workers were becoming less independent and more dependent upon a new, rising merchant class. Even though the agricultural West was developing rapidly, 28.2 percent of the population in 1820 were engaged in nonagricultural occupations; by 1840 this rose to 31.4 percent.[3]

As a result of increased white male suffrage during the 1820s, the new territories dispatched farmers as representatives to Congress. On the East Coast, the working classes of the growing industrial towns and cities likewise sent their kind to Washington. Educational opportunities were still denied to many, and a rising population of poorly educated urban workers and similarly poorly educated rural frontiersmen created an atmosphere ripe for a savvy political leader, one who could take advantage of the relative naïveté of these new voters.

In March of 1829 Andrew Jackson took the office of President of the United States.[4] He was the first president from west of the Appalachians and the first since George Washington who was not a college graduate. The son of poor Irish immigrants, Andrew Jackson was assuming an office previously held by well-educated, cultured landowners. Jackson was truly a self-made man, and for the first time the ordinary citizen felt that he, too, might have unlimited opportunities. To become upwardly mobile, with an emphasis on self-fulfillment, became the goal of the common man. With the start of the Jacksonian presidency, criticism mounted among European travelers anxious to see, firsthand, the American experiment in democracy. Among the various writers, Charles Dickens and Mrs. Trollope were two who found American manners sorely lacking, especially in the western parts of the nation. Many of these European writers did not take into consideration the facts that the land had to be cleared and crops planted and harvested, as well as the constant problem of Indians to be solved, before the correct method of holding a fork could even be contemplated. However, internal criticism also intensified throughout the United States. As part of the campaign to overcome these objections and in an effort to encourage this new class to become "gentlemen," an astonishing number of books dedicated to self-improvement were published between the late 1820s and 1850. The so-called Jacksonian rudeness generated at least twenty-eight manuals in the 1830s, thirty-six in the 1840s, and thirty-eight in the 1850s, not including reprints and new editions of manuals previously published.[5] Many of these publications were thrust westward by publishers who did not consider whether or not ideals of behavior, arbitrated by British authorities or the established urban centers of Boston and Philadelphia, were appropriate to the settlers of the new territories.

Andrew Jackson and his colleagues may have risen to the highest levels of government but not to the top of "society." This was unquestionably expressed in *The Laws of Etiquette* published in Philadelphia in 1836. "None are excluded from the highest councils of the nation, but it does not follow that all can enter into the highest ranks of society."[6] Criticism of the Jacksonian era continued to be a favorite topic in etiquette manuals, but the improved manners and formality of an increasingly ceremonious society eventually overcame Jacksonian rudeness.

Before the Civil War, a small number of established families emphasized good education and cultured manners rather than money and possessions, in an era when just over thirty Americans were known to be worth a million dollars. In the gilded era of untaxed wealth that began after the Civil War, not only did this number increase to over three thousand families, but some, such as the Vanderbilts and the Astors, were worth over two hundred and fifty million dollars. Marriages between America's rich and the aristocracy of Europe reinforced the status of these American families in an ever-widening class system: Henry Huntington's daughter married the prince of Hatzfeldt; President Ulysses S. Grant's granddaughter married Prince Michael Contaciozen of Russia, and Consuelo Vanderbilt married the Duke of Marlboro.

As other families began to ascend into the realm of the newly wealthy during the last quarter of the century, those of "old money," the accepted leaders of America's established "aristocratic society," were determined to distinguish themselves from the nouveaux riches. The various levels of society were clearly understood in older cities like Boston and Philadelphia, but guest lists for balls and parties in New York were screened. By 1890 a list of four hundred socially acceptable families was established by Ward McAllister. However, ostentatious furnishings continued to fill the lodgings of those not fortunate to be included in the "400." Large numbers of etiquette manuals were aimed at this class of the newly rich, published to provide solutions to such dilemmas as "Managing the House with One Servant, "Managing the House with Two Servants," and "The House with Many Servants." In her chapter "The Modern Dinner Table," Mrs. John Sherwood shared with her readers the following tips for setting a dinner table: "The appointments of the modern dinner-table strikingly indicate that growth of luxury of which the immediate past has been so fruitful. Up to twenty years ago a dinner, even in the house of a merchant prince, was a plain affair."[7]

Mrs. Sherwood continued with nearly three pages of description regarding the perfect table setting for a party. The following is but a small portion:

The open-work, white table cloth lies on a red ground, and above it rests a mat of red velvet, embroidered with peacock's feathers and gold lace. Above this stands a large silver salver or oblong tray, lined with reflecting glass, on which Dresden swans and silver lilies seem floating in a veritable lake. In the middle of this long tray stands a lofty vase of silver or crystal, with flowers and fruit cunningly disposed to it, and around it are placed tropical vines. At each of the four corners of the table stand four ruby glass flagons set in gold, standards of beautiful and rare design. . . . [8]

None but the most wealthy could afford such luxurious table settings, but anyone could attempt smaller-scaled festivities. As well as reading the popular manuals that were available to all, everyone followed the activities of America's self-proclaimed aristocracy and the wealthy in the increasingly popular society columns such as *Andrews' American Queen.*

In 1830, 23 thousand immigrants began new lives in the United States, and by 1890 this number had risen to 1.2 million.[9] Most of the new European arrivals had escaped from political upheavals, economic disasters, and pogroms. They settled into the destitute urban ghettos where, along with a growing population of formerly rural people, they were more and more excluded from established society.[10] In contrast to the 235 thousand families with average incomes of $187,000 in 1880, over eleven million had an average income of only $968.[11]

The task of assimilating into American society became a chief objective for the new arrivals, and during this time behavior became a required subject in many public schools. While a child's behavior was being enhanced at school, adults could purchase, at minimal prices, newly assembled manuals on etiquette and society or the many older titles that were going through reprint after reprint. *The Habits of Good Society,* originally published in 1860, saw fourteen reprints between 1863 and 1890. Whether or not the rules were practical to their circumstances, even the lowliest were expected to accept the etiquette norms set forth in these manuals.

Sex Roles in Society

A Scottish authoress once stated, "A party—a ball room—is woman's battlefield. There she sways her charming scepter, and although a bold man may disregard and disobey the most sacred laws and customs, he cannot—he dare not, disregard her influence, and the amiable woman rules the haughty man. Hence the business of a man is to govern the world, and the destiny of a woman is to charm and influence it, which she must do entirely by her accomplishments; and the greater these are, as well as her amiability and kindness, the more powerful and more successful will be her influence."[12]

The ballroom was an important part of a woman's domain. Here a lady could display the fine arts so often encouraged in her education: music and dance. In addition, a lady could show her abilities in all the facets required of giving a party or ball, including her taste in fashion.

Indeed, no discussion of dance or etiquette in nineteenth-century American society can be complete without an examination of the place in society and, ultimately, in the ballroom, of the men and women who danced.

During the eighteenth century, women were directly involved in all stages of the feeding and clothing of the family unit. Work was necessary and socially sanctioned; even single women and widows were expected to take care of themselves.

As the urban population increased, factories began to take over the tasks of spinning and weaving, work previously done by women in their homes. In 1810 virtually all the wool produced in the United States was domestic; by the 1830s, women in New England purchased rather than wove cloth.[13] During the first twenty years of the nineteenth century, noticeably fewer women were involved in small businesses than in the previous century. In the eighteenth century women had been silversmiths, upholsterers, butchers, and gunsmiths, among other occupations.[14] Furthermore, during this era of a newly expanding medical profession, women who had previously played important roles as healers and midwives, were now restricted to the pursuit of nursing, a task considered to be an extension of one's home duties.[15]

The 1820s and 1830s were a time of change in status for middle-class women, and, ironically, during the decades of expanding democraticization, only white males profited. As it was no longer socially sanctioned, middle-class women stopped working outside the home and thus joined upper-class women in the pursuit of becoming "ladies."[16] The "cult of the lady" elevated ideals of femininity to which all women aspired, and by 1840 a woman's aspirations centered on the activities of her home. Many etiquette and home-aid manuals were written for the express purpose of easing the transition from the outside world to one centered in the kitchen and parlor. One such manual was Mrs. Lydia Child's *The American Frugal Housewife, Dedicated to those Who are not Ashamed of Economy* (1829), which had an enormous circulation both here and in England. To ease similar transitions in England, *The Workwoman's Guide* (1838) was written by a "Lady" and dedicated to the "Inexperienced in Cutting Out and Completing those Articles of Wearing Apparel which are Usually Made at Home." The message was clear: it was not beneath a "Lady" to sew and to take advantage of multifarious tips designed to keep her home clean and her family contented and entertained.

Aimed specifically at women, etiquette manuals of the 1830s began to reflect home-centered domesticity by encouraging a smaller sphere of duties. *The Young Lady's Friend,* written in 1836 by a "Lady," devoted an entire chapter to "Domestic Economy."[17] As late as 1853, Mrs. Manners asked her readers, "Is Work Degrading? Is it *vulgar* to be usefully employed?" She concluded, "I call the *pride* which disdains such things *vulgar,* and the indolence which fears the effort contemptible."[18] *The Young Lady's Friend* also contained a chapter entitled "Improvement of Time," which included a discussion on "Thinking and Sewing." Other home-centered topics covered in this manual were: "Nursing the Sick," Behaviour of the Sick," "Dress," and "Means of Preserving Health," which encouraged women to exercise and to refrain from tight lacing and tight shoes. Other subjects included the treatment of domestics and workwomen and how to give dinner and evening parties.[19]

Also glorifying home duties were fiction writers who contributed stories to the numerous periodicals that circulated around the country. The readers of *Lady Godey's* and *Peterson's Ladies' National Magazine* were inundated with articles proclaiming women to be heroines who waged and won the battles of home life and domestic duties.

On the other hand, *The Young Man's Own Book,* published in Philadelphia in 1832, incorporated very different issues geared to business and the outside world. Chapters included: "The Necessity of Being Well Informed," "Advantages of a Variety of Studies," and "Debt and Credit." A long chapter entitled "Principles Necessary to be Observed by Those Young Men who are not Yet in Business for Themselves" included discussions on dishonesty, lying, frugality, sots, false complaisance, and bonds and securities. In "Advice on Entering Upon Business," young men were indoctrinated with such topics as "Important Affairs to be managed in Person," "Caution in setting up," and "Great Rents." Under the matter of "Entering Upon Business," was advice on "choice of wife." Writing in the same tone he employed in the rest of the manual, the author advised young men, "let her be of a family not vain of their name, or wealth, or connexions; those additions on her side, being certain matters of insult to defects on yours." Concerning "beauty" in a potential wife, "let her also be alike free from deformity and heredity diseases." And, under the topic of "Poor Relations," the author suggested that when a young man considers a wife "let him at least take care that she is not surrounded with hungry relatives; for if she is, they will throng about you like horse-leeches; and, by the connivance, artifice, or opportunity of your wife, either beg, borrow, or steal your substance, till they have plucked you as bare as the jay in the fable."[20]

During the nineteenth century women assumed the responsibility of being the arbiters of conduct, an activity believed to be in accord with the leisurely life of urban middle-class women. Women, reigning from their parlors, became the "queens" of family etiquette. It was a woman's responsibility to maintain the comfort and the decency of her family. "It is she who makes etiquette, and it is she who preserves the order and the decency of society. Without women, men soon resume the savage state, and the comforts of the home are exchanged for the misery of the mining camp."[21]

To support this responsibility, more and more literature was addressed specifically to women; thus, the reading of self-help manuals and periodicals, as well as novels, became an important pastime. Manuals on how to arrange tableaux and theatricals, song books, instructions for card games, and books on fortune-telling were available to assist a lady with the activities taking place in her parlor. Of great importance to this audience, of course, were dance manuals intended to assist with the planning and organizing of diverting evenings of dance. Cookbooks and manuals devoted to setting the table, folding napkins, and which fork to use at mealtimes, were targeted at the other half of woman's domain, the kitchen and the dining room. Additional self-help books on fashion, beauty tips, and manners were in constant demand by a female audience that cut across all classes.

With the major exception of ladies' academies run by such educational stalwarts as Emma Willard and Mary Lyon, learning for women during the nineteenth century centered on subjects considered suitable for a lady's temperament: sewing, music, dancing, painting, literature, history, and perhaps a foreign language.[22]

Traveling through the United States between 1859 and 1862, I. J. Benjamin II stated that American women were "very bright in conversation, always vivacious, and passionately love music, singing and dancing."[23] Forty years earlier, Giovanni Grassi commented about American women, "The education of girls rarely permits them to handle well the needle and the spindle, but never lacks instruction in the dance."[24]

"The stranger will always be surprised by the place occupied by women in American society, by the respect and the deference of which they are the objects."[25] Indeed, many foreign travelers, as well as American manuals, commented on the "special" treatment of women in the United States. Much of this had to do with the relative shortage of the female sex during the colonial era and in the West as the nation expanded. During her 1835 trip to Milwaukee, Harriet Martineau noted that out of four hundred citizens only seven were women.[26] This scarcity enhanced a position, thus described by *The American Code of Manners*:

In America we have the foundation of good manners, in the great chivalry of the men. No men have so profound a respect for women. . . . From the captain of a western steamboat to the roughest mines in California, from north, south, east and west, we hear but one voice. Women are to be protected, respected, supported and petted. There is no such paradise for women as the United States of America.[27]

Also important in the dissemination of information on self-help and culture was the development of the lyceum movement. Each week a different topic and speaker would be presented to members who paid a membership or admission fee, and the subscribers frequently had access to a library. Although mainly social in nature, the lyceum contributed to the goal important to many Americans: self-improvement. The founder of the institution of the lyceum, Josiah Holbrook, stated, "A Town Lyceum is a voluntary association of individuals disposed to improve 'each other' in useful knowledge."[28] The popularity of this format, where information was "brought within the comprehension of the most untutored minds,"[29] also presented opportunities for events that included entertainment. By the late 1830s there were more than three thousand active lyceums throughout the United States.[30]

The most fashionable amusement at Boston this year consists in lectures, which are delivered by literary men (even those of the greatest eminence, such as, for instance, Mr. John Quincy Adams), upon all sorts of subjects. The proprietors of the Lyceum, or some other great room, undertake the speculation, engage the lecturer at a certain price, and make a change for admission proportionate to his popularity. . . . Ladies often attend two or three in one evening; and so necessary is excitement and variety considered, that one lecturer is seldom allowed to give a "course," there must be a fresh hand every night.[31]

Etiquette books often devoted entire chapters to behavior appropriate at these lectures. *The Young Lady's Book* commented that lectures were "generally well attended by ladies" and suggested that, prior to the lecture, they obtain a copy of "the composition which is the subject of discourse," in order to "refer on the spot to the passages and particular effects cited by the lecturer."[32]

One of the most complete descriptions of the lyceum and its required code of manners is found in Mrs. Farrar's *The Young Lady's Friend*, published in 1836.

The admirable institution of Lyceum lectures should be held in great esteem by women, if it were only for the good they do those who would otherwise never quit the narrow round of household chores; and who have no access to libraries, or to cultivated society; as well as to those who think they have no time to drink at those fountains. To such, even the sprinkling of a Lyceum lecture is refreshing, and sometimes leads to a draught from other streams.

It suggests useful topics of conversation, and promotes sociability among neighbors; it affords opportunity for learning, to respect the rights of strangers, and to behave courteously and delicately to all.[33]

When attending the lyceum, Mrs. Farrar advised ladies not to wear large hats, not to whisper, never to oblige a gentleman to give up his seat ("which he has fairly earned"), not to arrive late, and, upon leaving, not to tread on peoples' clothing while going down the stairs.

As the lower classes began to embrace the popularity of the lyceum, its status faded among the middle and upper classes, and by the 1860s women were turning to "clubs" for study, discussion, social work and philanthropy. Many women organized for temperance, abolition, suffrage, public health, education, or caring for the poor—activities that were a natural extension of their home spheres.

As women socialized more and more with each other and in the outside world, the popularity of men's-only clubs also flourished. Serving as a refuge from the stresses of social life, the first organized gentlemen's club in the United States was the Adelphia Club (later to be called the Philadelphia Club), founded in 1834.[34] New York's Union Club was launched in 1836, the Somerset of Boston in 1851, and San Francisco's Pacific Club was founded in 1852.

Whenever you call on a lady, speak of having "just come from the club," and dwell with pride upon the amount of time you spend there, because all ladies have great faith in the happy influence of such places as "clubs" upon a young man, in not only teaching him the polite accomplishments of "chewing" and "drinking," and a great many coarser habits, but they get him into the pleasant way of late hours, and of spending all his leisure time away from home. There is no sensible lady who will not jump at the chance of marrying one of these "clubmen," for she knows that she will be relieved of his company nearly all the time, and that she will furthermore, have the great pleasure of sitting up to welcome him home at the poetical hour of midnight. What a charming prospect for domestic happiness![35]

Men's clubs and lodges were extremely popular during the last quarter of the nineteenth century, and numerous writers commented that gentlemen became more and more isolated from society. Abby Buchanan Longstreet grumbled that "club life among gentlemen tends more and more to postpone marriage."[36] The rising popularity of men's clubs also paralleled the steady decline of the number of men who attended dancing schools, and writers during the last quarter of the century frequently commented that gentlemen were more and more out of place in many social situations, including the ballroom.

And I could particularly note the difference in character between the two sexes, a difference so great that one might suppose them members of two different races. The men have a rigid temperament; they speak lit-

tle. . . . In the salon the American male is a fish out of water; not one of them will deny that his true place is the office, the countinghouse, or the political meeting.[37]

The author of these observations, Carlo Gardini, also observed dancing during the 1880s in Saratoga, a popular end-of-century summer society gathering locale. He noted that few men participated.

Numerous dance and etiquette manuals also commented that, when attending balls, the gentlemen did not always live up to the expectations of their hostesses. *The Hand-Book of Etiquette* declared: "If gentlemen go to balls, they should dance. It is a great breach of etiquette to stand idling and sauntering while ladies are waiting for an invitation to dance."[38] *Mixing in Society* felt that "a gentleman should not go to a ball unless he has previously made up his mind to be agreeable . . . to enter into the spirit of the dance, instead of hanging about the doorway."[39]

Florence Howe Hall complained about young men who "have an odious and selfish habit of not dancing if they cannot secure just the partners they want, and of standing, a black-coated and dismal group, like so many crows, around the doorway."[40] More cheerfully expressed, Ingersoll Lockwood reminded the P.G. (Perfect Gentleman) that he attended a ball

by courtesy of his hostess and his own free will, not so much to enjoy himself in the dancing as to play the part of "dancing man." . . . He is there with business in hand, to wit: to dance with the partners whom his hostess may provide for him, to aid her with all his strength of body and mind in preventing the growth of that genus of plant, y[c]lept "wall flower."[41]

While women continued to attend dancing schools and organize balls and parties, men, for the most part, did not follow suit. Without formal study of the latest ballroom dances, a man was frequently ill-equipped to dance with wall flowers. Customarily, a gentleman also faced the prospect of spending many hours performing the German, a party game where he could be humiliated or made the object of jokes. It is no wonder manuals and foreign visitors noted that many men gravitated further to the periphery of a dancing society.

Book Publishers, Manuals, and Their Audience

As early as 1810 Giovanni Grassi noted "trade in books is brisk."[42] In fact, there were 385 publishing houses in America by the mid-nineteenth century.[43] Due to the absence of an international copyright law, early book publishing in the United States was based heavily on the pirating of English books. Pirated works did not require financial negotiations with an author or publisher, and much of the courtesy literature published during the eighteenth and early nineteenth centuries was, in fact, British.

"There is no country where there are so many people asking what 'is proper to do,' or, indeed, where there are so many genuinely anxious to do the proper thing, as in the vast conglomerate which we call the United States of America,"[44] and a large portion of the titles circulating in the nineteenth century dealt with self-help or entertainment. Some publishers, such as D. Appleton & Co., Harper & Bros., Hurst & Co., and Dick & Fitzgerald, catered exclusively to a growing population searching for shortcuts to self-improvement. The majority of these readers were women, and publishers took advantage of the home-centered status of their audience. Instructions for activities in the home formed the basis for many a publisher's inventory.

As noted, the lyceum movement also encouraged reading, and many lyceum centers contained libraries for their members. In 1854 the city of Boston opened a library designed not just for scholars but for everybody, and by 1875 there were 185 public libraries in the United States.[45] Self-help and entertainment books now circulated to the general public.

Book and periodical publishing profited greatly in 1869 when the Union Pacific Railroad and the Central Pacific Railroad joined at Promontory Point, Utah. A transcontinental rail system meant that books arrived at the farthest points of the United States in a matter of weeks instead of months.

Inexpensively produced paperback books were issued by publishers in the 1870s, and some introduced a "Library Series." Many of these reprints of previously published materials were titles concerned with dance and etiquette. New printing technology enabled printers to produce up to twelve thousand pages an hour, and Frank Leslie's "Home Library," Beadle and Adams's "Fireside Library," and Harper's "Franklin Square Library" took advantage of a growing demand for these inexpensive paperbacks. The distribution of this information was also aided in no small measure by a postal rate of only two cents a pound.

Of course, publishers were often influenced by the economic problems which beset the nation, and the Panic of 1833 put many booksellers out of business. Overexpansion of credit with new western ventures caused many banks to fail in the Panic of 1837, causing additional problems for the publishing business. The decade of the seventies was extremely unstable because of the complications of reconstruction and inflation, and the Panic of 1873 caused numerous delays in the publishing community—with the exception of the reprinting of etiquette manuals, which cascaded into the marketplace as usual.

The earliest dance manual quoted in this work is Saltator's 1802 Boston manual, *A Treatise on Dancing*. Acknowledged to be "collected from many eminent writers," as were most nineteenth-century dance and etiquette manuals, its contents continued to reflect eighteenth-century thinking. Fully half of the book is devoted to dissertations on how behavior reflects one's morals as opposed to setting forth the rules for the ceremonious aspects of life. Addressed to the "Younger Classes of Society," Saltator provided his readers with long, detailed discussions on numerous subjects:

On the Employment of Time: *If we divide the life of many, perhaps most men into twenty parts, we shall find nineteen out of the twenty of them to be mere gaps and chasms, which are neither filled with pleasure nor business.*

Consideration of Company: *The love of company and of social pleasures is natural, and is attended with some of the sweetest satisfactions of human life: but like every other love, when it proceeds beyond the limits of moderation, it ceases to produce its natural effect, and sinks into disgusting satiety and discontent.*

Observations on Behaviour: *This is the token of dignity, by which, we are raised above the inferior tribes of groveling beings.*[46]

Other topics were "Choice of Companions," "View of the Passions," and four sections devoted to the art of dancing: "Observations," Short History of Dancing," and "Lessons in Dancing," which included instructions for bows and curtseys, proper deportment, dance steps, and descriptions for figures of English country dances and cotillions. "Management in an Assembly" was the manual's fourth and concluding section.

Early nineteenth-century etiquette manuals covered a similar range of material. The English manual, *The Mirror of the Graces,* published in New York in 1813, contained twenty-three chapters on such topics as "Preliminary Observations on the Subject Including Opinions of the Epicureans and Stoics." This section included separate discourses on "Female Charms, Their Use and Abuse," "Affectations," "Modesty," "Religion and Morality," and "Duty to a Husband." A chapter called "On the Female Form" discussed "Temperance" and "Exercise." The chapter "General Thoughts on Dress; On the Peculiarities of Dress" acquainted the young lady with "Good Sense," "Taste," and the "Bosom." "On Deportment" included a section entitled "Peculiarities in Carriage and Demeanor," which instructed the reader on how to walk, sit, stand, and dance.

The large number of self-help manuals that were published between 1820 and 1850 reflected changes in society and dispensed with the sentimental language of the eighteenth century. It became common to establish categories of precise rules which, directed at the uninitiated, left nothing to chance, and to use terminology everyone could understand. *True Politeness* reduced the tomes of etiquette to a series of numbered rules, none more than two sentences long. Diatribes against such themes as dirty linens and hands, spitting, and picking the nose were found in many mass-produced manuals, available for as little as ten cents.[47]

By the 1820s, etiquette manuals began to devote more attention to the ceremonial details of life: suitable attire, proper pronunciation, acceptable topics for conversation. Also, rules governing the rituals associated with the home begin to emerge: how and which foods to serve, which fork to use while eating, the proper mode of delivering calling cards, and how to give parties and balls. Throughout this period, dance manuals also reflected a shift of emphasis to the formal rituals of society by eliminating long dissertations on deportment and morals. Although Charles Durang stated that "dancing and etiquette are inseparable,"[48] his 1856 *The Fashionable Dancer's Casket* opened with a relatively short chapter entitled "Etiquette, or Preliminary Instructions to Dancing," which covered a myriad of discussions on dress for ladies and comments on the ballroom. The treatise concluded with additional short sections on proper ballroom dress for gentlemen, the etiquette of the ballroom, and a glossary of French terminology used in dancing. The majority of the manual was, in fact, devoted to descriptions of dances and dance steps.

After the Civil War, dance manuals contained markedly less information on etiquette or hints for giving balls. *The Ball Room Guide; or, Dancing without a Master,* published in 1875, contained five chapters: "How to Organize a Ball," "Ballroom Toilette," "Etiquette of the Ballroom," "Dances," and "Glossary of French Terms."[49] The longest chapter was on the dances themselves.

By the 1880s, the reduction of information on etiquette and rules for giving balls in dance manuals was even more marked. *Wehman's Complete Dancing Master and Call Book* of 1889 devoted less than one page to "Hints for the Organization and Management of Balls, Parties, Soirees, &c.," and an additional page-and-a-half to music for balls and calling quadrilles. Allen Dodworth's 1885 *Dancing and Its Relations to Education and Social Life* contained no discussion of etiquette at all, stating that "information upon the subject may be found in many excellent publications of the day."[50] Society now turned exclusively to etiquette manuals for their manners.

The American Catalogue, which compiled a list of books printed and for sale in 1876, contained twenty-two titles of dance manuals, ranging in price from ten cents for *Beadle's Ball-Room Companion* to DeGarmo's more expensive *Dance of Society* for a dollar fifty. The average price for a dance manual was only thirty-eight cents, considerably less than that for an etiquette manual.[51]

One popular etiquette manual entitled *Blunders in Behaviour Corrected* was advertised in 1858 by Dick & Fitzgerald for twelve-and-a-half cents. Twenty years later a similar manual, *How to Behave,* was offered for twelve cents. Most etiquette manuals, however, were more expensive. *The American Catalogue* listed sixty-six etiquette manuals, as well as an additional forty-three on related subjects such as conversation, table talk, and dining. They averaged ninety-seven cents in price, with over 40 percent costing a dollar or more. These manuals ranged in price from ten cents to a five-dollar version of Chesterfield's letters, which could also be purchased in a special volume for ten dollars!

After the Civil War, the readership for these manuals included, not only the middle class and the uninitiated, but a new class of nouveau riches who could afford to emulate, at least in possessions and in throwing lavish parties, the practices of those with "older" wealth. No longer content with the basic comforts of life, all classes took aim at materialism and set forth goals to acquire luxuries.

And indeed, the manuals surged forth to answer the needs of "young ladies in the West and East; from young housekeepers who are beginning, far from the great cities, the first arduous attempts at dinner giving; and from young men who are rising in the world . . . from elderly people, [to] whom fortune has come late. . . . "[52]

Good Manners, published in 1888 by the Butterick Publishing Company, had similar aims:

In preparing this volume we have kept in mind a large class of our patrons who have applied to us for information on matters of social etiquette as practiced in those circles whose members, by right of inheritance or acquirement, have assumed or had bestowed upon them the position of leaders in social affairs; and also, of a still larger class whose surroundings and circumstances do not permit of the adoption of the same rules that apply to the conduct of social life in large cities or in localities where popular taste may be safely counted upon to harmonize with individual preferences.[53]

The "unfortunates who have been reared at remote distances from the centres of civilization" could find assistance in Abby Longstreet's *Social Etiquette of New York.*[54] Even the British manuals, upon which most American publications were based, pointedly aimed their conversations, not at the titled but at a growing middle class. Charles William Day's 1834 London publication, *Hints on Etiquette and the Usages of Society,* formed the basis for this shift in attitude by assisting the uninitiated on matters of etiquette. Day's guide was very popular and the text was copied or paraphrased in numerous other works, both in the United States and England.

These manuals, diffused to all parts of the United States on the rapidly expanding rail network and aimed at the large group of people striving to become middle-class or better, were not "devised to meet the requirements of any particular locality but to suit America at large."[55] *The Ball-Room Instructor* of 1841 was targeted at those who had "neglected, or have not had an opportunity of attending dancing-schools," as well as to those who "are paying for a quarter's tuition," for they could practice at home and not be subjected to the "gaze of an assembly."[56]

With the availability of so many manuals, publishers were compelled to promote the preeminence of their books, even if the contents were acknowledged to be borrowed from other sources. In 1848 Turner & Fisher declared their manual, *The Ball-Room Bijou and Art of Dancing,* to be "the only legitimate and really artistical work on the subject published in America."[57] Reinforcing the authority of their contents, dance and etiquette manuals were entitled *The Laws of Etiquette* or, *The Scholars' Companion,* suggesting legal and academic clout. "Foreign" influence on American manuals was important, and Henry Whale's *Hommage à Taglioni* stated in its title that it contained "the only correct figures . . . introduced at the Court Balls in Europe." Scientific authority was the basis for Donald Walker's *Exercises for Ladies,* which was "Founded on Physiological Principles." Manuals were often authored by "A Gentleman" or, by "A Member of the Philadelphia Bar," and ladies' manuals were often written by "A Lady" or, worthier, "A Lady of Distinction."

Since the beginning of Jacksonian democracy, the concept of the self-made man was often reflected in the titles of dance manuals: it was thought possible, for example, to learn to dance without the aid of a master. In the late 1820s, E. H. Conway offered *Le Maître de Danse, or the Art of Dancing Cotillons . . . without a Master* and capitalized on two popular ideas: the vogue for French dancing and the opportunity to learn it on your own. *Offenbach's Dancing without a Master* of 1876 was advertised to the public as "a complete self-instructor in the art of dancing." This emphasis on learn-it-yourself, without the aid of a professional instructor, reached an almost ridiculous apex in George E. Wilson's 1884 *Wilson's Ball-Room Guide and Call Book.* Wilson stated that the best way to learn to dance was to "stand up and try it." He criticized dancing schools as places "where a company of bashful people congregate." Thus, his manual was meant to arm the reader with the theory, after which one was instructed to attend a ball with a "good partner by your side." The final result was that "you will become a finished dancer before those in the school have made their first attempt."[58]

Dance and etiquette titles were often published to improve upon information already available. *Cartier and Baron's Practical Illustrated Waltz Instructor* complained that many books on dance were lacking in "the want of simple explanations, suitable to those who are beginning the practice of dancing."[59] Critical of the state of teaching in the late 1860s, the author of *"The Prompter"* declared that his book was meant to counteract masters of the art who "have not kept pace with the public demand for more thorough instructions."[60]

Another large group of dance manuals were authored by actual dance masters. These manuals were aimed at the students of the various authors and, although many, such as Edward Ferrero's *The Art of Dance,* went into mass circulation, these manuals were generally the most coherently written. Although virtually none was an "original" manual, the various dance instructors seemed to take more care in assembling their books than is evident in a majority of the publisher-produced dance manuals.

Music and Dance

Included in this collection are a number of references to music, playing for balls, and compositions of dance music. The manuals also incorporated dialogues concerning rules of deportment and etiquette for ladies and gentlemen while playing an instrument or in singing for one's peers. Etiquette and dance manuals also discussed the kinds and numbers of instruments and musicians to use for a ball. Remarks, almost always critical if not completely scathing, concerning the behavior and performance of hired musicians can be found in numerous sources. In addition, dance manuals frequently provided suggested tempos for dance music and often included musical examples in their treatises.

"It is a matter of prestige for the ladies to be able to say they have studied music, drawing and French."[61] The ability to play an instrument, usually the piano, or to sing for one's companions were accomplishments much akin to the necessity of presenting one's self tolerably in a quadrille. It was not uncommon, during an intimate evening that included dancing, for the guests to play and sing for each other. Also, music was an important part of a "lady's" education and, as one of the refining, decorative elements, made her more desirable to a potential husband. Mrs. Hale hoped, however, that a woman would consider music something other than a "showy accomplishment" and would continue to use music "as a means of brightening and enlivening her home" after matrimony.[62]

Etiquette manuals warned that "a lady who can do nothing 'without her notes,' or who cannot read music, and play at sight, is scarcely enough of a musician to perform in a large company."[63] *Social Etiquette and Home Culture* pleaded with amateur violinists, who had studied but a few months, not to "harass society with their cat gut exasperations."[64]

Etiquette manuals were critical of the zest and emotion frequently displayed in performance. "A Lady of Distinction" criticized the contortions and facial expressions of young women and feared that an abundance of these antics would cause the listeners to think the young lady "impure." Actions and grimaces—which included heads swinging to the right and left, quivering lips, rolling eyes, and panting—were condemned by "A Lady of Distinction," and the author of *Social Etiquette* warned ladies against a similar variety of "don'ts" while playing the piano, among them "digital fireworks" and "throwing themselves to the right and left, as if preparing for the trapeze."[65]

Much of the piano music published during the nineteenth century was intended for these amateur performers. Publishers of manuals on "how to" play the piano often accompanied their teaching methods with volumes of music, which frequently included music for social dances. Having a piano in one's parlor was an important status symbol for both middle- and upper-class society, and the manufacture of pianos in the United States during the nineteenth century was significant: Steinway, Knabe, Mason and Hamlin, and Chickering all were successful instrument makers. The *American Catalogue* contains 175 titles of pedagogical methods and music collections available in 1876.

Once asked to sing by the host or hostess, lady readers were admonished by Mrs. Hale to accept at once, but not to hurry "as if glad of an opportunity to show off."[66] In the eyes of the author of *Social Etiquette*, "the little farcical comedy of insincere excuses and pretended apologies in which some indulge is an insult to the hostess and her company."[67] Mrs. Hale also spoke sharply against incorrect pronunciation in singing. "There is nothing so unpleasant as broad French, mincing German, or lisping Italian."[68] *Social Etiquette* requested that its readers sing only once in an evening, because the audience "will secretly be conscious of a sense of weariness,"[69] and *True Politeness* requested that ladies not "sing songs descriptive of masculine passion or sentiment."[70]

Discussions regarding accurate tempos and playing the correct number of refrains were important elements in many nineteenth-century dance manuals. For example, Thomas Wilson reminded musicians to play only the correct number of refrains because, if not, "blame will certainly fall on the Composer of the Figures though in Reality it is caused through neglect or oversight of the Musicians."[71]

The problem of dancing to the chosen tempos of the dance band was, not unlike today, a major topic of conversation, and nineteenth-century authors repeatedly complained about tempos played by hired musicians at balls. One dancing master felt that playing incorrect tempos "impedes or embarrasses the performance of the steps," and consequently it made the dancer appear "faulty" when he was not.[72] E. Woodward Masters wrote a stinging attack apropos the "uneven tempo of the different orchestras," and concluded that the leaders were "very inferior musicians."[73]

Concerning appropriate musical accompaniment for balls, *The Ball-Room Guide, a Handy Manual* advised the hostess, when choosing a pianist, not to leave her guests to "the mercy of chance players, while it happens that those who oblige out of courtesy would prefer taking part in the dance."[74]

Although early-nineteenth-century dance music was frequently composed for a single melodic instrument, usually the violin, the piano became increasingly popular for private, at-home dance parties. However, music for small ensembles, such as the piano and one or two other melodic instruments, was written by a number of popular composers.[75] Other dance manuals also suggested combinations for larger gatherings that could utilize mixed ensembles and brass bands. Elias Howe's manual, *Howe's Complete Ball-Room Hand Book* (see pages 129–30), gives one publisher's opinion of appropriate instrument combinations. Dance music for these mixed ensembles was circulated by numerous publishers.[76]

Group Dances

The English Country Dance

The English country dance is a progressive longways dance for "as many as will" first popularized by John Playford in his manual, *The English Dancing Master,* in editions from 1651 to 1728.[77] References to the performance of English country dances are found in plays of the early 1560s, and Queen Elizabeth is known to have enjoyed dancing several. The English country dance is performed by two lines of dancers, men facing women, with a top couple designated as "couple number one." As the first couple moves down the set one position each time the figure is performed, the other couples move up one position. Eventually, the first couple works down to the bottom of the set and the last couple moves up to the top of the set. Extremely popular in the early part of the nineteenth century, country dances eventually gave way to cotillions and quadrilles: dances for eight performers standing in a square formation. Manuals frequently commented that country dances, referred to as "those never-ending still beginning performances,"[78] continued to be performed throughout the century in rural areas or other informal settings.[79]

In his 1802 manual, Boston writer Saltator described ornamental steps that would be appropriate for country dances or cotillions and stated that these steps were "performed altogether by springs, hops or leaps."[80] However, there apparently was confusion regarding proper steps for English country dances, as can be observed in the following opinions. *The Mirror of the Graces* disagreed with Saltator and stated that "the English Country Dance and French Cotillion require different steps."[81] Along these same lines, Barclay Dun commented that "to use steps fitted for the English country dance or Scotch reel to French music, would be as incompatible as speaking the French language with the Scotch or English accent."[82] On the other hand, Francis Peacock said, in describing a reel step called "Minor *Kemkóssy,*" that the step "is an easy familiar step, much used by the English in their Country Dances."[83] Performers of early-nineteenth-century English country dances most likely used steps from the cotillion vocabulary and adapted them as necessary. The steps and step combinations were related to those utilized in late-eighteenth-century French contredanses, and, as itinerate dancing masters spread throughout the rural areas, steps and combinations would have been modified to fit the abilities of the constituency. After the 1830s, many of these steps and step sequences most likely were simplified or dancers would have simply walked through the figures.

Cotillion and Quadrille

The eighteenth-century French contredanse, performed in a square formation by eight dancers, was a French version of the English country dance. Eventually the contredanse was exported back to England where it was known as a "cotillion." In 1770 Giovanni-Andrea Gallini described the English cotillion, which was performed in the same formation as its relative, the French contredanse.[84] The "figure" of the dance was alternately performed with "changes." Saltator furnished the following definition of the cotillion, a dance that was popular during the first two decades of the nineteenth century: "The Figures of Cotillions, consist of two parts, the one is termed the change, the other the figure. There are ten changes, which are the same in all regular cotillions, but every cotillion has a different figure, which is performed between every change, and once after the last change."[85]

Appearing a bit later than the cotillion was a similar group dance called the "quadrille." The quadrille was a series of figures, usually five, performed without changes as in a cotillion but maintaining the square formation of eight performers. Growing in popularity after the first decade of the nineteenth century, the quadrille coexisted with the cotillion for at least ten years. The close association of the two dance forms was noted by numerous dancing masters, and *A Selection of Favorite Quadrilles* stated, "The modern French dances termed Quadrille, are a specie of cotillions in their style and composition."[86] Thomas Wilson described the quadrille as "entirely of French origin, and only differs from the well-known Dance, the Cotillion, by leaving out the changes."[87] In 1827 Mrs. Frances Trollope attended a ball in Cincinnati and declared, "Americans call their dances cotillions instead of quadrilles."[88] As late as 1846, the *Ball-Room Preceptor* stated, "The 'cotillion,' that once universal favorite in the ball-room has now also, in great measure been superseded, at least in name . . . its figures have been cut up to form new quadrilles."[89]

As with English country dances, all cotillions and quadrilles through the 1820s utilized a series of steps and step sequences that had an enormous range of technical difficulty. It was common for authors of dance manuals to list, if not fully describe, appropriate steps. Steps, in their suggested combinations for one quadrille figure, are presented in this collection by Alexander Strathy on pages 142–43. A French author, known as Gourdoux-Daux, also devoted a manual to the subject of steps and step combinations for cotillions or quadrilles.[90] The level of skill in early-nineteenth-century ballrooms was astonishingly high, and to get a full sense of the range of technical possibilities, the reconstructor is urged to consult Gourdoux-Daux's later 1819 and 1823 manuals.[91]

By the late 1840s dance technique had modified and few were attempting to perform technically difficult steps. Edward Ferrero noted in 1859 that the "quadrille of former times was adopted as a medium for the display of agility," and by the 1840s ladies and gentlemen were encouraged to walk or glide their way through the figures.[92]

"Calling" the figures, done by the master of ceremonies or dance band member, became a standard feature of quadrille performance. In 1827 Mrs. Trollope mentioned that the figures were "called from the orchestra in English, which has a very ludicrous effect on European ears."[93] Also critical of the practice, C. H. Cleveland, Jr., speculated, "It is to be hoped that the time will come when 'calling' will be obsolete in our ballrooms and parlors; and when the gentlemen who manage our social affairs will *all* be competent to conduct themselves and their partners through the mazes of the fashionable and popular dances without the assistance of a prompter."[94]

Many dance manuals throughout the century include directions for calling figures of quadrilles, and this collection includes quotations from *Howe's Complete Ball-Room Hand Book* on the art and rules of calling (see pp. 145–46).

An additional type of quadrille found in nineteenth-century ballrooms was the mazurka quadrille. The improvisitory nature of the original Polish or Russian mazurka made the dance unsuitable for nineteenth-century urban American ballrooms during an era when rules mandated that ladies and gentlemen look, act, and dance alike. However, put into the context of a quadrille, the mazurka became a very popular group dance. Danced with a variety of special steps, including those called *pas glissé, pas de basque, pas boiteux,* and *pas polonaise,* as well as the figures *kolo, tur sur place,* and *holubiec,* the mazurka quadrille utilized familiar quadrille figures as well as specialty figures. Descriptions of the steps and figures are available in Henry Cellarius's manual, *The Drawing Room Dances;* however, for additional information on the performance of steps and figures, the reader should consult P. Gawlikowski's *Guide Complet de la Danse* (Paris, 1858). Many nineteenth-century American manuals contained figures for the mazurka quadrille, including Charles Durang's *The Fashionable Dancer's Casket* and Edward Ferrero's *The Art of Dance.* This collection includes comment and a mazurka quadrille figure from an 1836 manual entitled *Hommage à Taglioni* (see p. 144).

The Cotillion, German Cotillion, or the German

During the 1840s, a new category of group dance became increasingly popular. Called "cotillion" (but not to be confused with the earlier dance of the same name), the dance was also known as the "German Cotillion," and eventually as the "German." The dance was a series of party game figures, led by a conductor or leader and played to a prescribed set of rules. Performed predominately to waltz music—although polka, mazurka, and galop music were also sometimes used—many figures were extracted from quadrilles; but other figures were games in the sense that there frequently was a "winner" or a "loser." A good description of the cotillion is given by Cellarius on pages 181–83. A number of cotillion figures, such as the Hoop (pp. 185–86), reveal that the decorum of the ballroom was often violated by extremely physical conduct during the performing of this dance.

The Ball-Room Preceptor gave but a single figure entitled "waltz cotillon" (p. 181); however, in 1847, Henri Cellarius provided 83 figures. At the height of the cotillion's popularity in the 1880s, Allen Dodworth supplied 250 figures to the readers of *Dancing and Its Relations to Education and Social Life*.

The importance of the leader or conductor was strongly emphasized in a number of dance and etiquette manuals. It was the leader's responsibility to organize the figures, choose the couples, and maintain order. Cellarius stated that the "fate of the cotillion is in a great measure in the hands of the conductor."[95] To deal with unruly participants, *Prof. Baron's Complete Instructor* advised the leader to "be firm and immovable and restore order to his ranks in a quiet but decisive manner."[96] William B. DeGarmo encouraged his readers to acquiesce to the leader, "however stupid or unadvisable" the commands might be.[97]

The primary venue for performing the German was at private parties, where "all should be upon terms of familiarity."[98] Some dance manuals suggested figures that would be appropriate at larger gatherings, but most authors felt that the German was "adaptable only to the performance of a limited company of intimate acquaintances, where merriment and even a little choice humor would rather advance than check the general enjoyment."[99] Many times this "choice humor" was at the expense of the gentlemen players. In describing a figure called "La Kangaroo" (also known as "The Fan"), C. H. Cleveland, Jr., asserted, "The figure is intended to create a hearty laugh at the expense of one gentleman at a time. . . . "[100]

The popularity of the German increased during the last quarter of the century, and it almost always appeared on the programs of private balls. Sometimes the German began after midnight, in which case the hostess was instructed to provide a "second supper of some sort."[101] On other occasions it was the only "dance" on the program.

The custom of giving favors to luncheon and dinner guests during the last twenty-five years of the century was also reflected in the German. Florence Hall stated, "It is the correct thing for a hostess to provide favors and bouquets for the german."[102] In awarding favors, William DeGarmo advised the leader not to give them all "to the beautiful and good dancers," but to "glance around and 'favor' those who seem to have been over looked."[103] Agreeing with this advice, Abby Longstreet stressed that it was the hostess's responsibility to "observe if any timid or unattractive guest receives a noticeably small number of these trifles."[104]

Mrs. John Sherwood, in her 1884 manual *Manners and Social Usages*, devoted eight pages to the subject of favors and some of her suggestions included: "White boxes covered with silk, in eight and six sided forms, with panel let in, on which are painted acorns and oak leaves, rose buds or lilies, and always the name or the cipher of the recipient. The opulent offer pretty satin fans painted with the recipients' monogram or else a fan which will match flowers and dress." In concluding her comments, Mrs. Sherwood stated, "Fans of lace, and of tortoise-shell and carved ivory and sandal-wood, are sometimes presented, but they are too ostentatious."[105]

Nevertheless, ostentatious favors appear to have been popular:

> *The German among ultra fashionable people of our larger cities at one time exercised an objectionable influ-*

ence on young people, from this extravagance of rivalry in the costliness of the "favors" presented during the performance of certain figures. Diamond rings and studs; fans of ivory and ostrich plumes, inlaid with gold and set with jewels; lace handkerchiefs, opera-chains, toilet-slippers, smoking-caps, and an infinity of other costly trifles,—were offered and accepted between ladies and gentlemen, who in many cases had no other excuses for the extravagance than those of purse pride and personal vanity.[106]

In any attempt to reconstruct and perform English country dances, cotillions, quadrilles, and the German, careful thought must be given not only to the social significance of each dance, but to the time frame of each dance's popularity. For example, the English country dance, with its capacity for a larger—namely, more democratic—participation, created an opportunity for participants to dance with everyone in the set. Therefore, it was more popular during the early nineteenth century, before class distinctions became more vigorously emphasized. The quadrille and early cotillion, on the other hand, offered the possibility of being more selective about one's dance partners. For many quadrille and cotillion figures, it was necessary, in fact, to dance with just an opposite or facing couple. *Manners and Tone of Good Society*, published in London in 1879 and available in the United States in 1880, described clearly how stewards, the representatives of each "class," would make sure that persons of differing stations in society were not placed facing each other, or presumably even in the same square.[107] *True Politeness, A Hand-book of Etiquette for Ladies* stated that, in attending public balls, it was "desirable to make up a party sufficiently large to render you independent of the introductions of the master of ceremonies, as, in spite of his best efforts, objectionable individuals will gain access to such."[108]

The German presents another set of dilemmas for the reconstructor. Dance and etiquette manuals placed great emphasis on decorum and deportment in carriage as well as admonishing participants to dance with ease, no matter how complicated the steps or figures. Contrasted with this protocol are requirements of many figures that included possible humiliation for men (The Fan, p. 182) and embarrassment for women (The Ladies Mocked, p. 182). Choice of partner for women, which was difficult under "normal" ballroom etiquette, was demonstrated in the figure, The Mirror (p. 186). An example of humor at the expense of the gentlemen's feelings was The Cushion (p. 182). Physical and possibly unbecoming ballroom demeanor would have been evident in The Rope (p. 185); The Race (p. 185) gave authority and dominance to women (as well as possibly inflicting physical pain on their gentlemen partners).

The lasting popularity of the German dictates that certain figures would have been appropriate at different times. The place of men and women in society and their attitudes toward each other changed with the decades. For example, the figure called The Race would not have been seen in the ballrooms of the 1840s during a time when women were considered delicate and in need of protection, and figures requiring elaborate props or ostentatious favors would have been appropriate only after the Civil War.

To a twentieth-century audience, many of the figures might be considered silly or quaint. (No doubt, with its props of whips and reins, The Race could be viewed today as very bizarre.) The German, however, was a true reflection of a changing society, and any reconstruction of its figures must take into serious consideration the time, place, and persons who performed it.

The Waltz

The biggest revolution in Western social dancing took place when the waltz broke away from the confines of the French contredanse during the last years of the eighteenth century, leaving men and women dancing together face to face. The term "valse" was used in 1778 to name a figure in several French contredanses, and this use of a turning motif within the context of group dances is the vehicle through which the waltz was introduced.[109]

During the 1790s music, titled "waltz" and usually composed in 3/8 meter, was published in France, England, and the United States. Although the waltz, as a separate dance, was known to have

been popular in New Orleans within the first few years of the nineteenth century, throughout most of the United States and England it continued to be performed as a figure of cotillions or country dances, well into the first decades of that century.

Once the waltz broke away from the context of group dances, round dancing in general, and specifically waltzing, were objected to for the indelicacy of the position. There were, however, other reasons. This "new" form of dancing did not require a viewing audience as did the "danses à deux" popular until the end of the eighteenth century; and, unlike English country dances, cotillions, or quadrilles, it did not seem to require any of the rules of social intercourse that governed the nineteenth-century ballroom.

The author of *The Mirror of the Graces* stated, "There is something in the close approximation of persons, in the attitudes, and in the motion, which ill agrees with the delicacy of women. . . . "[110] Most of the criticism regarding the waltz was, in fact, qualified; and a group of women designated as "delicate" were frequently urged not to participate: "There are, however, several dances that should be abandoned by very delicate women, on account of their causing too violent emotions or an agitation which produces vertigo and nervous symptoms."[111] Dio Lewis, founder of a school for women of "delicate constitution" in Lexington, Massachusetts, in 1866, advocated dancing, but not round dances, because "the rotary motion is injurious to the brain and spinal marrow."[112]

During the first forty years of the nineteenth century, walzing couples turned clockwise as partners while traveling counterclockwise around the room. This constant spinning, never reversing, could and did produce a feeling of euphoria—or, worse, vertigo—that could result in a loss of control. Vertigo and its effects on women while walzing were discussed by Donald Walker in 1836.

Vertigo is one of the great inconveniences of the waltz; and the character of this dance, its rapid turnings, the clasping of the dancers, their exciting contact, and the too quick and too long continued succession of lively and agreeable emotions, produce sometimes, in women of a very irritable constitution, syncopes, spasms and other accidents which should induce them to renounce it.[113]

Other writers did not object to the waltz so much in principle; but, just exactly *who* should experience the dance was often clearly defined: "Unmarried ladies should refrain from it altogether, both in public and private; very young married ladies, however, may be allowed to waltz in private balls, if it is very seldom, and with persons of their acquaintance."[114]

Along these lines, the author of *The Illustrated Manners Book* stated: "Those who believe that a woman should never come into any near personal contact with any gentleman but a near relation, or a probable or actual husband [while waltzing], must still object to this and all similar dances."[115] The author of this manual concluded with the following advice: "A woman especially ought to be very sure that the man she walzes with is one worthy of so close an intimacy; and one who understands her nature and relations well, will not waltz with any other."[116]

An excellent description of the early-nineteenth-century waltz was provided by Thomas Wilson in his 1816 treatise, *A Description of the Correct Method of Walzing, the Truly Fashionable Species of Dancing*. Wilson's descriptions clearly indicate that, by this date, the waltz in England was a fully developed dance. Wilson described two kinds: "French" and "German" waltzing. Under the category of French waltzing he noted three different "classes": The Slow French Waltz, The Sauteuse Waltz, and The Jette or Quick Sauteuse Waltz. (Wilson's Slow French Waltz is quoted on p. 158.) The footwork for Wilson's Slow French Waltz, a 5-step combination turning one-half revolution every three counts, provided the framework for numerous descriptions found throughout the nineteenth century. (See, for example, Edward Ferrero's 1859 description of "The Step of the Waltz," p. 159.) It should be noted that a 6-step variant was also included in a number of nineteenth-century manuals during the first half of the century, and Carlo Blasis's 6-step waltz is given for comparison on pages 158–59. The 5- or 6-step waltz was performed in a strict configuration: couples danced in a large circle that moved counterclockwise around the room.

By the 1840s ballroom dance technique was growing simpler and the 5- or the 6-step waltz, both now commonly called the "valse à trois temps," was gradually replaced by a new variation called the "waltz à deux temps." In 1847 Cellarius allowed that the "Waltze à Deux Temps" was "more generally adopted" and regretted that the "old waltze should have so fallen into disuse."[117] Essentially a chasse or galopade step, it appears to have been easier to master than the valse à trois temps and was most likely often performed by the more untutored ballroom dancers. For this popular 6-step waltz, Cellarius gives the following straightforward directions for the footwork: "to glissade with one foot, and to chasser with the other."[118] This waltz, which turned on the chassé, could reverse direction, thereby availing the dancers of the ability to make left-hand turns. (The valse à trois temps turned only to the right.) Also, since it was no longer necessary to make a complete revolution every 6-counts, the valse à deux temps allowed couples, if they so desired, to turn less often as well as to dance in all parts of the ballroom. They were no longer confined to the strict circle of couples dictated by the valse à trois temps.

There were, however, criticisms, and *The Ball-Room Guide* made the following comments on the "Valse à Deux Temps": "Unfortunately, there are few dances which have amongst their pledged admirers such a vast assemblage of bad dancers as the Valse à Deux Temps. Its rapid *temps* induces many youths [to drag] their partners round in a wild scramble, with a total disregard of time and step."[119]

In 1885 Edward Scott commented that the deux temps was "little else than a galop performed to waltz music; it is rarely heard and we are fortunate in being rid of such an ungraceful movement."[120]Allen Dodworth also echoed this late-century criticism in referring to the deux temps as the "Ignoramus Waltz."[121]

A new element began to appear in the waltzes of the 1860s, an exaggerated bending of the legs, later referred to as "dipping." *The Ball-Room Guide and Call-Book,* in describing the "Glide Waltz," stated, "with the exception of the bending motion, it is identical with the plain waltz."[122] The same manual describes another dance, "The Boston Dip," as "an exaggeration of the Glide Waltz, each glide being accompanied by a considerable bend of the knee, which causes the whole body to sink down."[123] Although frequently criticized by writers (*The Ball-Room Guide and Call Book* felt the movements of the Boston Dip to be ungraceful and ungainly), the dance's popularity increased, and most likely it was taught by all dancing masters. For example, though dancing master Allen Dodworth commented that the Boston Dip is a "childish form of waltzing, scarcely worthy of adults,"[124] he does give a cursory description of it in his manual.

During the 1840s there were a great number of step variations for the waltz, some of which retained popularity to the end of the century. Many of these variations were based on ballroom mazurka steps, which enriched the waltz with interesting rhythmic patterns. This collection quotes directions from Edward Ferrero's 1859 manual for the polka redowa, polka mazourka, and zingirella (see pp. 162 and 170).

Despite changes of step and style and endurance of criticism, the waltz retained its essential identity throughout the century. In 1885 Allen Dodworth summed up the signature dance of the nineteenth century:

> *We have now arrived at the culmination of modern society dancing, the dance which has for fifty years resisted every kind of attack, and is today the most popular known. From palace to hovel its fascination is supreme, and it is truly worthy of this universal love, for no other dance so fully gratifies the sense of rhythmical motion as the modern waltz with its poetic time and phrasing.*[125]

Fashion

Women

New printing technologies, aided by a developing railroad system, enhanced the popularity of inexpensive fashion magazines, which carried illustrations and descriptions of the latest Parisian fashions to ladies throughout the United States. Mechanical improvements—such as the early-century English invention of a lace-making machine known as the Jacquard loom, Elias Howe's mid-century invention of the sewing machine, as well as the Mays sewing machine, which created a market for ready-made shoes—all contributed to the creation of an enormous market for inexpensive yet fashionable clothing. Stylish clothing that could be made at home with factory-made or entirely store-bought fabrics was well within the financial means of many Americans by the end of the first half of the nineteenth century.

"Gentlemen and gentlewomen do not array themselves in garments that are not appropriate," proclaimed Abby Longstreet.[126] Indeed, proper attire was a battle cry that echoed throughout all etiquette manuals published after the first quarter of the century, and the importance of appropriate dress for particular times of day or evening was clearly defined. "The difference between morning and evening dress should be distinctly marked,"[127] and fashion guidelines mandated differences be-

Figure 2

tween morning dress, dress for afternoon or promenading, and dress for visiting. Evening dress was often divided between correct dress for dinner and that correct for a party or ball.

The importance of clothing classifications, as well as late-nineteenth-century emphasis on opulence, was dramatically documented in John H. Young's 1879 *Our Deportment.* His chapter on dress included twenty-four separate discussions regarding appropriate garments for: evening dress, ball dress, full dinner dress, dress of hostess at a dinner party, dress for receiving calls, carriage dress, visiting costumes, dress for morning calls, morning dress for street, the promenade dress, opera dress, riding dress, walking suit, dress for ladies of business, ordinary evening dress, dress for social party, dress for church, dress for theater, dress for lectures and concerts, croquet, archery, and skating costume, bathing costume, traveling dress, wedding dress, and mourning dress.[128]

Regarding the ladies who summered in Saratoga during the 1880s, Italian visitor Carlo Gardini declared, "The alpha and omega of their daily routine is to rise, to eat, to talk, to change their costumes three or four times and to sleep."[129] Although few but the very rich could afford to change their attire several times a day, advice such as is found in *Our Deportment* and other manuals reinforced and established unequivocal aspirations for middle-class ladies.

During the nineteenth century fashion fell totally within a woman's sphere and, in an era when styles changed frequently and rapidly, only two elements remained constant: the outline of a lady's dress was shaped by petticoats, crinolines, or bustles, and her silhouette was molded by a corset.

1800–1820

[See figs. 3 and 4]

During the late eighteenth century dress styles attempted to imitate Greek and Roman statues, and early-nineteenth-century dress and hairstyles continued to reflect the general curiosity about the civilizations of antiquity. Early-nineteenth-century

Figure 3

Figure 4

dresses had ankle-length skirts, medium-high waists, short sleeves, and low, V-shaped, round, or square necks. Trains or demi-trains were frequently found on ball dresses, although *The Mirror of the Graces* commented that they were "too cumbrous an appendage to dance."[130]

Hairstyles were modeled after Greek, Roman, even Egyptian fashions, with light curls on the forehead and the fullness behind the head or short hair with ringlets or curls. Twisted and flat curls or braids were popular toward the end of the first decade, and hair ornaments for balls included jewelry, bandeaux, turbans, and wreaths of grapes.

After 1810, dress waistlines rose higher and shortened skirts became A-shaped; sleeves were small and puffed. Borders of ribbon, pleats, and flounces ornamented dress hemlines. During the early teens, many ball gowns were also made with over-dresses of net or fine lace. Ball dresses were made from stiffer fabrics in contrast to the softer muslins and cottons of earlier years.

Long hair became increasingly popular and full ringlets began to appear near the sides of the face. Hair ornaments for balls included flowers, turbans, and ostrich feathers.

Evening shoes for the first twenty years of the century were flat and made of satin, soft leather, or silk. Gloves were long, ending above the elbow.

Although a few fashionable women may have chosen not to wear corsets during this era, it seems likely that the majority felt more comfortable wearing something to assist in molding the narrow, thin silhouette which characterized these fashions.

1820–1830

[See fig. 5]
The predominant fashion alteration during this decade was a gradual lowering of the waistline. Sleeves for ball gowns, while remaining short, grew wider. Skirts became very full and were supported by numerous petticoats. Skirt pleating was concentrated at the back of the dress and was occasionally supported by rolls of cotton attached to an under-petticoat.

By 1827 the descending waistline reached its natural level and corsets became short and heavily boned and worn by all fashionable women.

Figure 5

To balance the ever expanding skirts and sleeves, hairstyles for evening consisted of long, large loops placed on the top of the head. Ornaments included flowers, bows, and feathers. Flat shoes, with square toes by the end of the decade, were laced with ribbons. Gloves were elbow-length or slightly shorter.

1830–1840

[See figs. 6 and 16]
Necklines in the 1830s continued to be high and set straight across the upper chest. The skirt lengthened and increased in width, and by the mid-1830s, dress bodices were pointed at the waistline. Ball-dress sleeves, which had grown more ample by 1830, decreased in size and were shortened; some sleeves simply drooped halfway down the upper arm.

Figure 6

Mrs. Alexander Walker, in her 1840 Americanized version of a British beauty manual, *Female Beauty* (pp. 67–68), gives an excellent description of three versions of ballroom attire worn in the late 1830s.

Foreign visitors to the United States often commented on the splendor of the ladies' garments, as did Isidore Löwenstern during his 1837 tour of North America: "The Philadelphia ladies are always luxuriously dressed, whether it be to go out to parties in the evening, or just to stay at home. The every day garments, even of the middle classes, are made of silks and of the richest cloths. As for the wealthy, they shine in the most elegant dresses, particularly their evening gowns."[131]

Fashion styles throughout the nineteenth century were dominated by French tastes, as Löwenstern observed, "They make it a point to follow the Paris fashions exactly."[132]

By the mid-1830s hair for evening parties and balls was worn close to the head with curls in front or parted with plaited braids behind. Curls at the sides of the face and back knots were increasingly found throughout the thirties and the use of false hair gained in popularity. Evening hair ornaments included combs, ribbons, feathers, and jewelry.

Beginning in the 1830s, criticism began to mount in etiquette and beauty books regarding the perils of wearing a tightly laced corset. *The Young Lady's Friend* felt that "few girls are aware of the force they employ when they lace their corsets,"[133] and *The Art of Good Behaviour* stated in no uncertain terms, "No woman who laces tight can have good shoulders, a straight spine, good lungs, sweet breath or is fit to be a wife and mother."[134] English writer John Robert Godley also commented on the tight-waisted fashions of the late 1830s and 1840s:

> *The Parisian fashions of the day are carried out to their extreme, detestably ugly as they are. Really the modern European (and American) costume gives a woman the appearance of something between a trussed fowl and an hour-glass . . . she is compressed in the waist, and puffed out above and below it, to such an extreme that one expects her to break off in the middle at the slightest touch.*[135]

But in spite of continuing condemnation, a tightly laced corset remained a standard part of women's clothing throughout the century.

1840–1850

[See figs. 7, 20, and 21]

Early in the 1840s a new method was devised for pleating and attaching straight sections of fabric to a dress bodice, which created the distinctive bowl-like look that prevailed throughout the decade. As skirts became fuller, ladies increasingly made use of multiple, stiffened petticoats. Hemlines reached the floor and evening shoes were elongated but kept their square toes. The elaborate skirt ornamentation so popular in the twenties and thirties was modified and simplified, but after the mid-forties flounces of matching fabric or lace began to appear. Bodice drapings of light-weight fabric,

Figure 7

known as "berthas," were popular on ball gowns, which had necklines cut low and off the shoulder. Sleeves were short and set well below the shoulder, making arm movement difficult. Ball dresses were frequently made in plain, light-colored fabrics, and short gloves completed the ensemble.

Evening hairstyles were smooth with center parts. Side hair was looped over the ears or worn in long ringlets. The back hair was wound into a knot, which moved down toward the back of the neck as the decade progressed; artificial hair continued to be popular. The 1840s also saw an increased use of artificial paints and powders for the face.

A twentieth-century author has described the 1840s as an era characterized by "modesty and reticence,"[136] and another fashion historian contends that the decade was the "dullest . . . in the history of feminine dress."[137] Certainly the political turmoil that plagued France and the rest of Europe during this period had little influence on Parisian fashion statements. It is important to note that however bland these fashions may seem to twentieth-century writers, in an era characterized by sentimentality the simple lines and minimal dress and hair ornamentation were meant to symbolize the inner purity and sincerity of the wearer. During a time when socioeconomic trends had forced women to redefine their domestic responsibilities and place in society, a dependence on others was certainly reinforced by the clothing of this decade. Tightly laced corsets under bodices, which now fastened in the back, as well as sleeves that allowed little arm movement, made it next to impossible for a woman even to dress herself.

1850–1860

[See fig. 8]

Flounced skirts with an ever-increasing width characterized evening dresses of the 1850s and created a more dynamic and solid look, in contrast to the frailty of the 1840s. Many stiffened, quilted, or horsehair petticoats were required to support the expanding skirts, and in 1856 the crinoline, a petticoat of rigid hoops in the form of a wire cage, was introduced. Although impractical for sitting, walking through doors, and getting in and out of carriages, the crinoline dominated the shape of skirts for the next ten years. At the peak of its popularity, dress circumferences were reported to be more than twenty feet.[138] Sarah Hale, author of *Manners; or Happy Homes and Good Society*, commented that although the crinoline had been carried to an extreme, it did have the rare virtue of preventing dresses from dragging on the floor. Mrs. Hale did suggest, however, that women wear smaller hoops when walking or getting into carriages to "thus prevent much inconvenience to . . . fellow travellers."[139]

Short, small sleeves continued to dominate

Figure 8

evening dresses, and bodice bottoms retained their points. Gloves remained wrist-length.

By 1852 elaborately waved side hair replaced ringlets, but the center part and back knot remained. During the mid-1850s, short curls began to trail down the back of the neck and wreaths were common ornaments for evening hairstyles. Although flat shoes continued to be worn with evening wear, small heels of one inch or less appeared in the early 1850s and became even more popular after the introduction of the crinoline. Fashion was enhanced by newly developed aniline dyes, which made colorful evening dresses popular by the early 1860s.

1860–1870

[See fig. 9]

During the early 1860s the shape of the crinoline was modified by flattening in the front and the skirt once again became A-shaped. Double skirts were popular and the lower skirt frequently extended into a train. To augment the growing emphasis of fabric at the back of the dress, some fashions dispensed entirely with the crinoline and utilized small hoops to support just the back of the dress.

The fascination with false hair, fashionable since the 1830s, reached the height of its popularity in the elaborate hairstyles that dominated the late 1860s. Back hair was frequently wound over pads, with two long curls hanging down the back, and stiff, pinned curls were popular for evening. Gloves for evening increased in length and, by the end of the decade, evening shoes had heels of an inch-and-a-half.

1870–1880

[See figs. 10 and 11]

A bustle or horsehair pad dominated dress shapes of the 1870s. By 1874, bodices had lengthened and fit snugly over the hips, resulting in the reintroduction of long corsets. Sleeves remained short,

Figure 9

and necklines were usually rounded, low, and off-the-shoulder. The backs of the dresses often cascaded down into trains, and hooks or bunches of artificial flowers were frequently utilized by ladies to hold them up while they were dancing. At the same time, many dancing masters recommended that ball dresses be made without trains. For example, Professor Bland stated in 1870 that "in having dresses made long, care should be taken that they be not so long as to touch the ground."[140] *Offenbach's Dancing Without a Master* declared, "Dresses should be short enough to clear the ground. We would ask [ladies] whether it is not better to accept this slight deviation from an absurd fashion, than to appear for three parts of the evening in a torn and pinned-up skirt?"[141] C. H. Cleveland, Jr., stated that a gentleman "should understand the engineering of 'trains' in all their most extravagant curves, lengths, and contortions." (He also reminded gentlemen to "always apologize when you step on a lady's train.")[142] The author of *Manners and Tone of Good Society* commented that it was a breach of decorum for a lady to "permit her partner to assist her in holding up her dress while dancing."[143]

Elaborate hairstyles continued to be popular

Figure 10

Figure 11

during the early years of the decade, but by the mid-1870s, evening hairstyles consisted of a large knot at the back of the head, with loose curls or braids falling on the neck. Headdresses of flowers and ferns as well as combs were popular ornaments. By the end of the decade, short curls enhanced by heat or chemicals embellished the forehead, with an emphasis on very curly front hair. Elbow-length gloves and heeled shoes completed a lady's ballroom ensemble.

1880–1890

[See figs. 12 and 13]

The slimmer outline continued into the early 1880s, when another form of bustle was introduced. Producing a much harsher profile, this bustle increased in size until 1887, then began immediately to shrink, and by 1889 had disappeared altogether. Colors for evening dresses intensified, and dressmakers frequently combined several color combinations. Suggested colors for an evening dress included one of purple, scarlet, blue, yellow, and black, and another of mulberry, yellow, silvery gray, and light green.[144]

Pointed toes became standard on evening shoes, with one-and-a-half to two-inch French heels (set close to the arch of the foot). Hair was simple in the 1880s with little emphasis on false hair. Variations on forehead fringe with back knot were ornamented by asymmetrically placed flowers, combs, or ostrich feathers to harmonize with the sometimes asymmetrically draped dresses. Gloves were elbow-length or longer.

Dress and Dance

The changing shape and volume of dresses were directly related to the ease with which a lady could dance, and the waltz can be used as an example of parallel changes in fashion and dance.

At the end of the eighteenth century skirts were full and the tempo of the waltz was rapid. The tempo slowed down after the first years of the nineteenth century and a lady's dress was tubular and narrow. The slower tempo of the "Slow Waltz," described by Thomas Wilson in 1816 (p. 158), complemented the architecture of the narrow skirts. Fuller skirts, which began appearing at the end of the teens and reached their height of fullness in the fashions of the 1830s through the early 1860s, paralleled the increasing tempo of the waltz and also complemented the circular nature of the whirling dance. As full skirts gave way to the trains and bustles of the later 1860s through 1880s, whirling in rapid circles yielded to a more pendulum-like box-step waltz.

Likewise, the shorter length of the dresses during the first three decades, as well as the tight pantaloons worn by the men, enabled dancers fully to maneuver their legs and feet in performing intricate quadrille, cotillion, and reel steps. After the

Figure 12

Figure 13

1850s, when feats of agility were discouraged in the ballroom, crinolined, trained, or bustled ladies glided or walked their way through the figures of a dance, laced tightly into restrictive corsets.

Gentlemen

As was the case with women's fashion, nineteenth-century men's clothing was based on European ideals; but, unlike women's dress, ballroom costume for men remained static and conservative. Plain, dark clothing was already an accepted standard by 1800, and while women's dress changed decade by decade, one fashion observer noted that men's fashion maintained a "republican simplicity."[145]

"The dress of a gentleman should be such as not to excite any special observation, unless it be for neatness and propriety,"[146] declared Edward Ferrero; and the author of *Mixing in Society* stated, "a gentleman should always be so well dressed, that his dress shall never be observed at all."[147] Simplicity of ballroom dress was best summed up by *The Ball-Room Guide, a Handy Manual*, when it stated that a gentleman "shall always be attired in a black dress suit in the evening, only allowing him a white waist-coat as an occasional relief to his toilet."[148] (In an unusual criticism of the standard ballroom attire for gentlemen, Abba Woolson felt that men's fashions were "compact, simple, and serviceable," but that they were "an insult to woman's aesthetic tastes" and there was "no excuse for intruding it upon elegant, social assemblies.")[149]

As with women's fashions, etiquette manuals also stressed the importance of appropriate cloth-

Figure 14

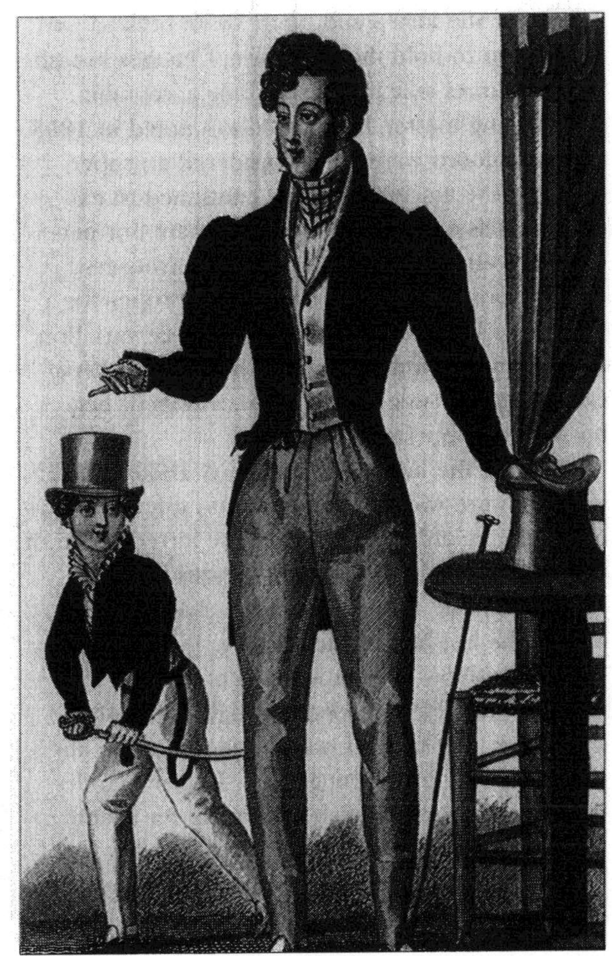

Figure 15

ing for men. However, gentlemen dressed only in morning or evening attire. *Our Deportment,* which presented women with twenty-four categories of clothing, concurred with those two choices for men. In addition, manuals were usually straightforward in their instructions: "Wear frock-coats in the streets, dress-coats in the dining or drawing room."[150] "Don't wear evening dress in the morning, or on any occasion before six o'clock dinner."[151] *Manners, Good and Bad* elaborated only slightly: "a man must wear a dress suit at an evening party, or when calling and never by day. . . . A frock coat, or cutaway, the former preferred . . . is the visiting and afternoon or morning reception dress in good society."[152]

During the first fifteen years of the century short knee-breeches were gradually replaced by close-fitting, ankle-length pantaloons. By the midteens, pantaloons, called "trousers," reached to the top of the instep and, until 1850, utilized an understrap to hold them in place. Changes in fashion sometimes take time to become acceptable, and dancing master Thomas Wilson noted in 1808 that pantaloons were not "considered a proper dress for the assembly."[153] He continued to express criticism in 1816: "Gentlemen are not permitted to enter the Ball Room in . . . trousers . . . nor are loose pantaloons considered proper for a Full Dress Ball."[154] While there was little variation in trouser-leg width during the period, *The Art of Good Behaviour* was critical of "extravagant bell bottoms and puckered waists."[155]

During the late 1850s and early 1860s, black trousers were wider at the waist and gradually narrowed to the ankle. Other than the introduction of the fly front in 1850 and pant creases in the 1890s, the style of men's trousers changed little during the last half of the century.

The swallowtail coat was accepted dress for both day and evening wear through the 1840s. Thereafter, the tailcoat was considered to be appropriate only for evening dress. In some circles the dinner jacket was also acceptable for evening wear during the 1880s.

Reflecting the shape of women's fashions, tailcoats had high waists with snug pantaloons during the early years of the nineteenth century. As women's sleeves became fuller in the 1820s, tailcoats countered with fuller shoulders balanced by wider pants. Waistlines rounded in the 1860s, and this style remained for the rest of the century. Dark blue, green, brown, and black were worn until the 1860s, when black became the standard color for evening.

The frock coat, sometimes called a riding coat, appeared during the mid-teens and soon became a popular option for day wear. Frock coats were occasionally worn in the ballroom but were considered unacceptable by most writers. *The Gentleman and Lady's Book of Politeness* stated, "a gentleman who would appear in a riding coat and boots would pass for a person of bad *ton.*"[156] Another author declared that "frock coats and boots may be worn by spectators . . . but should a gentleman attempt to dance with either, he would probably be requested to withdraw from his position in the set."[157] *The Art of Good Behaviour* elaborated on frock coats, which it said were to be "worn in the morning, riding or walking, but never at evening visits, or at weddings, balls, parties, or the opera."[158]

Single-breasted vests, frequently referred to as waistcoats, were long with pointed fronts through the 1840s. By 1860, the waistlines were shorter, reflecting the cut of the tailcoat. Shirts were made of linen with high collars, and after 1850 tucks or pleats replaced ornamented front-openings. *The Art of Good Behaviour* warned gentlemen to "avoid all finical bosoms, ruffles, and lace-work fopperies."[159] Until the 1840s a white evening tie was folded and wrapped around the neck. While there was a vogue for wearing black ties with evening wear during the 1840s, a white tie was reestablished by the 1850s. For the remaining years of the nineteenth century, a narrow, sometimes tapered, one-inch white cravat was tied into a bow or knotted.

Low-heeled black shoes or pumps were traditional for evening wear. During the early years of the century, boots were popular for day but not considered appropriate for ballrooms. "No person is permitted to Dance in Boots or Gaiters."[160] In *An Analysis of Country Dancing* Thomas Wilson also admonished, "No gentleman must enter the ballroom with whole or half boots."[161]

"Balls and parties require white or light kid

gloves."[162] "Never be seen without gloves in a ballroom."[163] Indeed, gloves were the most frequently described accessory for men during the nineteenth century, and *A Gentleman's Book* suggested that gentlemen carry two pairs to a ball, "as in the contact with dark dresses, or in handling refreshments, you may soil the pair you wear . . . and will thus be under the necessity of offering your hand covered by a soiled glove, to some fair partner."[164] Abby Longstreet stated that when a gentleman was to dance, "the wearing of gloves is *de rigueur*,"[165] and *Our Etiquette* pointed to practical reasons for wearing gloves. "The perspiration on the hand from dancing will ruin a lady's dress when gloves are not worn. . . . "[166]

Daniel R. Shafer's treatise *Secrets of Life Unveiled; or Book of Fate*, which included standard comments on etiquette as well as discussing such subjects as "The Significance of Moles," and "Dreams, with Their True Interpretations," includes "Glove Flirtations." As if there were not already enough rules to remember, Shafer suggested that by learning this "language," one could communicate such emotions as "I wish to be rid of you very soon," by biting the tips of the gloves, and "I hate you," simply by turning the gloves inside out."[167]

Conclusion

To a twentieth-century audience, much of nineteenth-century dance and its surrounding ceremonies and customs can appear innocent or quaint. But this view results from judging one age by the expectations and experiences of another. As we draw toward the end of our own century, we have only to view Hollywood movies or attend the ever-popular Renaissance fairs to see that interpretations of past eras are distorted by contemporary idealizations of them. For example, Renaissance dance is usually seen as having been "slow and stately." Highly developed eighteenth-century dance is usually represented only by country dances, which are merely walked through without any notion of style, step, or technique. Most performances are given in costumes that rarely approximate the proper cut, boning, and style of that age. Many modern "interpretations" of these dances require that partners hold their arms shoulder high, and are thus oblivious to or choose to ignore the constraints often imposed by the costume of the time. (Ironically, this was *exactly* how ladies and gentlemen of the late nineteenth century interpreted these Renaissance and Baroque dances!)

Within the past fifteen years or so, interest in "recreating" nineteenth-century balls has flowered. Like the dance of previous centuries, that of the nineteenth century was fully integrated into its society and culture. It existed in and interacted as part of its culture rather than as an independent system. Studies of nineteenth century dance are not complete until they take into account the culture as a whole. Just as one could never fully appreciate the swimming abilities of a fish by observing it only on dry land, never in its proper environment, and would, as a result, find its flopping about and wide, gaping mouth quaint, odd, or amusing, so would one fail to appreciate nineteenth-century dance if one were to limit oneself only to a list of dances and steps—or, worse, to a "feeling" of how it might have been performed.

With this in mind, I have chosen for this volume not only materials concerned directly with dance, but also materials ancillary to it, in the hope and expectation that nineteenth-century dance will, as a result, be understood more as those who practiced it understood it. In other words, I have tried to keep the fish in water.

On with the dance! let joy be unconfined;

No sleep till morn, when Youth and Pleasure meet

To chase the glowing Hours with flying feet . . .

Lord Byron, *Childe Harold's Pilgrimage, Canto III, st. 22*

"Oh! my dear Mr. Bennet," as she entered the room, "we have had a most delightful evening, a most excellent ball. I wish you had been there. Jane was so admired, nothing could be like it. Every body said how well she looked; and Mr. Bingley thought her quite beautiful, and danced with her twice. Only think of that *my dear; he actually danced with her twice; and she was the only creature in the room that he asked a second time."*

Jane Austen, *Pride and Prejudice*

"Do you waltz?" she asked me suddenly.

"I do," I replied, a little taken aback.

"Well, come along then—come along. I'll ask my brother to play us a waltz. Let us imagine that we are flying, that we've grown wings."

She ran into the house. I ran after her, and a few moments later we were spinning round in a narrow room to the sweet sounds of a Lanner waltz. Assya waltzed beautifully, with enthusiasm. . . . For a long time afterwards my hand felt the touch of her yielding waist; for a long time I heard her quickened, close breathing; for a long time I imagined I could see her dark, immobile, almost closed eyes in a pale but animated face, sharply outlined by fluttering curls.

Ivan Turgenev, "Assya," from *First Love and Other Tales*

Dancing, the Most Enchanting of Human Amusements

Part 1: The Utility of Dancing

I am an advocate for dancing, because it has a tendency to refine the manners and behaviour of young people, and I am persuaded that if the art is kept under proper regulations, it would be a mechanic way of implanting insensibly into minds, not capable of receiving it so well by any other rules, a sense of good breeding and virtue.

Saltator,
A Treatise on Dancing
(Boston, 1802), 34–35

In short, Dancing is the most enchanting of all human amusements, it is the parent of joy, and the soul and support of cheerfulness; it banishes grief, cheers the evening hours of those who have studied or laboured in the day, and brings with it a mixture of delightful sensations which enrapture the senses.

Any pleasure carried to an extreme is dangerous, and ought to be checked; for, whether dancing, music, theatricals, drinking, gaming, hunting or shooting, it is no matter if it causes us to neglect those concerns on which our happiness or prosperity depends.

But Dancing in itself is as harmless as the frisking of the infant lamb across its native fields, it is merely action accompanied to time; not but jumping or running might answer all the good purposes resulting from Dancing as an exercise; but mankind, naturally indolent, are rarely tempted to rise from any sedentary employment to run or jump, independent of the ridicule that would attend such conduct; but Dancing being accompanied by music has such attractions, is such a stimulus to action, that between the fascination of sound, and the fear of being thought incapable, we can begin and continue to Dance, without feeling ourselves in any degree tried, twice the time we could employ ourselves in any other way, divested of the charms that amusement affords us.

T. Wilson,
An Analysis of Country Dancing
(London, 1808), vi-x

As dancing is the accomplishment most calculated to display a fine form, elegant taste, and graceful carriage to advantage; so towards it our regards must be particularly turned: and we shall find that when Beauty in all her power is to be set forth, she cannot choose a more effective exhibition.

By the word *exhibition*, it must not be understood that I mean to insinuate any thing like that scenic exhibition which we may expect from professors of the art, who often, regardless of modesty, not only display the symmetry of their persons, but indelicately expose them, by most improper dresses and attitudes, on the public stage. What I propose by calling dancing an elegant mode of showing a fine form to advantage, has nothing more in it than to teach the lovely young woman to move unembarrassed and with peculiar grace through the mazes of a dance, performed either in a private circle or public ball.

The Mirror of the Graces,
By a Lady of Distinction
(New York, 1813), 164–65

Dancing, however unscientifically it may at present be cultivated, is in reality the first of the fine arts, or that which involves the general and actual use of the muscular motions of the body, which are imitated by sculpture and painting. Scientifically practised, it is obvious that this art would not be inferior in expression to those which are merely imitative.

Dancing contributes greatly to improve the figure. When habitually practised, it increases the strength, the suppleness and the agility of the body. The shoulders and arms then fall farther back; the limbs become stronger and more supple; the feet turn more outward; and the walk assumes a particular character of firmness and lightness.

Dancing also renders the deportment more easy and agreeable, and the motions more free and graceful. Those, indeed, who learn to dance when very young, acquire an ease of motion that can be gained in no other way; and if a habit of moving gracefully is then acquired, it is never lost.

To be useful to health, dancing must not be engaged in immediately after a meal, nor be continued whole nights, nor in places confined in proportion to the number of dancers. In these places, there is frequently a great quantity of dust, which, joined to animal exhalations, and carried with the atmospheric air into the lungs, contributes with the slightest cause, the least chill, to create irritation in these parts. These become the more serious, because, young people, especially of the female sex, are very careful to conceal the commencement of these affections, lest they interfere with their views of pleasure.

Dancing is an excellent exercise for females, because it powerfully counterbalances the injurious effects of their sedentary occupations. It is particularly suited to females in whom ennui and inaction have produced habitual indisposition, to those who are of a lymphatic temperament, but more especially to young persons in whom the appearance of the phenomena peculiar to their sex and age is slow, who are subject to irregularities, and even to symptoms of chlorosis. In this case, more confidence may be put in dancing than in the list of formulas that ignorance and quackery set forth. Indeed, this exercise of the dance, to which young females resign themselves sometimes with great difficulty, forms, in addition to a tonic regimen and delicate attentions, the most suitable treatment for chloratic affections.

Donald Walker,
Exercises for Ladies
(London, 1836), 116, 145–48

It would be to no purpose to enlarge upon the necessity of dancing, for the general and extensive practice of it, in all ranks of society, stands as the best proof of its need. In the ages of chivalry, when the knights-errant made woman the day-star of their wanderings and hardships, their whole and long-sought reward was the laurel of the chosen queen of beauty at the tournament, and the ball in the evening was the field in which the man of glory received his honour in the approving look of a woman. Christianity raised woman from slavery, and placed her on an equality with man; and chivalry, by the tournaments and balls, to commemorate victories, raised her above man to the loftiness and nobleness almost of a divinity. Balls and parties then became the fields where woman wields her mighty influence. There she appears vested with the splendour of her mighty power—there she *reigns*; her reign is one of beauty and modesty—there she inspires with tenderness, elegance, and gentleness. She appears there as a messenger to dispel man's gloom and sorrow, her presence bringing all hearts with an endearing tie, adds vivid colours to the pleasures of the evening. She appears there—what she is born for—a gentle soother throughout the transient joys and sorrows of this life, and a noble guider to faith, hope and happiness.

Every victory, every glorious achievement, every great invention, enterprize or reform, is always now solemnized by a ball, and the greatest *point*, then, is to have plenty of ladies. "What world this would be without woman?—a world without the sun!" Let therefore the sun shine upon us brightly in all his mighty splendour, and let women remember that, as they cannot command nor rule it, they must charm and influence it, which they only can do by availing themselves of all those lively and innocent accomplishments, through means of which they may exert their influence. Dancing thus stands as one of the most important accomplishments, not so of itself, but because it draws, invisibly and gently after it, other accomplishments, which are indispensable in the highest and educated spheres of society.

Madame Zuingle,
Petits Secrets of Dancing
(Edinburgh, 1848), [5]–8

Ease, gentleness and dignity of carriage are necessarily the accompaniments of motion, when the mind has been rightly directed, and its impulses regulated by a refined conception; whilst from a false one, or where the ideal standard is low, uncouthness and *gaucherie* are the only results. Thus it cannot be considered surprising that dancing has become so essential a characteristic of modern education, however rarely the high tone here suggested has been impressed upon the pupil, so much conducive to a pleasing exterior being involved in its cultivation. Its tendency to elevate the mind, whilst it invigorates the energies of the body, renders it a fit medium for the display of the high animal spirits and mental buoyancy so natural to youth, and therefore the worthiest amusement for relaxation from severe studies and occupations.

Francis Mason,
A Treatise on the Use and Peculiar Advantages of Dancing
(London, 1854), 7–8

It may be prejudice, perhaps, but we know of no more pleasing spectacle than a well appointed ball; we, of course, allude to select private assemblies, where refinement and courtesy prevail; where elegant dressing and fine taste are apparent, and where grace and easy carriage are the predominating characteristics.

Edward Ferrero,
The Art of Dancing
(New York, 1859), 74

There are few amusements more enjoyable than an evening spent at an evening party. There is however one accomplishment that is essential because a large part of the time is devoted to it, that is dancing. We are well aware that there are those who object to dancing, on moral grounds. This is not a proper place to discuss its right and wrong but as it is now countenanced and looked upon as an innocent amusement by all fair minded people and in as much as no one can appear well in society without some knowledge of it, we recommend it most highly.

Hudson K. Lyverthey,
Our Etiquette and Social Observances
(Grand Rapids, Mich., 1881), 56–57

Part 2: Acquiring the Steps

With regard to the dance of society, the manner of it is very much altered in this country. Formerly, for example, they danced cotillons, allemands, minuets and ballets, the modern practice is confined to the reel, country-dance and jig. It would appear quite unfashionable to introduce any kind of cotillon-step in the present stile of dancing; a quick movement must therefore be adopted, in order to accord in time with the rapidity of the music. A multiplicity of steps or violent exertions must also be avoided, as they would only tend to fatigue the dancer, render him weak and incapable of continuing any length of time.

James P. Cassidy,
A Treatise on the Theory and Practice of Dancing *(Dublin, 1810), 62–63*

Extraordinary as it may seem, at a period when dancing is so entirely neglected by men in general, women appear to be taking the most pains to acquire the art. Our female youth are now not satisfied with what used to be considered a *good dancing-master*; that is, one who made teaching his sole profession; but now our girls must be taught by the leading dancers at the Opera-house.

The consequence is, when a young lady rises to dance, we no longer see the graceful easy step of the gentlewoman, but the laboured, and often indelicate exhibitions of the posture-mistress—Dances from *ballets* are introduced; and instead of the jocund and beautifully-organized movements of hilarity in concord, we are shocked by the most extravagant theatrical imitations.

The chaste minuet is banished; and, in place of dignity and grace, we behold strange wheelings on one leg, stretching out the other till our eye meets the garter; and a variety of endless contortions, fitter for the zenana of an eastern satrap, or the gardens of Mahomet, than the ball room of an English woman of quality and virtue.

French dances, which include minuets, cotillions, and all the round of *ballette* figures, admit to every new refinement and dexterity in the agile art; and while exhibiting in them, there is no step, no turn, no attitude within the verge of maiden delicacy that the dancer may not adopt and practise.

In short, in addressing my fair country-women on this subject, I would sum up my advice, in regard to the choice of dances, by warning them against the introduction of new-fangled fashions of this sort. Let them leave the languishing and meretricious attitudes of modern *ballette* teachers to the dancing-girls of India, or to the Circassian slaves of Turkey, whose disgraceful business is to please a tyrant for whom they can feel no love.

Let our British fair also turn away from the almost equally unchaste dances of the southern kingdoms of the continent, and, content with the gay steps of France, and the active merriment of Scotland, with their own festive movements, continue their native country balls to their blameless delight, and to the gratification of every tasteful and benevolent observer.

The Mirror of the Graces,
By a Lady of Distinction
(New York, 1813), 168–75

Every lady should desist from dancing the moment she feels any difficulty of breathing; for oppression, overheating and perspiration render the most beautiful dancer an object of ridicule or of pity for the time.

It is not, however, only this momentary fatigue that should be avoided, but also lasting fatigue. When its gradual approach is felt, dancing should be left off; for it no longer affords either charm or pleasure. The steps and attitudes lose that easy elegance, that natural grace which bestow upon dancers the most enchanting appearance. The dance is nothing without grace: leave off before gracefulness leaves you.

There are, however, several dances that should be abandoned by very delicate women, on account of their causing too violent emotions, or an agitation which produces vertigo and nervous symptoms. Dances which require these violent shocks and the forcible employment of the muscles, are obviously unsuitable to females, in whose movements we look for elegance instead of strength, and in whom those violent and difficult efforts which we admire at the theatre, would create much more astonishment than delight.

Donald Walker,
Exercises for Ladies
(London, 1836), 144–48

There are many unacquainted with dancing, who labor under an erroneous impression, that "the steps" are all that are necessary to be learned to fit a person for the ball-room. In our modern assemblies, scarcely one person in ten is acquainted with them; and if they are, they make use of steps to please their own fancy, or intersperse them with those they have been taught. A person well skilled in graceful and classic steps, and unacquainted with figures, would certainly make a ridiculous appearance, beside confusing others in the set; while one thoroughly acquainted with figures, would go through without difficulty—strict attention to good dancers being only necessary for an acquirement of movement, of which scarcely two can be found alike; and which even those who attend schools acquire more by practice and observation than by tuition.

The Ball-Room Instructor
(New York, 1841), 6–7

Be not ambitious of doing steps with the pedantry of the school-room, lest you be taken for a dancing master.

Let no one essay to *teach him or herself* this difficult art. Let every one, therefore, who would pass muster in the Ball Room, take lessons from a Professor, and then *practise at home*; and let him take opportunities of attending professional Balls, so as to fit for himself for bearing his part, without effort, in every society where Dancing may prevail.

The New Ball-Room Guide
(New York, 1844), 12, 18

If any one will compare the physiognomy of a ball of the present day with a *réunion dansante* of only five or six years ago, he will, doubtless, be struck with the happy change that has taken place in the enthusiasm of the dancers.

Formerly, the lady of the house succeeded in organizing a quadrille only with considerable difficulty, after being reduced to the necessity of individually soliciting the dancers; a few cavaliers only deciding from time to time, to draw as many timid girls from their seats, and to walk, or rather drawl, with an ill grace, through the dance, almost without troubling themselves to preserve its figures.

Now, on the contrary, what animation has suddenly succeeded to this languor in our assemblies! The choice of a partner, the comparative merit of each waltzer, the movement of the orchestra, the organization of a mazurka, the arrangement of a cotillon; all these details, formerly so indifferent but now so important, have sufficed to resuscitate the Ball.

Unfortunately, the study of the dance has for years been neglected. Nothwithstanding its antiquity, this art, so eminently national, has been considered as a trifling accessory, or as a superfluity which might be excluded from a finished education with impunity.

The consequence of this neglect of the dance has been, and continues to be, that, in our lessons and classes, the most ungraceful forms present themselves daily; legs and arms of a despairing rigidity, which are to be taught steps and positions, the execution of which requires so much ease and grace.

We are, therefore, reduced, except in the very rare cases of a great natural disposition for the dance, to teach the mechanism of the steps, rather than the steps themselves, for, can it be expected of the master to create, in a few lessons, elastic legs, arms detached from the body, a head which moves with freedom on the shoulders, and many other natural requisites of dancing, of which they form the chief merit?

Nevertheless, when I state that it is useful, and even indispensable, to study the principles of dancing before attempting to acquire its novelties, I do not wish to frighten parents, or, above all, pupils who might be tempted to judge us, in these days, by the methods of the ancient professors.

The professor now seeks to accommodate the preparatory exercises to the disposition of his pupils, and to the taste of the time. I need not here enter into details; but there exists a great number of steps fitted to give suppleness and ease to the limbs of the pupils, and which may be varied so as to avoid *ennui*, that greatest of ills attending the study of any art.

There was a time when the dancing-master undertook to teach his pupil to sit down, to walk, to cross a drawing-room, to descend from a carriage, to fan herself, &c.; all which has, doubtless, contributed to render dancing ridiculous, and to cause it to be considered as a puerile and pretentious art, which was exercised at the expense of good taste and common sense.

Henri Cellarius,
Fashionable Dancing
(London, 184–), [5]–6, 12–15

Those ladies who have witnessed the choreographic displays of the Operas, will, I feel sure, agree with me that it is high time a strong line of demarcation should be drawn between Stage and Room Dancing. The former has doubtless great attractions, owing to the ability of celebrated artistes; but, however calculated to excite our wonder on the stage, it has most assuredly nothing in it to invite us to imitate it in our Drawing Rooms.—while the largeness of the movements, the unceasing pirouetting, the ungracefulness of many of the attitudes, the unnatural turning out of the legs, and the absence of story or meaning in many of the "pas," all tell, in my opinion, a sad tale of the decline of the art which has been called the "poetry of motion." Many of these extreme positions are still taught in Room Dancing by those professors who have been on the stage, and by many who have not; hence the objection often raised, that it is quite unfitted to impart to children the bearing of ladies and gentlemen, and that it is worse than uselessness as a means of preventing or removing bad habits or personal deformity. In this way the art is condemned and its teacher discarded.

Mrs. Alfred Webster,
Dancing as a Means of Physical Education
(London, 1851), 4–5

The writer's academy at the Hanover Square Rooms affords facilities for those pupils whose convenience enables them to attend, for fully entering into the routine of the ball-room with grace and ease, and it is referred to simply as supplying the opportunity to become familiar with the more promiscuous intercourse which characterises it.

The advantages of the public and private lesson are separate and distinct in their characters. In the private lesson, alone, or when it is shared with two or three other pupils, slight peculiarities of carriage, conduct, or manner, may be commented on or corrected without inflicting pain or distress, and with more pointedness and effect; whereas in the large class only the general conduct can be conveniently and advantageously observed. The value of the private lesson principally manifests itself in the facility it affords for the attainment of any specific object; say the correction of any slight deformity, or, of any peculiarity of awkwardness requiring more particular attention to grace and deportment is, in the writer's estimation, of the greatest interest, and of the gravest importance.

Francis Mason,
A Treatise on the Use and Peculiar Advantages of Dancing
(London, 1854), 41

The notion is very generally entertained that dancing can be picked up by attending the balls, and the figures from observation—a most absurd conclusion. The instruction of amateurs is even to be distrusted.

The Illustrated Manners Book
(New York, 1855), 407

Rules for Hillgrove's Academy

Where persons may be instructed privately or in classes at any hour not pre-occupied.

Parents sending their children may rest assured that every pain will be taken to make them easy and graceful dancers; and no expense will be spared to secure for the pupils of this academy every possible advantage that can be obtained.

Private Dancing

Many of the votaries of this accomplishment are impressed with the idea that the art and figures of dancing can be acquired without the aid of a master, as diagrams of figures are published, with a sort of description, impressing the belief that the whole can be imparted for a few cents. This is a radical error. . . . The proposition that a person can acquire any more than the figures without a proper knowledge of the principles of dancing, is too ridiculous for refutation.

Thomas Hillgrove,
The Scholars' Companion and Ball-Room Vade Mecum
(New York, 1857), [4], 19

Hints to Gentlemen or the Art of Fascinating

As *heels* are of more importance to men than *heads*, you will of course, spend all of your earlier days in learning to dance, and when you are perfected in the art, you cannot do better than spend the rest of your time in dancing. Fail not to convince a lady that your *real existence* is in the ball-room, and that during all the intervening time your godlike faculties are simply taking their natural sleep. You must not dance as a mere pastime and as a occasional amusement, but you must devote yourself to it as a business and a religion for which you wish to live or dare to die.

Dance with all the might of your body, and all the fire of your soul, in order that you may shake all melancholy out of your liver; and you need not restrain yourself with the apprehension that any lady will have the least fear that the violence of your movements will ever shake anything out of your brains.

Madame Lola Montez,
The Arts of Beauty
(New York, ca. 1858), 113–14

The Dancing Academy

Concerning the architectural requirements of a private dancing-academy, there can be but one opinion,—that it should be built with every convenience necessary to the accommodation of pupils of all ages and both sexes; with not less than two large, comfortable, and well-furnished dressing-rooms, each supplied with all the accessories to the toilet that might be required in emergencies.

Abundant ventilation, to be secured by large, well-shaded windows on four sides, and by a dome with air-valves and frosted or colored glass sky-lights in the centre, should be a prominent consideration in building.

If the hall should be on the second story (which would be preferable), broad stairways with wide steps should lead in and out at both ends of the building; and the seating-capacity of the hall, independently of the open floor, should be double that required for dancing, so that during the intervals between dances, not only spectators, but participants, might find comfortable resting-places. I have seen and danced in many of the largest halls North and South, and have never found in any of them this self-evident necessity supplied.

The formation of a floor for dancing should also be carefully considered. The foundation should be solid and firm, and perfectly level and smooth, with water-tight seams and joints. In areas for a private academy, sixty feet by eighty of clear space for dancing may be regarded as sufficient; while the galleries and chair-ways should contain seats each distinct from the other, and yet sufficiently near together to admit of conversation, in modulated tones, between those who sit next each other.

The stage or stand for musicians should be raised at least as high as the heads of the dancers, and placed half-way between the head and foot of the hall, so that the music may not be torn by mingling with the company, but float freely over all, equally distinct in all parts of the room.

The head of a dancing-room is usually opposite to the main entrance; but in my own experience, I have found it more convenient to designate the end opposite the musicians as head, in order to have the first or leading couples in square dances facing the music and its director of ceremonies.

Believing, as I do, that the dancing-academy is an "*alma mater*" to its specific purposes, and not, as some people regard it, a place where men, women, and children are taught only to hop and "cut capers," I consider its location and surroundings to be of paramount importance.

It should be situated apart from the business thorough-fares, away from the neighborhood of bar-rooms, beer-salons, and other places of public resort; and under no circumstances, except for the most select social and amateur entertainments should it be devoted to other than its legitimate uses; so that the patrons and pupils, especially ladies and children, might visit it at any hour, without fear of being rudely stared at, and perhaps approached by dissolute characters, or of having their delicacy shocked by vulgar language.

And here I cannot lose the opportunity to deprecate the custom of setting up bar-counters and beer-stands in the building on the occasion of balls or other social entertainments. The custom is prevalent with the Germans; but with them it is both national and natural. By taste and temperament they are moderate and economical drinkers; and the rule, as applied to them, is different in effect to that which should govern the habits of the nervous and impressionable Americans.

It is no compliment to a lady to take her to a ball, and then resort to beer, wine, or alcohol for that inspiration and pleasure which her society and conversation should afford.

Children

With regard to the art of dancing particularly, it may be asserted that early training and constant practice are absolutely essential to insure ease and proficiency. It may be imagined—often it is imagined—by those who form their opinions from casual observation, that to teach dancing is an easy, pleasant, almost frivolous pursuit. To all such as indulge these views, there can be but one answer,—"Try it."

C. H. Cleveland, Jr.,
Dancing at Home and Abroad
(Boston, 1878), 11–13, 45

Many books have been written on the subject of dancing, some of which lie before us at this moment. The great defect with all of them is the want of simple explanations, suitable to those who are beginning the practice of dancing. They are full of learned disquisitions, but barren of any real help to those who are beginning this most graceful study.

This little book which we herewith give to the press is designed to supply a practical want in this respect. There is nothing original in it, simply because we have not attempted to invent dances—only to render easy the acquirement of those which already exist.

Clinton T. De Witt,
Cartier and Baron's Practical Illustrated Waltz Instructor
(New York, 1879), [3]

No matter what teachers of dancing may assert, the most expedient and certainly the best way to learn to dance is to stand up and try it; no one can ever learn by sitting quietly and looking on.

Dancing-school is a place where a company of bashful people congregate, who are fearful of being laughed at by those who really know how to dance. They are charged eight or ten dollars a quarter, buy a book from the professor (?), for which they pay two dollars more, listen to his lectures at every lesson, and some time after they make an attempt to dance, which is a failure, because none of the others are any better off—no one in the school knows how to dance, except the professor (?), and maybe one or two of his assistants. But attend a few good balls or parties with the theory in your mind, a good partner by your side, and you will become a finished dancer before those in the school have made their first attempt.

George E. Wilson,
Wilson's Ball-Room Guide and Call Book
(New York, 1884), 11–12

To be really healthful, the exercise of dancing should never be indulged in longer than four hours at a stretch, for beyond the evil effects of over exertion, the air in the ball-room, however well ventilated it may be, is certain to become more or less violated as the night wears on. One of the effects of exercise, is, we know, to quicken the respiration, and just think how many gallons of carbonic acid may be drawn into the lungs after midnight. Think also, of the number of miles that may be waltzed between the hours of ten and four, by legs which can scarcely be induced to walk a single mile in the morning sunshine!

Is it not wonderful what heroic feats of this description are sometimes performed by delicate little bodies, under the influence of excitement and champagne.

Each hour spent at a ball after midnight is, metaphorically speaking, a draught drawn on the Bank of Beauty—a bank in which few of us are fortunate enough to possess a large balance—and if nothing afterwards be paid in, as it were, in the way of refreshing sleep and morning breezes, it is astonishing how soon, by continuing the cheque-drawing process, we shall discover that the fund is exhausted.

Edward Scott,
Dancing and Dancers
(London, 1888), 9–10

Col. Grangerford was a gentleman, you see. He was a gentleman all over; and so was his family. He was well born, as the saying is, and that's worth as much in a man as it is in a horse, so the Widow Douglas said, and nobody ever denied that she was of the first aristocracy in our town; and pap he always said it, too, though he warn't no more quality than a mud-cat himself. . . . His hands was long and thin, and every day of his life he put on a clean shirt and a full suit from head to foot made out of linen so white it hurt your eyes to look at it; and on Sundays he wore a blue tail-coat and brass buttons on it. . . . There warn't no frivolishness about him, not a bit, and he warn't ever loud.

Mark Twain, *Adventures of Huckleberry Finn*

There is always a best way of doing everything, if it be to boil an egg. Manners are the happy ways of doing things; each once a stroke of genius or love,—now repeated and hardened into usage.

Ralph Waldo Emerson, *The Conduct of Life*

Thoughts on Society

Part 1: The Spirit of Social Observances

[Description of a ball in Cincinnati in 1829]

I was really astonished at the *coup d'oeil* entering, for I saw a large room filled with extremely well-dressed company, among whom were many very beautiful girls. The gentlemen also were exceedingly smart, but I had not yet been long enough in Western America not to feel startled at recognising in almost every full-dressed *beau* that passed me, the master or shopman that I had been used to see behind the counter, or lolling at the door of every shop in the city. The fairest and finest *belles* smiled and smirked on them with as much zeal and satisfaction as could feel no doubt of their being considered as of the highest rank. Yet it must not be supposed that there is no distinction of classes: at this same ball I was looking among the many very beautiful girls I saw there for one more beautiful still, with whose lovely face I had been particularly struck at the school examination I have mentioned. I could not find her, and asked a gentleman why the beautiful Miss C. was not there.

"You do not yet understand our aristocracy," he replied; "the family of Miss C. are mechanics."

"But, the young lady has been educated at the same school as these whom I see here, and I know her brother has a shop in the town, quite as large, and apparently as prosperous, as those belonging to any of these young men. What is the difference?"

"He is a mechanic; he assists in making the articles he sells; the others call themselves merchants."

The arrangements for the supper were very singular, but eminently characteristic of the country. The gentlemen had a splendid entertainment spread for them in another large room of the hotel, while the poor ladies had each a plate put into their hands, as they pensively promenaded the ballroom during their absence; and shortly afterward servants appeared, bearing trays of sweetmeats, cakes, and creams. The fair creatures then sat down on a row of chairs placed round the walls, and each making a table of her knees, began eating her sweet, but sad and sulky repast. The effect was extremely comic; their gala dresses and the decorated room forming a contrast the most unaccountable with their uncomfortable and forlorn condition.

This arrangement was owing neither to economy nor want of a room large enough to accommodate the whole party, but purely because the gentlemen liked it better. This was the answer given me, when my curiosity tempted me to ask why the ladies and gentlemen did not sup together, and this was the answer repeated to me afterward by a variety of people to whom I put the same question.

In America, with the exception of dancing, which is almost wholly confined to the unmarried of both sexes, all the enjoyment of the men are found in the absence of women. They dine, they play cards, they have musical meetings, they have suppers, all in large parties, but all without women.

Mrs. Trollope,
Domestic Manners of the Americans
(London and New York, 1832), 129–31

The great error into which nearly all foreigners and most Americans fall, who write or speak of society in this country, arises from confounding the political with the social system. In most other countries, in England, France, and all those nations whose government is monarchal or aristocratic, these systems are indeed similar. . . . But in America the two systems are totally unconnected, and altogether different in character. In remodeling the form of the administration, society remained unrepublican. There is perfect freedom of political privilege, all are the same upon the hustings, or at a political meeting; but this equality does not extend to the drawing room or the parlour. None are excluded from the highest councils of the nation, but it does not follow that all can enter into the highest ranks of society. In point of fact, we think, that there is more exclusiveness in the society of this country, than there is in that even of England—far more than there is in France. And the explanation may perhaps be found in the fact which we have mentioned above. There being there less danger of permanent disarrangement or confusion of ranks by the occasional admission of the low-born aspirant, there does not exist the same necessity for a jealous guarding of the barriers as there does here. The distinction of classes, also, after the first or second, is actually more clearly defined, and more rigidly observed in America, than in any country of Europe. . . . [We] know from observation, that there are among the respectable, in any city of the United States, at least ten distinct ranks. We cannot, of course, here point them out, because we could not do it without mentioning names.

The Laws of Etiquette,
By a Gentleman
(Philadelphia, 1836), 9–11

Etiquette is the barrier which society draws around itself as a protection against the offenses the *law* cannot touch—it is a shield against the intrusion of the impertinent, the improper, and the vulgar—a guard against those obtuse persons who, having neither talent nor delicacy, would be continually thrusting themselves into the society of men to whom their presence might (from the difference of feeling and habit) be offensive, and even insupportable.

Besides, in a mercantile country like our own, people are continually rising in the world. Shopkeepers become merchants, and mechanics manufacturers; with the possession of wealth, they acquire a taste for the luxuries of life, expensive furniture, gorgeous plate, and also numberless superfluities with the use of which they are only imperfectly acquainted. But, although their capacities for enjoyment increase, it rarely happens that polish of their manners keeps pace with the rapidity of their advancement; hence such persons are often continually reminded that wealth alone is insufficient to protect them from the mortifications which a limited acquaintance with society entails upon the ambitious.

Etiquette, or, A Guide to the Usages of Society
(Boston, 1844), [3]–4

I have looked over the shelves of more than twenty book-stores, in this, the greatest city of America, without being able to find one single plain, straightforward, common sense book, teaching what all young people, whatever their condition, are properly ambitious to know, what is really important to their welfare and happiness, but what they are generally left to pick up by themselves, either with no instruction, or that which is worse than none.

I know that there are numerous books on etiquette, fashion, dress, &c. &., by male and female writers from Chesterfield to Willis, and they are all more or less adopted for the class for which they are intended. For an educated person, with a large fortune, and nothing to do but make and receive visits, give and attend parties, and whose life is a perpetual round of amusement, they contain admirable directions, but nine tenths of those for whom I write would, by attempting to follow these "guides," make themselves ridiculous.

In this free land, there are no political distinctions, and the only social ones depend upon character and manners. We have no privileged classes, no titled nobility, and every man has the right, and should have the ambition to be a gentleman—certainly every woman should have the manners of a lady. But an easy carriage, tasteful dressing, graceful deportment, and polished manners, do not come by nature, though doubtless more easily acquired by some than by others. They must be taught directly, or learned by observing and imitating others. Where one has the advantage of having parents, teachers and companions, who are graceful and accomplished, and whose lessons are constantly enforced by their example, these things seem to come of course, though they are in reality the result of careful training. But the people of this country, up to the present time, have had but little opportunity to study polite accomplishments, and it therefore becomes the duty of the rising generation to educate itself.

The Art of Good Behaviour
(New York, ca. 1845), vii–ix

We possess an undeniable right to ordain a social code of our own, and we confess frankly and thankfully that we have imitated whatever we have considered wisest and pleasantest in the habits of French, English, and other nations. As the formality of social matters is less heavy and more graceful than it is in England, New York, which is admitted to be the metropolitan city of America, has discreetly chosen its customs largely from the former, modifying and adapting them to accord with our national conditions.

True Politeness. A Hand-Book . . . for Ladies,
By an American Lady
(New York, 184–), 12

To live comfortably in the world, it is not only necessary to adopt the style of dress and the manners of the circle in which you habitually move, but to be able to adapt both to a more elevated one, and to exhibit neither stiffness nor *mauvaise honte.* Study therefore the dress, habits, and manners of the best society to which you are admitted; you will either privately, or in public places and conveyances, have many opportunities of seeing good models.

True Politeness, a Hand-Book . . . for Gentlemen,
By an American Gentleman
(New York, 1847), 17

Letter IX

My Dear Nephews: Though accomplishments are a very poor substitute for the more substantial portions of a thorough education, no one should be so indifferent to the embellishments of life as wholly to neglect their cultivation.

With Europeans some attention to this subject always makes part of a thorough education, but among a *new people,* differing so essentially from the nations of the Old World in social habits, the leisure and inclination that induce such a system of early discipline are both still wanting—speaking generally. It is not the lack of wealth—of that we have enough—but of a cultivated, discriminating taste, the growth of time and favoring circumstances, which is not yet diffused among us. But, though our young men, even of the more favored class, do not enjoy the carefully elaborated system of early training, common abroad, personal effort will produce a result similar in effect, if well-directed and steadfastly pursued, and the best of all knowledge—that most beneficial in its influence upon character—is acquired by unaided individual exertion. Young Americans, above the men of all other countries, should lack no incentive to add, as occasion may permit, tasteful polish to the more essential solidity of mental acquirements.

Henry Lunettes,
The American Gentleman's Guide to Politeness
(New York, 1857), 286–87

The next kind of bad society is the vulgar, in which the morals may be good, but the manners are undoubtedly bad. What bad manners are in detail, will be shown in the course of this work; but I shall now take as the distinguishing test of this kind of society—a general vulgarity of conduct. Until the end of the last century, the word vulgarity was confined to the low, mean and essentially plebeian. It would be well if we could so limit it in the present day, but the great mixture of classes and the elevation of wealth, have thrust vulgarity even into the circles of good society, where, like a black sheep in a white flock, you may sometimes find a thoroughly vulgar man or woman recommended by little but their wealth, or a position gained by certain popular qualifications. Where the majority of the company are decidedly vulgar, the society may be set down as *bad*.

Apart from coarseness and familiarity, vulgarity may be defined as pretension of some kind. This is shown prominently in a display of wealth. I remember being taken to dine at the house of a French corn-merchant, who had realized an enormous fortune. It was almost a family party, for there were only three strangers including myself. The manners of everyone present were irreproachable, and the dinner excellent, but it was *served on gold plate*. Such a display was unnecessary, inconsistent, and therefore vulgar. A display of dress in ladies comes under the same head and will be easily detected by inappropriateness. The lady who walks in the streets in a showy dress suitable only to a *fête*; who comes to a quiet social gathering with a profusion of costly jewelry; the man who electrifies a country village with the fashionable attire of Rotten Row or reminds you of his guineas by a display of unnecessary jewels; the people, in short, who are always over-drest for the occasion, may be set down as vulgar.

The Habits of Good Society
(New York, 1860), 46–47

Nowhere is "class" more brought into prominence than at a "Country ball," where there is a recognized though unwritten law, which every one obeys, to infringe which would be a breach of etiquette, and argue a want of knowledge of the social code observed at Country balls, where each class has its own set, and where a member of the one set, would be foolish were he or she to attempt to invade another or a higher set. Thus, a couple belonging to say the professional set, or strangers in the town attending the ball, would not take their places in a quadrille at the top of the ball-room—which is always appropriated by the aristocratic element, head stewards, and titled patronesses—under the risk of being mortified by some act of avoidance on the part of those whose set they had so indiscreetly invaded. The *vis-à-vis* under such circumstances would either silently walk away, or a gentleman would remark superciliously to the offending couple—"*We have a vis-à-vis, thank you*"—or make some such cutting speech.

At some public balls a cord is drawn across the ball-room to render the upper end unassailable, but this extreme exclusiveness is not often resorted to, "clique" and "class" being thoroughly maintained without its aid.

Manners and Tone of Good Society,
By a Member of the Aristocracy
(London, 1879), 124–25

We can, at best, but remotely fix the manners of the time we live in; people differ about trifles. . . . There will never be a faultless code of manners *written*, although it may be spoken, understood and felt. We have a thousand refinements and fashions now which were to our ancestors unknown. We have lost, too, much which they had gained. Our hours, dress, houses, are vastly different from theirs. Their bows and courtesies were better than ours, and our children's children, again, will have another set of manners and customs differing from ours.

The American Code of Manners
(New York, 1880), iv

tention of any man or any woman. They will carry a stranger farther up the heights of social ambition than money, mental culture, or personal beauty. Combine elegance of manner with thoughtfulness and any other of the three powers, and the world is vanquished.

Etiquette is the machinery of society. It polishes and protects even while conducting its charge. It prevents the agony of uncertainty, and soothes even when it cannot cure the pains of blushing bashfulness. . . . It is like a wall built up around us to protect us from disagreeable, underbred people, who refuse to take the trouble to be civil.

Social Etiquette of New York
(New York, 1879), [7]–9

Part 2: The Importance of Etiquette, or Mischievous Tendencies Corrected

To enter a social circle without being familiar with its customs and its best usages is like attempting to dance a quadrille without knowing its forms. It is claimed that kindliness of heart and gentleness of manners will make rudeness impossible. This is very true, but the finest and the sweetest of impulses, combined, fail to produce graceful habits or prevent painful awkwardness. An intimate acquaintance with the refined customs and highest tones of society insures harmony in its conduct, while ignorance of them inevitably produces discord and confusion. Fortunate are those who were born in an atmosphere of intelligent refinement, because mistakes to them are almost impossible. They know no other way than the right one in the management of their social affairs.

As to the unfortunates who have been reared at remote distances from the centres of civilization, there is nothing left for them to do but to make a careful study of unquestionable authority in those matters of etiquette which prevail among the most refined people. High breeding may be imitated, and a gentle courtesy of manner may be acquired through the same processes by which other accomplishment is perfected. Even a disagreeable duty may be so beautified by a graciousness that it will appear almost as if it were a compliment. Elegant manners should not be considered beneath the at-

The editor of *The American Queen,* like many another editor of a fashionable journal, has been for some time the recipient of innumerable letters, all of which have for their burden the request that he will enlighten the writers as to some vexed question of etiquette. These letters come from young ladies in the West and East; from young housekeepers who are beginning, far from the great cities, the first arduous attempts at dinner giving; from young men who are rising in the world, and who are beginning to aspire toward that knowledge of society from which they have been debarred by a youth of industry; from elderly people, to whom fortune has come late, but whose children begin to wish to know how to take their places in the gay world; from all parts of the country, in fact, come these letters, too many of them to be answered individually. Therefore, in order not to ignore them, but to answer them collectively, he has caused to be written a series of articles, called "The American Code of Manners." . . .

Books of etiquette may be divided into three classes—those which are writtten by people who know nothing of society, or who, at best, have only been permitted a glimpse of its coarser manifestations at a watering-place; or by those who seek to avenge their anger at not having been admitted to the arena, by abusing it; or those which are written by people who know so much of society, that they forget the steps by which they have risen, and who fail, as some grammarians do, to give the learner the *first principle,* without which all subsequent teaching is in vain.

Many books of etiquette are as useless as Ollendorff's French Grammar which gives the scholar phrases which he can never use, as "Have you the cotton nightcap of the shoemaker," instead of telling him how to ask for his dinner, or teaching him how to form a sentence. The experts of society are, on the contrary, as certainly skilled in the laws which govern that great world as are the officers of the army in the regulation code. Officers of the army know not alone the art of war, but they know the *etiquette of the camp*—the proper dress, the salute due to each officer. It is a study. No man can enter the army from the ranks of civil life, without committing some flagrant solecism which, to a regularly-educated officer, would be impossible.

So with the uninformed writers upon fashion—their errors are endless and ridiculous. Nor would we claim that a book of etiquette can be written which *shall be perfect,* even by an expert; for etiquette is cumulative, changeful and uncertain. "The fashion of this world passeth away."

The mischievous tendencies of our society are many, and always tend to lower the tone of good manners. The vulgar worship of wealth, the imitating of foreign vices and follies, contempt of the domestic virtues, impoliteness of young men, and the fast and immodest manners of young women, should all be taken into consideration in the efforts which some well-intended people are making to introduce a perfect American Code of Manners. Until these faults are wholly mended, we need never hope to have an elegant society. The aristocratic code in Europe retains always a certain semblance of decency, no matter how dissolute and vicious society may be. With us, the manners of our people must proceed from their morals; and, as we have no queen, no court, no observance, to set our fashions, we must set them ourselves.

As everything in a republic is chaotic and uncertain at first—as it is, from its very inception a "new departure"; as we are just now beginning to test the virtues and the evils of universal suffrage, so it is not astonishing that our observance of etiquette has been chaotic, uncertain and occasionally absurd. It would naturally be the last thing to right itself in a nation so vast as ours, with a population made up of every other nationality, and with that "glittering generality" incorporated into our Declaration of Independence "that all men are created equal."

For no greater mistake was ever penned than that last statement. A man may be born to great freedom as to his political opinions, but he is not free; he may be equally trammeled by riches as by poverty. He is not the equal of some other man who has more brains, more health, more vigor than he has. The world is always full of inequalities. We may call it luck, or tact, or knack, or fate, or what we will—some people are always superior to some other people, and always will be. As we look at the world through eighteen Christian centuries, we see that in every capital, every town, there has been a high, well-to-do, distinctive class, setting the fashions, holding the power, being looked up to; and we see, also, another class—those who are looking up. Of course, the distinctions of rank, title and grade are abolished in this country. And here we have our own great distinction, which is that every American man and every American woman can, if they are educated, refined, and know how to behave themselves, enter on an equality the society of princes. Still the fact remains that, until they do achieve a certain knowledge of the rules of etiquette, they are not presentable in the drawing-room of a well-bred lady in any part of the world.

Etiquette in America is resolving itself into a system, and the best sign of the times is the growing interest in the subject. Every American citizen is interested in the best way of doing everything, and a man of true character and self-respect is always willing to learn. The people who make the most mistakes are the conceited and the half-learned. "A little learning is a dangerous thing" in any branch; in none more so than in society. Some people go about a great deal without apprehending the proprieties; they dress badly and out of season; they are too showy at one place, too plain at another. . . .

Etiquette settles many a disputed point, and brings comfort to many a mind, in new positions in which we find ourselves placed toward foreigners. Many Americans are suddenly afflicted with a crude prosperity which they do not know how to use gracefully. To them etiquette should be defined as a code of laws. It is a convenience.

[O]ur great man, Andrew Jackson, thought that he showed his Americanism by receiving the French Minister, who came in full uniform to present his credentials, in a ragged dressing-gown and smoking a corn-cob pipe. He called up his French cook, Deni, to translate for him. The result of this proceeding was to send the French Minister home to write to his Government that he had been insulted. It required all the tact of Mr. Van Buren to explain away the conduct of the eccentric President.

The American Code of Manners
(New York, 1880), [i]–v, [7]–8, 13–19

Another great difficulty which confronts all writers upon American etiquette is, that many matters of detail are not definitely settled in our social code. About the great general principles upon which all really good manners are founded, no difference of opinion exists. But we are pre-eminently a freedom-loving people, and every man claims liberty of conscience as in a right to dictate to us what our conduct shall be. In European countries it is a part of the privilege of the court to lay down an absolute law on all matters of etiquette, and the social culture and training, hereditary and traditional in a royal house for centuries, give its members a certain moral right to prescript what shall and what shall not be considered good breeding. Whenever we may think of a monarchical and aristocratic form of government, we must at least acknowledge that in countries where it is allowed to exist at all it may reasonably claim the privilege of, and a special fitness for, social jurisdiction.

Our political rulers are often men of no special culture or early advantages. For those who set themselves up as our social rulers are often utterly deficient in the important social prerequisite of grandparents; and the man whose ancestors came over in the "Mayflower" will not submit to dictation in matters of conduct from the man who had a rag-picker for his grandfather.

Florence Howe Hall,
Social Customs
(Boston, 1881), vi-vii

There is no country where there are so many people asking what "is proper to do," or, indeed, where there are so many genuinely anxious to do the proper thing, as in the vast conglomerate which we call the United States of America. The newness of our country is perpetually renewed by the sudden making of fortunes, and by the absence of a hereditary, reigning set. There is no aristocracy here which has the right and title to set the fashions.

But a "reigning set," whether it depend upon hereditary right or adventitious wealth, if it be possessed of a desire to lead and a disposition to hospitality, becomes for a period the dictator of fashion to a large number of lookers-on. The travelling world, living far from great centres, goes to Newport, Saratoga, New York, Washington, Philadelphia, Boston, and gazes on what is called the latest American fashion. This, though exploited by what we may call for the sake of distinction the "newer set," is influenced and shaped in some degree by people of native refinement and taste, and that wide experience which is gained by travel and association with broad and cultivated minds. They counteract the tendency to vulgarity, which is the great danger of a newly launched society, so that our social condition improves, rather than retrogrades, with every decade.

Our political system alone, where the lowest may rise to the highest preferment, upsets in a measure all that the Old World insists upon in matters of precedence and formality. Certain immutable principles remain common to all elegant people who assume to gather society about them, and who wish to enter its portals; the absent minded scholar from his library should not ignore them, the fresh young farmer from the countryside feels and recognizes their importance. If we are to live together in unity we must make society a pleasant thing, we must obey certain formal rules, and these rules must conform to the fashion of the period.

There are, however, faults and inelegances of which foreigners accuse us which we may do well to consider. One of these is the greater freedom allowed in the manners of our young women—a freedom which, as our New World fills up with people of foreign birth, cannot but lead to social disturbances. Other national faults, which English writers and critics kindly point out, are our bumptiousness, our spreadeagleism, and our too great familiarity and lack of dignity, etc.

Mrs. John Sherwood,
Manners and Social Usages
(New York, 1884), [3]–5

Part 3: Addressed to Women

Is Work Degrading?—May I claim your attention again, young friends, to a subject which is often very erroneously considered by persons of your age? I have referred to it frequently; it is based on the golden rule, and it is for the consideration of the girl in the embroidered muslin, as much as for her in the calico dress with check apron.

Is Service Degrading?—By *service* is meant any kind of aid or assistance which can be rendered to those around us. Is it *vulgar* to be usefully employed? Is it menial to take care of your own room, to aid in keeping the house neat, even to go into the kitchen to cook, if necessary; or to iron, or to clear-starch your own muslins, when you get old enough for such things? *I* think not. *I* call the *pride* which distains such things *vulgar*, and the indolence which fears the effort contemptible.

Mrs. Manners,
At Home and Abroad; or How to Behave
(New York, 1853), 128

Speech on Strong-Minded Women—In their coarse and clamorous demand to be allowed to mix in elections, how unlike virtuous and exemplary Madame de Longueville, who, when she was advised to appear at Court in order to set the courtiers an example, replied, "I cannot set a better example than to stay at home, and not to Court at all." For women past their prime, for old termigants, or those of a cracked reputation, women's-rights meetings are natural places enough; not, for a fair and virtuous young girl to be seen there, is as ungraceful a sight as it would be to see a bunch of June roses growing in the midst of the *geese* and *pigs* of a barn-yard.

The Perfect Gentleman,
By a Gentleman
(New York, 1860), 39

Certain enfranchised women think that they gain fame and power by abolishing good manners, but this is a mistake so profound, so deep and so lasting that it will right itself without further comment. The power of a woman is in her refinement, gentleness and elegance; it is she who makes etiquette, and it is she who preserves the order and the decency of society. Without women, men soon resume the savage state, and the comfort and the grace of the home are exchanged for the misery of the mining camp.

In America we have the foundation of good manners, in the great chivalry of the men. No men have so profound a respect for women; and this is the beginning of the best etiquette. Politeness, which Sidney Smith said was one of the Christian graces, should flow from the heart, and a tenderness and protection, extending from the weaker to the stronger, is the corner-stone of good manners. From the captain of a western steamboat to the roughest mines in California, from north, south, east and west, we hear but one voice. Women are to be protected, respected, supported and petted. There is no such paradise for women as the United States of America.

In Paris, the headquarters of elegance, the rottenness of an old civilization has undermined this loyalty to the ideal woman. In London there is a brutality and coarseness, perhaps partly underlying the English character, perhaps proceeding from overcrowded streets and tenements, which descend with heavy hand upon the poorer women, and which reach by atmospheric pressure the women of every grade.

There is no doubt that the American girl is somewhat of a spoiled child. She forgets to be polite, to be deferential, to thank a gentleman for giving her his seat in an omnibus or car. She has received so much politeness that she now takes it as her right.

This is a great mistake. No woman can afford, be she ever so beautiful, or so flattered, or so well placed, to disregard the solvency of her position. She must pay her debts, bow politely, thank heartily, receive graciously all the well-meant and the chivalrous attentions of men.

It is to be feared that American women, as a class, have disregarded etiquette in Europe too much; but this must be the subject of a separate paper, as it is a most important one.

The American Code of Manners
(New York, 1880), 10–14

A young lady should not attend parties and balls while engaged in educational pursuits. The proper serving of two such masters as learning and the gay world, is an utter impossibility, especially at the age of seventeen, when the fascinations of a ball possess charms that are never experienced in after years. Going to school is an old, well tried experience, going to a ball is a new and delightful one, and it is not hard to tell which would engross the entire thought of a young girl.

Social Mirror
(St. Louis, 1888), 17

Part 4: The Supper Table

Of Children's Behavior When at Home

Make a bow always when you come home, and be instantly uncover'd.

Children's Behavior at the Table

Come not at the table without having your hands and face washed, and your head combed.

Ask not for anything, but tarry till it be offered thee.

If thou wantest any thing from the servents, call to them softly.

Make not a noise with thy tongue, mouth, lips, or breath, in eating or drinking.

Stare not in the face of any one (especially thy superiors) at the table.

Crease not thy fingers or napkin more than necessity requires.

Dip not thy meat in the sauce.

Spit not, cough not, nor blow thy nose at the table, if it may be avoided: but if there be necessity, do it aside, and without much noise.

Lean not thy elbow on the table, or on the back of thy chair.

Blow not thy meat, but with patience wait until it be cool.

Sup not broth at the table; but eat it with a spoon.

Spit not forth any thing that is not convenient to be swallowed, as the stones of plums, cherries, or the like; but with thy left hand neatly move them to the side of thy plate.

Foul not the table-cloth.

Foul not the napkin all over, but at one corner.

Pick not thy teeth at the table unless holding up a napkin before thy mouth with thine other hand.

Of Children's Behavior When in Company

Spit not in the room, but in the corner, or rather go out and do it abroad.

Spit not upon the fire, nor sit too wide with thy knees at it.

Before superiors, scratch not thy head, wink not with thine eye, but modestly look straight before thee.

The School of Good Manners
(New London, Conn., 1801), 6, 8–12, 14

Your first duty at the table is to attend to the wants of the lady who sits next to you, the second, to attend to your own. In performing the first, you should take care that the lady has all that she wishes, yet without appearing to direct your attention too much to her plate, for nothing is more ill-bred than to watch a person eating. If the lady be something of a *gourmande*, and in over-zealous pursuit of the aroma of the wing of a pigeon, should raise an unmanageable portion to her mouth, you should cease all conversation with her, and look steadfastly into the opposite part of the room.

The Laws of Etiquette,
By a Gentleman
(Philadelphia, 1836), 90–91

Never *use your knife to convey your food to your mouth,* under any circumstances; it is unnecessary, and glaringly vulgar. Feed yourself with a *fork* or *spoon, nothing else*—a knife is only used for cutting.

Ladies should never dine with their gloves on—unless their hands are not fit to be seen.

Finger glasses, filled with *warm* water, come on with the dessert. Wet a corner of your napkin, and wipe your mouth, then rinse your fingers; but do not practise the *filthy* custom of gargling your mouth at the table, albeit the usage prevails amongst a few, who think that *because* it is a foreign habit, it cannot be disgusting.

Etiquette, or, A Guide to the Usages of Society
(Boston, 1844), 15–17

It is unseemly to stuff your mouth full when you are eating, and to speak while your food is in your mouth, or to eat fast. It is ill-bred to smack your lips while you are eating, or to make any unnecessary noise with your teeth or lips—to soil your mouth, or your fingers or the table cloth—to take up your food dripping with gravy—to overload your plate—to take so much more than your appetite requires, that you leave your plate half full when your meal is finished. You may almost know a neat, well-bred person by his plate, when he has finished his meals.

Miss Sedgwick,
Morals of Manners
(New York, 1846), 24

If you have acquired the habit of drinking tea and coffee, do not pour them out into the saucer to cool; saucers were made to hold the cup; they are not properly shaped for drinking. Never blow your tea, or coffee or any of your food; it sends your breath into the faces of those near you.

Be especially careful to make as little noise as possible with your lips, or teeth, or throat, while eating or drinking, or swallowing, particularly if eating an apple, or anything hard. . . .

Again, I have met persons who suck the air through their teeth with a loud noise. This is done by such as have hollow and decayed teeth, and particles of food lodge in them, and trouble, or give them pain; but they should find some way of removing the annoyance, without disturbing their neighbors with it. I have actually heard this done in company, and in church.

Others are in the habit of removing with the tongue food which has lodged about the mouth, in the cheek, or under the tongue itself. Eating is so entirely a sensual, animal gratification, that unless it is conducted with much delicacy, it becomes unpleasant to others. To open the mouth wide, pick the teeth at the table, or roll the tongue or the food about, is inexcusable, unless the napkin is used as a shield, which can be done in cases of great necessity.

Mrs. Manners,
At Home and Abroad; or How to Behave
(New York, 1853), 15–16, 26

Where it is possible, a tea-room, separate from the supper-room, is thrown open at a ball, provided with tea, frozen coffee, claret or fish-house punch, sandwiches, plain cakes, and, later in the evening, bullion and hot coffee. Where this is not possible, punch and cakes are served from a side table, at the end of a hall, and this is quite sufficient where the invited are in the habit of arriving two hours after they are asked.

The supper-room is thrown open generally at twelve o'clock. The table is made as elegant as beautiful china, cut glass and an abundance of flowers can make it. In Europe the suppers are generally cold, and the dishes that are served vary with the customs of the people. In our cities, they are always hot, with a few cold dishes, such as boned turkey, *boeuf à la mode*, chicken, and lobster salad, salmon *mayonnaise* and raw oysters. The hot dishes are oysters stewed, fried, broiled, and scalloped, chicken sweetbread and oyster croquettes, sweetbread and green peas, terrapins and game. . . . *Bullion* and ices are then sometimes served in the refreshment room, or passed during the cotillion, if the ball is a late one. It is not in good form to hand cigars at balls, nor to ask for anything that is not served with the supper.

Mrs. H. O. Ward,
Sensible Etiquette of the Best Society
(Philadelphia, 1878), 224

For a ball, all the appointments must be very handsome; there must be a first-class supper as well as good music, good floors, plenty of illumination. Usually a wealth of floral decoration is an important feature of a modern ball-room; people turn their city mansions into temporary greenhouses, and waving palms, with every variety of potted plants and choice flowers, make a veritable Eden for the time being.

Supper may be served continuously during the evening, or it may take place at a stated hour,—twelve or one o'clock, for instance. If the latter plan is adopted, it is advisable to have punch, bouillon, and other light refreshments placed where they will be easily accessible throughout the evening. Bouillon and ices are sometimes handed among the company at intervals. Those who dance the german will need a second supper; or, if that is not provided, bouillon and ices should be passed to them.

Oysters—fried, creamed, escalloped, and raw,—salads, croquettes, cold salmon served whole and handsomely ornamented, boned turkey, terrapin, birds, ices of the most expensive forms and varieties,—such as frozen pudding, bombe glacée, café mousse, etc.,—wine jellies and charlotte russeé, fresh and candied fruits, bonbons, tea and coffee and endless quantities of cake, are found on the supper-tables. Champagne and other wines are usually provided; and alas! it is sometimes wiser for ladies not to visit the supper-table very late in the evening, unless they wish to run the risk of meeting there young men who have drunk more than is good for them.

The quantity of silver plate, gold spoons, etc., displayed by some rich families on these occasions is very great, and detectives in evening dress are sometimes employed to watch the supper-table. Other entertainers do not use all their best plate and china at a crowded ball, but hire their supplies from the confectioner, thus giving themselves greater ease of mind than they could possibly have, were so much of their worldly wealth exposed to loss or destruction.

Florence Howe Hall,
Social Customs
(Boston, 1881), 133–34

It Is the Correct Thing—At a ball, to serve supper throughout the evening, or to serve it at a stated hour; in the latter case, a second supper of some sort will be needed for those who dance the german.

It Is Not the Correct Thing—To give a ball or dancing-party and provide meager or insufficient refreshments. The hostess who should do so would excite the wrath of dowagers and dancers alike, since dancing makes people very hungry, and the lookers-on—from sympathy, no doubt—usually become hungry also.

The Correct Thing in Good Society
(Boston, ca. 1888), 115

Part 5: Tobacco, Spitting, and other Violations of Decency

Pulling out your watch, in company, unasked, either at home or abroad, is a mark of ill-breeding. If at home, it appears as if you were tired of your company, and wished them to be gone: if abroad, as if the hours dragged heavily, and you wished to be gone yourself. If you want to know the time, withdraw; besides, as the taking of what is called French leave was introduced, that, on one person's leaving the company, the rest might not be disturbed, looking at your watch does what that piece of politeness was designed to prevent: it is a kind of dictation to all present, and telling them it is time, or time to break up.

Spitting on the carpet, is a nasty practice, and shocking, in a man of liberal education.* Were this to become general, it would be necessary to change the carpets, as the tablecloths; besides, it will lead our acquaintance to suppose that we have not been used to genteel furniture. . . .

The American Chesterfield,
By a Member of the Philadelphia Bar
(Philadelphia, 1827), 172–76

*Spitting upon a carpet, might have been occasionally practised in England *in the time of Lord Chesterfield*; though the Editor supposes that he here alludes to France. Such a violation of decency, is never witnessed, *now* in England, even amongst the rudest clowns.

If you are so unfortunate as to have contracted the low habit of smoking, be careful to practise it under certain restrictions; at least, so long as you are desirous of being considered fit for civilized society.

The tobacco smoker, in *public*, is the most selfish animal imaginable; he contaminates the pure and fragrant air, careless whom he annoys, and is but the fitting inmate of a tavern.

Etiquette, or, A Guide to the Usages of Society
(Boston, 1844), 20

Never scratch your head, pick your teeth, clean your nails, or worse than all, pick your nose in company; all these things are disgusting. Spit as little as possible, and never upon the floor.

If you are going into the company of ladies beware of onions, spirits and tobacco.

The Art of Good Behaviour
(New York, ca. 1845), 31–32

Quiet manners are every where a mark of good breeding—at home and abroad, in the house and in the street. If you hear men or women in the street, or in company, in a car, or a steamer, talking much and loudly of themselves and their own affairs, set them down as ill-bred. They may wear fine clothes, and be in high company, but believe me they are ill-bred.

If there are any among my readers, who are in the practice of jumping up behind omnibuses, and other carriages, I beg them to discontinue it, for it is dangerous as well as vulgar. It is a small fraud and may lead to a greater, and is often the first step in *rowdyism*.

The general and excessive use of tobacco leads to extreme ill-breeding—to vulgarity. . . . Smoking in the street is a vulgar practice. It is forbidden in some of our cities, and not practised in New York, except by foreigners and under-bred people. . . .

Do not amuse yourself by hacking the woodwork of your room,—do not lean your greasy heads against the wall, or the paper—and do not scratch, or in any way mar the furniture. All this might be classed under ill-manners; but it is also bad morals, and should be set in that serious light. It is bad morals, because it defaces and destroys property, increases unproductive and fatiguing labor, and has a tendency to provoke ill temper.

Miss Sedgwick,
Morals of Manners
(New York, 1846), 16–17, 25, 55–56

Always change your dress, after having been in a room where there was much smoking, if you are going into general society, and particularly if you have to meet ladies.

The filthy habit of snuff-taking destroys the voice, distorts the face, and by its *dirtiness* presents an effectual bar to its victim assuming the character of an *elegant*; and few would willingly place themselves out of the page of its assumption.

True Politeness, A Hand-Book . . . for Gentlemen, By an American Gentleman
(New York, 1847), 50

Sometimes people get a habit of spitting—which they do with much noise as though it gave them an air of importance. The inhabitants of the United States are notorious for it. It accompanies the bad custom of smoking, or chewing tobacco—and it is one of the disagreeable and painful consequences of a bad cold or of some diseases. That anyone, not suffering from these causes, should allow such a habit to grow upon them is very surprising.

Mrs. Manners,
At Home and Abroad; or How to Behave
(New York, 1853), 26

Loud conversation, profanity, stamping the feet, writing on the wall, smoking tobacco, spitting or throwing anything on the floor, are strictly forbidden.

The practice of chewing tobacco and spitting on the floor, is not only nauseous to ladies, but is injurious to their dresses. They who possess self-respect, will surely not be guilty of such conduct.

Thomas Hillgrove,
A Complete Practical Guide to the Art of Dancing
(New York, 1863), 29

He [Mr. Lapham] held out openly, but on his way home the next day, in a sudden panic, he cast anchor before his tailor's door and got measured for a dress-coat. After that he began to be afflicted about his waistcoat, concerning which he had hitherto been airily indifferent. He tried to get opinion out of his family, but they were not so clear about it as they were about the frock. It ended in their buying a book of etiquette, which settled the question adversely to a white waistcoat. The author, however, after being very explicit in telling them not to eat with their knives, and above all not to pick their teeth with their forks—a thing which he said no lady or gentleman ever did—was still far from decided as to the kind of cravat Colonel Lapham ought to wear: shaken on other points, Lapham had begun to waver also concerning the black cravat. As to the question of gloves for the Colonel, which suddenly flashed upon him one evening, it appeared never to have entered the thoughts of the etiquette man, as Lapham called him.

William D. Howells, *The Rise of Silas Lapham*

I have heard with admiring submission the experience of the lady who declared that "the sense of being well-dressed gives a feeling of inward tranquility which religion is powerless to bestow."

Ralph Waldo Emerson, "Social Aims" from *Letters and Social Aims*

Fashion

Part 1: The Fashionable Lady

Whatever the fashions may be, never be induced by them to violate the strictest modesty. No woman can strip her arms to her shoulders and show her back and bosom without injuring her mind and losing some of her refinement; if such would consult their brothers, they would tell them how men regard it.

The Young Lady's Friend.
By a Lady
(Boston, 1836), 368

The ball dress requires a union of beauty, elegance, lightness, and magnificence. All the required resources of the toilet must be lavished upon it. No trivial embroidery or ornaments of gold or silver must glitter there: their place is supplied with pearls, diamonds and other jewels.

As the degree of elegance varies much in ball dresses, we may make three divisions: 1st, plain; 2d, half-dress; 3d, full-dress.

For plain ball dress, black or prunella shoes; plain silk stockings; white taffety slip; a gauze or a muslin dress, trimmed with wide ribbon in puffs, or other slight ornament; sleeves and body plain; the last slightly showing the neck; the band with bows or clasp of the same colour as the trimming; the hair uncovered and ornamented with bows of ribbon or a flower; ear-rings and necklace or roman pearls; white gloves; and scarf of transparent material suited to the prevailing colour, which is generally rose or azure blue.

Figure 16

As the robe is always worn a little lower in the bosom than ordinary, the scarf or any other equivalent fichu, may be assumed in the intervals of dancing.

For half ball dress:—shoes of black or white silk; of the same colour as the dress; very fine silk stockings; white satin slip; a dress of white or coloured crape, trimmed with several rows of similar ruches; puffed trimmings of crape or satin mixed; draperies beneath which rise the puffs of crape; sometimes a bouquet of flowers raising the trimming on the knee; a bouquet similar at the cincture or elsewhere; a draped body showing the neck; cincture of satin or ribbon suited to the robe; sleeves decorated; headdress of flowers; earrings, necklace and other ornaments of roman pearl; white gloves; and scarf of lace, &c.

For full ball dress:—white satin shoes; very beautiful open work silk stockings; satin slip trimmed with blonde; dress composed of the most magnificent materials, such as lace elegantly worked in colonnades, with two rich flounces; figured blonde trimmed with blonde; similar materials plain but embroidered with variegated silks; the blonde trimmings raised up with flowers, and raised by a bouquet on the knee; body ornamented with draperies of blonde, fastened on the shoulders by ornaments similar to those of the trimming (except the flowers, for nothing is in worst taste than wearing flowers on the shoulders); a bouquet at the side; head-dress of flowers, pearl, amethyst, ruby, topaz, chrysolites, or diamonds; scarf or shawl of blonde.

At the present day, ladies dance in long sleeves *en giget*: nothing can be more unbecoming; and not even those who have ill-shaped arms should acquiesce in such a fashion. The short sleeves now worn, reaching nearly to the bend of the arm and finished with wide blonde sabots, conceal every defect.

Half-length gloves are much more becoming than long ones; but the arms or at least the forearms, must then be white and well-formed. It is the fashion to wear several pairs of bracelets over long gloves: this strange custom becomes still more whimsical if the dress is plain. But all kind of spangled embroidery, and ribbon glittering with tinsel, or flowers with tinsel leaves, are more suitable to a ballet at the opera, than to an assembly in good society.

It was formerly the custom to wear ball-dresses so low in front, as almost to amount to indecent exposure of those charms which cease to be attractive when unblushingly obtruded. The fashion has changed, and the ball-room no longer presents a collection of semi-nude female figures.

Through a light tissue of tulle or gauze, the skin appears much whiter, more beautiful, and it conceals the perspiration and redness, which often streak the skin and neck, in dancing. Besides the attraction of modesty, the most powerful charm that women possess, will make this simple fichu the most elegant part of dress.

A very beautiful embroidered handkerchief, and a fan, are the only things that may be carried in the hand in dancing.

In sending invitations to intimate friends, to an evening party, they must be made acquainted with the degree of ceremony and dress of the assembly. The invitation alone is a sufficient indication to persons who are not intimate, of the style of dress that will be requisite.

Whenever the mistress of the house receives company at home, her dress should be of an elegant simplicity, so as not to appear to rival that of the guests. If their dress is in any wise disarrayed, she should supply them carefully with the means of repairing it, but never give advice as to a better arrangement, even though it should to her seem urgent. She must never let them suppose that she does not consider them perfectly well dressed.

Mrs. A. Walker,
Female Beauty
(New York, 1840), 354–57

Ladies are allowed to consult fancy, variety and ornament more than men, yet nearly the same rules apply. Of course a lady's under clothes are not intended to be seen, but as we always imagine them to be faultlessly clean, and as an accident may at any time reveal their true condition, they always should be so. A man who would marry a woman, who wore a dirty stocking, or one with a hole in it, would be very likely to beat her in a month, and run away from her before a year was over. It is the mark of a lady to be always well shod. . . .

The Art of Good Behaviour
(New York, ca. 1845), 15

For ball dresses light and diaphanous materials are worn; silk dresses are not suitable for dancing. Black and scarlet, black and violet, or white are worn in mourning; but ladies in deep mourning should not go to balls at all. They must not dance, and their dark dresses look out of place in a gay assembly.

Mixing in Society
(London and New York, 1860), 119–20

America used to be looked upon as the country where excessive dress was a reproach. The magnificent silks, the foreign lace, and expensive evening dresses, have often been the theme of comment. But Paris at present stands pre-eminent for extravagance. The Empress Eugenie has been the originator of extreme richness and variety in dress; and her example has been only too closely followed, not alone in France, but even in England, where French customs are rarely adopted, and also in America.

The modern custom of wearing crinoline, in spite of the crusade waged against it, has many advantages. It is to be regretted that it should have been carried to such an extreme; but it cannot be denied that it shows off a dress, and preserves it from trailing on the floor, whilst it supports and lightens the weight of other clothing; thus possessing that rare virtue with any fashion, that it is in many cases a sanitary measure. Ladies should endeavor to wear smaller hoops, when going into cars, or in walking, than for evening dresses, and thus prevent much inconvenience to their fellow-travellers: we cannot desire that the practice should be entirely abolished, but simply that it be rightly regulated.

Mrs. Hale,
Manners; or Happy Homes and Good Society
(Boston, 1867), 238, 241

It is much to be desired, that the young ladies of our country would dress with more plainness and simplicity in the street and at church. A Frenchman who had just arrived in one of our larger cities, the first morning after his landing walked through the favorite street for promenading; on returning to his hotel, he inquired of a lady,—"Madam, where is the ball this morning?" "The ball! What Ball?" "I don't know what ball, but you Americans have one very strange custom; the ladies all go to the ball before dinner; some ride, more walk, all dressed for the ball; ha! ha! ha! republican vulgarity."

Mrs. L. C. Tuthill,
The Young Lady at Home and in Society
(New York, 1869). 166

It is because we believe in the picturesque, and that no human being has a right to ignore it even in clothes, that we cannot today admire the costume which woman adopts to-day. And, were it entirely satisfactory in this respect, we should then feel like remonstrating against that total disregard of beauty which is shown in the dress of the other sex. It is often asserted that they who preach dress-reform for women desire merely that they shall dress like men. Heaven forbid! is our response.

Abba Louisa Woolson,
Dress-Reform
(Boston, 1874), 197

Evening parties, balls and dinners are of a much more formal character than the entertainments which have been mentioned. They require evening dress; although for a dinner a lady's dress should be less elegant than for a ball, and she should wear less jewelry. French women often wear high corsage, with short sleeves. English women, who once never failed, even at family dinners, to appear *décolleté* (some of them distressingly so), now often wear gowns that are high, or cut square in the neck. Americans follow their own inclination, sometimes adopting one custom, sometimes another; but of late years evening dress is almost as much worn at grand dinners as at balls, only the material is not of so diaphanous a character. Lace and muslin dresses are out of place.

Mrs. H. O. Ward,
Sensible Etiquette of the Best Society
(Philadelphia, 1878), 200

No lady need be ashamed to dress plainly, or cheaply. She can, with the help of the modern guides of dress, "appear like a lady" on very little money. She can lay down three rules for herself: Never to *pretend* to anything, never to wear false jewelry, and *affirmatively*, always to be neat.

True womanhood includes all the delicate refinements that overflow in the perfect glove, the well-fitting shoe, the pretty stocking, the neat frills, the becoming bonnet. The American woman, to do her only justice, is a neat creature by instinct, and if she occasionally gives too much thought to dress, she is still to be admired and commended for her daintiness.

The American Code of Manners
(New York, 1880), 17

It Is Not the Correct Thing—For women with ugly, scraggy necks and shoulders, and arms, to display them in a way that is painful to the beholders.

It Is Not the Correct Thing—For any woman to wear a corsage cut so low as to cause general and unfavorable comment.

Florence Marion Hall,
The Correct Thing in Good Society
(Boston, 1888), 115, 117

A woman of business, an artist, or a physician must remember that the obligations of her calling alone justify many ways of doing things quite unusual and unnecessary among women who lead more secluded lives. Her manner should be serious, quiet, business-like—in fact, impersonal as far as it is possible to make it so. While her dress may very properly be of handsome materials, it should be quiet, plain, and severely lady-like.

Louise Fiske Bryson,
Every-Day Etiquette, a Manual of Good Manners
(New York, 1890), 32

A woman who is acquainted with the requirements of good society in matters pertaining to the toilet, respects its cannons. To be eccentric in dress, or even to be unusual, is impossible to her, as it would be, of course, painful, if she has delicate sensibilities. The usual is the appropriate, also the most attractive at the time of its popularity. Properly clothed men and women are at their ease in any society. If a well-bred woman finds herself overdressed she is more uncomfortable than if too simply attired.

Gloves are worn by women through all entertainments except at dinners, where they are taken off when seated, and drawn on again at the end of the dessert, or as soon as the drawing-room is reached. [For] "perpendicular refreshments," one glove may be removed should there be foods requiring use of the fingers. This, however, is a matter of personal preference and not of etiquette. One woman prefers risking a spot on the fingers of a glove to the unpleasantness of removing and putting it on again. It is not yet a custom, but in good society women with gloves reaching above their elbows have been seen unclosing a few glove buttons, and drawing out a thumb and finger, for use at a stand up supper, and thereby saving their gloves without wholly uncovering their arms.

It is bad form to emphasize one's advancing age by an attire that is excessively or in the least needlessly grave, either in its form or color. Cheerfulness is due the young, and the absence of it in dress, simply because the afternoon of life is reached, is either an affection or it is an evidence of morbid self-consciousness.

Abby Buchanan Longstreet,
Manners, Good and Bad
(New York, 1890), 52, 56–57

Part 2: The Properly Attired Gentleman

Gentlemen are not permitted to enter the Ball Room, in boots, spurs, gaiters, trousers, or with canes or sticks; nor are loose pantaloons considered proper for a Full Dress Ball.

Thomas Wilson,
A Companion to the Ball Room
(London, 1816), 220

Before going to a ball or party it is not sufficient that you consult your mirror twenty times. You must be personally inspected by your servant or friend. Through defect of this, I once saw a gentleman enter a ball-room attired with scrupulous elegance, but with one of his suspenders curling in graceful festoons about his feet. His glance could not show what was behind.

The Laws of Etiquette,
By a Gentleman
(Philadelphia, 1836), 29

For gentlemen, dress-coats, light vests, gloves, black hose, and pumps or gaiters: frock-coats and boots may be worn by spectators who do not participate in the amusement; but should a gentleman attempt to dance with either, he would probably be requested to withdraw from his position in the set.

The Ball-Room Instructor
(New York, 1841), 40

A clean, unrumpled shirt, coarse or fine, cotton or linen as you can afford, is of the first importance. If the choice is between a fine shirt or a fine coat, have the shirt by all means. . . . Let it be a whole, entire garment, too, and avoid separate collars, dickies, and all such hypocrisies. Never wear by day, a shirt you have slept in—if you must wear it two days in succession wear a night shirt, or sleep without any, rather than show a rumpled bosom or wristbands. Avoid all finical bosoms, ruffles, and lace-work fopperies.

Be as particular as you like about the cut of your pantaloons. Run into no extravagances of bell bottoms, or puckered waists. Buy strong cloth that will not be tearing at every turn, and if you consult economy and taste at the same time, let them be either black or very dark grey, when they will answer upon all occasions.

If you have but one coat, it will be a black dress coat, as there are occasions where no other will answer. Frock coats are worn in the morning, riding or walking, but never at evening visits, or at weddings, balls, parties, or the opera. . . . Most gentlemen wear a simple, plain, black silk cravat, neatly tied in a bow-knot before. Balls and parties require white or light kid gloves. Black, or very dark ones, of kid, silk or linen are worn upon all other occasions, except in driving, when buff leather gloves are preferable.

The Art of Good Behaviour
(New York, ca. 1845), 13–15

Let your dress also harmonize with your appearance: the same style of the hair, color of the cravat, or of the coat, may be preposterous in one individual, and appear elegant in another.

Wear frock-coats in the streets, dress-coats in the dining or drawing-room; dress-boots are admissible in the dressing-room, but shoes and silk stockings are in better taste.

Clean linen, white as snow, is indispensable, if you wish to support the appearance of a gentleman; a bad coat, hat, or boots, may be worn by a decayed gentleman, but dirty linen never; it would remove him from his order.

True Politeness, A Handbook . . . for Gentlemen, By an American Gentleman
(New York, 1847), 14–16

A gentleman should always be so well dressed, that his dress shall never be observed at all. Does this sound like an enigma? It is not meant for one. It only implies that perfect simplicity is perfect elegance, and that the true test of dress in the toilet of a gentleman is its entire harmony, unobtrusiveness, and becomingness. Displays should be avoided. Let a sensible man leave the graces and luxuries of the dress to his wife, daughters, and sisters, and not seek distinction in the trinkets on his watch-chain, or the pattern of his waist coat. To be too much in the fashion is as vulgar as to be too far behind it. No really well-bred man follows every new cut that he sees in this tailor's fashion-book. Only very young men are guilty of this folly.

Mixing in Society
(London and New York, 1860), 126

Never dance without gloves. This is an imperative rule. It is best to carry two pair, as in the contact with dark dresses, or in handing refreshments, you may soil the pair you wear on entering the room, and will thus be under the necessity of offering your hand covered by a soiled glove, to some fair partner. You can slip unperceived from the room, change the soiled for a fresh pair, and then avoid that mortification.

Cecil B. Hartley,
The Gentlemen's Book
(Boston, ca. 1860), 16

When a gentleman is invited out for the evening he need be under no embarrassment as to what he shall wear. He has not to sit down and consider whether he shall wear blue or pink, and whether the Jones' will notice if he wear the same attire three times running. Fashion has ordained for him that he shall always be attired in a black dress suit in the evening, only allowing him a white waistcoat as an occasional relief to his toilette. His necktie must be white or light-coloured. An excess of jewelry is to be avoided but he may wear gold or diamond studs, and a watch chain. He may also wear a flower in his button-hole, for this is one of the few allowable devices by which he may brighten up his attire.

Plain and simple as the dress is, it is a sure test of a gentlemanly appearance. The man who dines in evening dress every night of his life looks easy and natural in it, whereas the man who takes to it late in life generally succeeds in looking like a waiter.

The Ball-Room Guide, a Handy Manual
(London and New York, 186–), 25

The costume which men have chosen for all occasions is an insult to woman's aesthetic tastes. By what privilege, we ask, do they ignore their bounden allegiance to art, and daily afflict our sense of the graces of form and charms of color by the attire they adopt? Have not our eyes rights in this matter as well as theirs? If we have thus far sacrificed every thing to beauty, as we understand it, they have to-day sacrificed every thing to comfort, while we seek to retreat from our one extreme, let them retreat from theirs.

Who that ever sits in the gallery of a crowded ball-room, looking down on the whirling dancers below, is not struck with the ridiculous incongruity in their dress, as they glide in close couples over the floor? The ladies, huge and cylindrical in masses of vaporous tulle, appear smiling and radiant in jewels and garlands and festive array; while the poor little men, black as ebony and straight as clothes-pins, pirouette in bold relief against their unsubstantial edges with an anxious look, as if they felt that at any moment a sudden gust might puff them off into the air, or drag them out beyond their bearings. Did we not know the fashions of our modern world, we should suppose that a wedding procession had just broken into a funeral train, and whirled off the mourners to dance a jig. And, judging by their faces, the mourners never forget the bier left halting outside, even when skipping to the sound of the timbrel and lute in the merciless grasp of their captors. But, unlike clothes-pins, the men are not wooden-headed; for, when the music strikes up a quadrille, they show marvellous dexterity in piloting themselves through the vaporous lanes and around their huge partners; and, even in the swift interlacing of the grand-right-and-left, no one of them treads on the lowest, outlying ruffle of the tarlatan mists through which they pick their way. When the music stops with a long scrape from the violin, they are always found bowing in their right places, though they have had to circumnavigate great circles in their devious voyage, to look out for shoals and quicksands on every side, and to tack often in the face of gusty winds and through a chopped sea.

The masculine half of humanity do well to wear about their work a compact, simple, and serviceable dress; but they have no excuse for intruding it upon elegant, social assemblies, and thus robbing them of half their picturesque charm. If men enter such festive scenes, they should don a wedding garment. Nature has not rendered it impossible for them to assume those splendors of the toilet which they are so fond of in us. Once they made themselves magnificent with scarlet velvets slashed with gold, with embroidered ruffs, flashing knee-buckles, and long powdered hair. Why does not a full-dress occasion demand this of them today, as rigorously as it does the trains, the laces, the coiffures of our sex? If it be essential to the brilliancy of the drawing-room that the fall of silken draperies shall reveal their lights and shadows under the blaze of chandeliers,—why, the more of them the better. And if some people must agonize as lay-figures for the sake of others' eyes, let the suffering be equally divided. We will bear our half, let the men bear theirs! Though masculine coat-tails cannot offer us the sweep and shimmer of floating drapery, by trailing on the floor as we trail our robes, their wearers, on state occasions at least, might don the glittering and gorgeous apparel in which they were wont of old to present themselves at the courts of queens, and ever in the halls of our provincial assemblies.

While we bewail the imperfections of clothes, as now worn by men and women, we do not sorrow as those without hope. Already indications appear that man's attire has reached its acme of ugliness, and that the reaction towards adornment and color has begun. If the feather he sticks in his new hat-band is a very tiny one, and worn with a half-shamed air, it is still there, a veritable bit of color and grace, and useful for nothing else. It is but a line of piping, but it carries a streak of scarlet through the gray uniformity of his winter riding-coat; and the gay posy pinned into his button-hole is another step toward the happy mean which lies between mere comfort on the one hand and mere beauty on the other.

Abba Louisa Woolson,
Dress-Reform
(Boston, 1874), 149–52, 162–63

Ladies attending a State Ball at Buckingham Palace, would wear the usual full evening dress; but they would not wear court trains, or plumes, or lappets. Gentlemen attending state balls, would either wear uniform, or full Court dress—dress coat, breeches and silk stockings, shoes and buckles; trousers can only be worn as part of a uniform, and not with a Court dress as generally worn at a levee.

A gentleman intending to dance, would remove his sword, otherwise he would wear it the whole of the evening at a State ball. When the Court is in mourning, the ladies attending a State ball would wear mourning according to the official notice which regularly appears in the *Gazette,* and the gentlemen would wear crape on the left arm, which is supplied in the cloak-room of the Palace to those gentlemen who have forgotten to provide themselves with it, as it is imperative, when the Court is in mourning, that a band of crape should be worn at either State ball, State concert, or Levee.

Manners and Tone of Good Society,
By a Member of the Aristocracy
(London, ca. 1879), 135

A gentleman cannot be too careful not to spoil a lady's dress. Gloves are not worn to a ball for looks alone but serve a practical purpose as well. The perspiration on the hand from dancing will ruin a lady's dress when gloves are not worn, then the gentleman should hold his handkerchief in his right hand so that his hands will not touch the lady's dress.

Hudson K. Lyverthey,
Our Etiquette and Social Observances
(Grand Rapids, Mich., 1881), 63

Don't wear apparel with decided colours or with pronounced patterns. Don't—we address here the male reader—wear anything that is *pretty*. What have men to do with pretty things? Select quiet colours and unobtrusive patterns, and adopt no style of cutting that belittles the figure. It is right enough that men's apparel should be becoming, that it should be graceful, and that it should lend dignity to the figure; but it should never be ornamental, capricious, or pretty.

Don't wear evening dress in the morning, or on any occasion before six o'clock dinner.

Don't: A Manual of Mistakes,
By Censor *(New York, 1883), 16*

Gentlemen and gentlewomen do not array themselves in garments that are not appropriate to the occasion. This much respect all guests at entertainments ought to pay their hostesses when an invitation is accepted. If appropriate toilets are beyond reach, a hospitality must be declined. . . . Gloves are always worn with the day costume, but in the evening, it is a matter of personal taste whether or not gloves in light colors shall be used. In case a guest is to dance, however, the wearing of gloves is *de rigeur*. Neckties are matters of fashion rather than of etiquette, although a little white cambric, silk, or satin tie is never out of style and never of questionable taste at a party or reception, day or night. For daylight any tie of prevailing mode is appropriate, a cheerful becoming color always preferred.

A tall silk hat is usual, though if it is to be left in the hall or dressing-room, its style is of small consequence. Few men would carry a felt hat into a drawing-room, and the crush or opera hat appears to have had its day in good society. It was convenient in an orchestra stall at an opera or theatre, but as an ornament for the hand of a man at an evening party, its appropriateness, and especially its beauty, has always been doubted, except by those who doted upon it.

Abby Buchanan Longstreet,
Manners, Good and Bad
(New York, 1890), 53–55

Part 3: The Evils of Tight Lacing

Few circumstances are more injurious to beauty than the constrained movement, suffused complexion, and labored respiration, that betray tight-lacing. The play of intelligence and varied emotion, which throw such a charm over the brow of youth, are impeded by what ever obstructs the flow of blood from the heart to its many organs. In Greece, where the elements of beauty and grace were earliest comprehended and most happily illustrated, the fine symmetry of the form was left untortured.

But the influence of this habit on beauty is far less to be deprecated than its effects upon health. That pulmonary disease, affections of the heart, and insanity, are in its train, and that it leads some of our fairest and dearest to fashion's shrine to die, is placed beyond a doubt, by strong medical testimony.

We quote the following from Miss Sedgwick:—"One word as to these small waists. Symmetry is essential to beauty of form. A waist disproportionately small is a deformity to an instructed eye. Women must have received their notions of small waists from ignorant dress-makers. If young ladies could hear the remarks made on these small waists by men generally, and especially men of taste, they would never again show themselves till they had loosened their corset-laces and enlarged their belts."

Ladies' Vase,
By an American Lady
(Lowell, Mass., 1843), 83, 88

Above all, as you regard health, comfort, and beauty, do not lace too tightly. A waist too small for the natural proportion of the figure is the worst possible deformity, and produces many others. No woman who laces tight can have good shoulders, a straight spine, good lungs, sweet breath or is fit to be a wife and mother.

The Art of Good Behaviour
(New York, ca. 1845), 16

The waist should never be made to feel compressed. *The vital organs are too sacredly at work,* to be checked or injured by external *pressure.* The bodice should never be so tight, but that the hand can be easily placed under it.

The evils of tight dressing are yet to be written, but they are manifest, and what need of further argument or inducement when physiology has been our teacher? *Debility and displacement, and a thousand ills, must be the result.*

Mrs. L. G. Abel,
Woman in her Various Relations
(New York, 1851), 310

There is one very insidious aid to physical deformity—I mean stays. The evils resulting from them have been made so apparent by the pens of distinguished medical writers, that I shall only state that I invariably urge their wear being discontinued by all ladies, old and young, who come to me for lessons; and I am happy to say that the ease and comfort consequent on their removal give great hope that all those who have discarded them will never again resume them, or allow of their being worn where they have any influence.

The only "support" required is a close-fitting

body of stout jean made to lace up *in front*, as the act of reaching behind to lace ordinary stays is one of the causes of the right shoulder being so often larger than the left. Nature has given to us all the bones we require; and be assured, that to add others, is "to gild refined gold, or paint the lily." Let those bones act, and they will strengthen as the body grows; case them in stays and keep them constantly in inaction, and they become so enfeebled that, even with stays, they fail to preserve the body erect.

Mrs. Alfred Webster,
Dancing as a Means of Physical Education
(London, 1851), 37–38

Lacing the chest.—When the breathing is deep and full, the chest is expanded and rises, and the stomach is protruded during inspiration, while the chest falls and contracts, and the stomach recedes during expiration. Now what must be the effect of preventing these movements of the chest and stomach by means of a tight bandage? Why, the lungs can be distended no longer with air, the breathing becomes hurried by the least exertion, the natural functions of the organs occupying the interior of the body are hindered, and the free circulation of the blood impeded, constituting, altogether, ample causes of disease.

When the chest is scientifically laced as tight as can be borne, it often causes the blood to rush to the face, neck, and arms, on taking exercise or remaining in a heated room. Young ladies at parties frequently become so suffused from this cause, that they present the appearance of a washerwoman actively engaged over a tub of hot suds. Tight lacing also causes an extreme heaving of the bosom, resembling the panting of a dying bird.

Emily Thornwell,
The Lady's Guide to Perfect Gentility
(New York, 1856), 132–37

It Is the Correct Thing—To remember that a woman who is pinched in at the waist with tight corsets, throttled around the neck with a tight collar, and cramped as to her feet with tight, high-heeled shoes, will walk about as gracefully as a swan on a turnpike road.

Florence Marion Hall,
The Correct Thing in Good Society
(Boston, ca. 1888), 162

Part 4: Potatoes, Gin, and Other Concoctions for Cleaning

The following recipes have all been tried either by the Authoress herself, or by her immediate friends, and are thoroughly to be depended upon.

To Remove Common Ink From clothes, &c.—Rub the place immediately with lemon juice, and hot soap and water, and if this does not succeed, have recourse to slats of lemon, which seldom fails.

To Clean Silks and Cottons Without Injury to their Colour or Texture—Grate two or three raw potatoes into a pint of clean water, and pass the liquid through a sieve, when it has stood to settle, pour off the clear part, and it will be fit for use.

Dip a clean sponge in the liquid, and apply it to the silk till the dirt is well separated, then wash it in pure water.

The coarse pulp of the potatoes which does not pass the sieve, is of great use in cleaning worsted curtains, carpets and other coarse goods.

To Wash Black Silk and Crepe—Warm some small beer, and mix some milk with it, then sponge the silk with this liquid, and it will freshen the colour very much.

A strong decoction of fig-leaves, a little gin, or spirits of wine, will have an equally good effect.

To Wash Silk Handkerchiefs—These must be first washed in cold water, and the second lather must be only luke warm, then rinse them in cold water, dry them gradually, and send them to the mangle.

To Clean White Satin Shoes—Rub them with stale bread. Or rub them with a piece of new flannel dipped in spirits of wine.

To Wash Kid Gloves—Kid gloves, if they are good ones, and have never been touched by Indian rubber, may be washed so as to look new, in the following manner; and some will bear the operation more than once; it answers equally well both white and coloured gloves.

Lay the gloves on a clean towel, and with a piece of flannel dipped in warm water with a good deal of white soap, rub them thoroughly till all the dirt is removed; take care to use as little water as possible. Hang them up to dry gradually, at a distance from the fire, and the next morning, they will appear shriveled and yellow, pull them out the cross way of the leather, and they will soon resume their colour and shape.

Mode of Washing a Silk Dress—If the dress is made up, the seams need not be separated, but the body should be removed from the skirt, and the lining taken away from the bottom. Trimming and ornaments should be taken off.

If dirty, wet the dress by simply washing first in soft, cold clear water, and if black, a pint of gin should be added to every gallon of water, then proceed as follows:—

Lay the dress on a clean smooth table, a flannel should be well soaped, being made just wet enough with lukewarm water, and the silk rubbed one way, being careful that this rubbing is quite even. When the dirt has disappeared, the soap must be washed off with a sponge, and plenty of cold water. As soon as one side is finished, the other must be washed precisely in the same manner.

Observe that not more of either side must be done at a time, than can be spread perfectly upon the table, and the hand conveniently reach; likewise, the soap must be sponged off one portion of the dress, before the soaped flannel is applied to another.

The dresses should be hung up on a linen horse, in the shade, and when dry, if of a black, or dark blue colour, another sponging of gin, or whiskey, is highly advantageous.

Washed silks are spoiled if ironed with a hot iron, therefore use one of moderate heat, with a sheet of paper between.

The Workwoman's Guide,
By a Lady
(London, 1838), 217–18, 221–22, 224, 230–31

All the essentials were ready. Feet, arms, necks, and ears had been washed, scented, and powdered with peculiar care and readiness for the ball. Openwork silk stockings and white satin shoes with ribbons had been put on. . . . but Natasha, who had been busily looking after everyone, was behindhand. . . .

Madame Peronsky was ready and waiting [for the Rostovs]. In spite of her age and ugliness, just the same process had been going on with her as with the Rostovs, not with flurry, for with her it was a matter of routine. Her elderly and unprepossessing person had been also washed and scented and powdered; she had washed as carefully behind her ears, and like the Rostovs' nurse, her old maid had enthusiastically admired her mistress's attire, when she came into the drawing room in her yellow gown adorned with her badge of a maid-of-honour.

Leo Tolstoy, *War and Peace*

The Body: Detractions from and Complements Thereto

Part 1: The Vulgarity of a Foul Mouth and Unclean Hands

Beauty, without cleanliness may excite love, but it cannot secure it. An indifferent person kept clean, will make more conquests, than a beautiful slattern.

He who is not thoroughly clean in his person will be offensive to all with whom he converses. A particular regard to the cleanliness of your mouth, teeth, hands and nails, is but common decency.

A foul mouth and unclean hands, are certain marks of vulgarity: the first is the cause of an offensive breath, which nobody can bear, and the last is declarative of dirty work. One may always know a gentleman, by the state of his hands and nails.

The American Chesterfield,
By a Member of the Philadelphia Bar
(Philadelphia, 1827), 73

Wash very often, and rub the skin thoroughly with a hard brush.

Clean teeth in pure water two or three times a day; but, above all, be sure to have them clean before you go to bed.

Mrs. Child,
The American Frugal Housewife
(Boston, 1832), 88

No man can be considered a gentleman—no woman treated as a lady who neglects cleanliness. It is the first requisite to health, serenity, comfort, and beauty. A clean man is half a gentleman. The first process towards reforming a felon, is to give him a thorough washing.

Not merely the face and hands should be kept clean, but the whole skin should be subjected to frequent ablutions. There is water everywhere, and if desirable the means of heating it. If one has not a bathing apparatus, a wash-tub, a bucket—any thing will answer better than dirt. Better coarse clothes with a clean skin, than silk stockings drawn over dirty feet. Remember that dirt is the never failing sign of vulgarity, as cleanliness is of gentility.

Nothing is so favorable to the beauty of a clear transparent skin, a glowing color, a bright eye, as absolute cleanliness, external and internal; and though beauty strikes and fascinates us at first, sweetness and purity bind us the fastest. There is not a man in the world who would not prefer for his wife a woman of ordinary features and perfect neatness, to the handsomest slut alive. Plenty of cold or warm water and towels for the whole body, combs and brushes for the hair, a tooth brush with pure water, and a little fine soap if necessary, are all that are required for the first and most important outward requisites for personal cleanliness.

The Art of Good Behaviour
(New York, ca. 1845), 11–12

No one wishes to inspire others with disgust. No one ought to be willing, from laziness, inattention, or moroseness, to produce an unpleasant impression on any of the senses of those about him. No man can afford to cut himself off from human sympathy, the vital circulation of the social being, without which it withers and dies.

There are eccentricities of habit and manner, peculiarities of costume and deportment, that are harmless and even picturesque, though not strictly beautiful. The "Gent," the "Snob," the dandy of exaggerated finery, or the dandy of an equally affected and exaggerated coarseness and ugliness, we may tolerate; but a positive disregard to personal decency, ranks a man below all ordinary savageism.

The care of the person is the beginning of good manners. Everyone not only consults his own well being, his dignity, and enjoyment, by his care of himself, but he also fulfills a social duty. Everyone should do the best he can for himself, for his own sake, and to avoid giving pain to, or to promote the happiness, of others.

The first moral and physical duty of every human being is *to be clean*. Cleanliness, the apostle says, is akin to godliness. We would not give much for the godliness of any man or woman who was not cleanly. Filth is a violation of the rights of several of the senses. We see it; we feel it; sometimes we may be cheated into tasting it; and we smell it terribly. In all ways, and under all conditions, it is vile and bad, ill-mannered and immoral.

First of all, then and above all, as the prime condition of all excellence of character and beauty of life, oh, be thoroughly and perfectly clean! The human organism is so constituted that no person can be absolutely clean without washing the whole surface of the body every day. Millions of pores are constantly exuding waste matter from the body. This matter, if allowed to remain, is filth; in any considerable quantity it is poison. Retained in the system, it is matter of disease, and is the efficient cause of typhus, and similar diseases.

The Illustrated Manners Book
(New York, 1855), 23–25

Part 2: Rouge, Paints, Hair, and General Maxims for Health

Advocate as I am for a fine complexion, you must perceive that it is for the *real,* not the *spurious.* The foundation of my argument, *the skin's power of expression,* would be entirely lost, were I to tolerate that fictitious, that dead beauty which is composed of white paints and enameling. In the first place, as all applications of this kind are as a mask on the skin, they can never, but at a distinct glance, impose for a moment on a discerning eye. But why should I say a discerning eye? No eye that is of the commonest apprehension can look on a face bedaubed with white paint, pearl powder, or enamel, and be deceived for a minute into a belief that so inanimate a "whited wall" is the human skin. No flush of pleasure, no shudder of pain, no thrilling of hope, can be decried beneath the encrusted mould; all that passes within is concealed behind the mummy source. Perhaps the painted creature may be admired by an artist, as a well executed picture; but no man will seriously consider her as a handsome woman.

White painting is, therefore, an ineffectual, as well as dangerous practice. The proposed end is not obtained; and, as poison lurks under every layer, the constitution wanes in alarming proportion as the supposed charms increase.

Besides, while *all* white paints are ruinous to health, (occasioning paralytic affections and premature death,) there are some red paints which may be used with perfect safety.

A little vegetable rouge tinging the cheek of a delicate woman, who, from ill health or an anxious mind, loses her roses, may be excusable; and so transparent is the texture of such rouge, (when unadulterated with lead,) that when the blood does mount to the face, it speaks through the slight covering, and enhances the fading bloom. But though the occasional use of rouge may be tolerated, yet, my fair friends must understand that it is only *tolerated.*

Penciling eyebrows, staining them, etc. are too clumsy tricks of attempted deception, for any other emotion to be excited in the mind of the beholder, than contempt for the bad taste and willful blindness which could ever deem them passable for a moment.

Recipes, Useful and Ornamental

Fard

(This useful paste is good for taking off sunburnings, effects of weather on the face, and accidental cutaneous eruptions. It must be applied at going to bed. First wash the face with its usual ablution, and when dry, rub this fard all over it and go to rest with it on the skin. This is excellent for almost constant use.)

Take two ounces of oil of sweet almonds, ditto of spermaceti: melt them in a pipkin over a slow fire. When they are dissolved and mixed, take it off the fire, and stir into it one table spoonful of fine honey. Continue stirring till it is cold, and then it is fit for use.

Madame Recamier's Pommade

(This was communicated by this lady as being used in France and Italy, by those who professionally, or by choice, are engaged in exercises which require long and great exertions of the limbs, as dancing, playing on instruments, etc.)

Take any suitable quantity of *Axungia Cervi,* i.e. the fat of a red stag or hart; add to it the same quantity of olive oil, (Florence oil is preferable to any of the kind,) and half the quantity of virgin wax; melt the whole in an earthen vessel, well glazed, over a slow fire, and, when properly mixed, leave it to cool.—This ointment has been applied also with considerable efficacy in cases of rheumatism.

Wash for the Hair

(This is a cleanser and brightener of the head and hair, and should be applied in the morning.)

Beat up the whites of six eggs into a froth, and with that anoint the head close to the roots of the hair. Leave it to dry on; then wash the head and hair thoroughly with a mixture of rum and rose-water in equal quantities.

The Mirror of the Graces,
By a Lady of Distinction
(New York, 1813), 42–44, 47, 208, 211, 212

Too frequent use of an ivory comb injures the hair. Thorough combing, washing in suds, or New England rum, and thorough brushing, will keep it in order; and the washing does not injure the hair, as is generally supposed. Keep children's hair cut close until ten or twelve years old; it is better for health and the beauty of the hair. Do not sleep with hair fizzled, or braided. Do not make children cross-eyed, by having hair hang about their foreheads, where they see it continually.

Mrs. Child,
The American Frugal Housewife
(Boston, 1832), 88

In France they have a preparation of rouge called "vinaigre de Rouge de Maille," which is applied to the cheek by means of a bit of raw cotton and gentle friction. As it does not color until it begins to dry, great caution is necessary in its application. A humorous story is told of a young Englishwoman, who, ignorant of this quality of the vinaigre, applied an over-dose, and in her nervous anxiety to remove it, rubbed her cheeks with a towel and spread it all over her face, and in short, so be-rouged herself, that when she appeared in a ball-room, whither she was instantly hurried by the impatience of her companions, who were altogether ignorant of her mishap, every one stared at and shunned her. A report soon spread that she had been suddenly seized with a malignant scarlet fever. She was immediately hurried away—she had forgot all about the rouge, and so excited had her feelings become, that she seemed really threatened with the dreaded disease. On reaching home, however, the cause of her strange appearance was explained. The application of the wet towel to the half-dried rouge had streaked her face, so as to give a most singular look. As this preparation, when it once dries, cannot be removed by any application of soap and water, she was obliged to confine herself to her room for more than a fortnight; her humorous admirers, in the mean time, suffering unspeakable anxiety from the report that she was dying of a malignant fever.

The Art of Dress
(London, 1839), 55–56

Cosmetics and Cleanliness

Baths of Milk

Milk and cream are doubtless preferable to most other applications; but still they are dirty, clog the skin, and injure it in the end. Nature certainly never meant that people should plaster their food over the outside of their bodies.

Artificial Paints and Natural Complexion

Numerous are the preparations of white to improve the complexion, of black to dye the hair, of blue to define the veins, or red to colour the cheeks, of carmine to colour the lips, &c. The most remarkable is the paint which is meant to supply the place of the natural colour and the whiteness of the skin.

Of White Metallic Paint

For white mineral paints, the preparations of bismuth and lead are generally used, in spite of their deleterious properties and the disadvantages they labour under of changing colour when exposed to the contact of sulphuretted hydrogen gas, because these alone resemble the soft brilliancy of a beautiful complexion.

In the first place, however, they remain powdery on the parts to which they have been applied, or if they do not, they melt with the perspiration, and streak the face.

In the second place, being the product of acids of bismuth, or of lead, they are subject to rapid changes which frequently produce, to the great horror of the wearer, effects totally different from those intended.

The sulphureous exhalations with which the air is sometimes impregnated, suddenly turn these preparations black upon the skin; and this alteration remains as long as the exhalation from the pores continues.

This accident would be likely enough to take place in any theatre where chemical lectures are delivered, or wherever medicated baths are taken.

In the third place, this white paint obstructs the pores, tarnishes the skin, and in a short time furrows the face with ineffaceable wrinkles. If any chaps or fissures exist upon the skin, they greatly increase the dangerous effects of these substances.

Of Red Metallic Paint

Red mineral paint or rouge is composed of vermillion rubbed down with Briançon chalk.

This paint is very dangerous, if any portion of its poisonous substance be absorbed by the pores. It corrodes and loosens the teeth.

Every mineral paint, says the Dictionary of Medical Sciences, is a poison, and the smallest inconvenience it will cause, after the destruction of the skin, is the loss of the teeth and foul breath.

These paints, however, white lead and vermillion are now used chiefly at theatres.

Of Red Vegetable Paint

Vegetable rouge is generally obtained from the roots of orchanet, madder, sandal, and Brazil wood, and especially from the stamina of the Carthamus, and from the cochineal, an animal substance.

The rouge from the Carthamus, which is called Spanish rouge, because it was first prepared in that country, and rose en tasse, or pink saucer, because, as a precipitate, it is known under that name in trade, is now the principal basis of red paints. It is with this precipitate, which may be bought cheap at the grocers, druggists, and colour dealers, that different sorts of rouge are prepared.

It is used in powder, in pomade, in crepons or gauze, and in liquid.

For rouge in powder, they take talc reduced to an impalpable powder, and mix it with the rose en tasse, pounding this mixture carefully with a few drops of olive or ben oil, to make it soft and thick. The beauty and the value of rouge, in trade, depends upon the fineness of the talc, and the proportion of the rose en tasse. It is then placed in small gallipots in a very thin layer.

The powder is applied to the cheeks by means of a little bag or ball of cambric or muslin.

A pomade of this red paint is easily obtained, by adding a proper quantity of precipitate of carthamus to a mixture of white wax and soft pomade.

It is spread on the face with the finger, and rubbed in till it ceases to feel greasy: it will resist moisture and even a slight touch.

This is perhaps the most favourable and the most agreeable form in which this rouge can be used.

Liquid rouge heightens the colour of the skin, has the appearance of the natural complexion, and adheres a long time to the face.

This brilliancy, however, thus produced, is afterwards dearly paid for: this vegetable rouge is very injurious to the skin, in consequence of the acids which are employed in its composition.

The green red is simply rose en tasse poured, whilst still moist, into rouge pots, where, on becoming dry, it assumes naturally an olive green tinge, which changes to a lively red when it is moistened with a little fresh water.

As all these rouges preserve a portion of the juice of the citron employed in manufacturing them from the Carthamus, they dry and produce a contraction of the skin which prematurely destroys its freshness.

In addition to this, though this vegetable rouge is less pernicious than other rouges, it is still very injurious, because it is mixed with a sufficient quantity of talc and mineral white, to produce various shades of rouge.

The root of the Bugloss is used in the composition of many cosmetics. The rouge, of which it is said to be the base, is vaunted as the best and the least dangerous. It remains several days on the face without fading; water is said to brighten its brilliancy, as it does that of natural colours; and it is pretended that it does not so seriously injure the skin.

From some of these circumstances, it must be a dye, and cannot but be hurtful.

Of Paint for the Eyes, &c.

Many persons have been desirous of a tincture to dye the eyebrows and eyelashes without staining the skin instead of a powder or paste, which blackens the skin rather than the eyelashes. With this view, the following wash has been proposed: namely, one drachin of sulphate of iron dissolved in one ounce of gum-water and a teaspoonful of eau de Cologne. This is mixed well together and bottled; and, when it is required to be used, the eyebrows are first wetted with tincture of galls, and the wash is then carefully applied with a camel-hair pencil.

Mrs. A. Walker,
Female Beauty
(New York, 1840), 47–57

A good selection of cosmetics and kindred preparations is important for the completeness of a lady's toilette. As a general rule, to set off the complexion with all the advantage it can attain, nothing more is requisite than to wash the face with pure water; or if anything further occasionally be necessary, it is only the addition of a little nice soap. As to the use of paints, washes, &c., it is not for us to determine; but in giving the following receipts, we have endeavored to distinguish those which are most objectionable, on account of the deleterious articles which they contain. A knowledge of their manufacture will, therefore, prevent ill consequences, if it be productive of no other good.

White salve which may be used for paint.

Take four ounces of very white wax, five ounces of oil of almonds, one ounce of very pure spermaceti, one and one-half ounces of white lead washed in rose-water, and an ounce of camphor. Mix the whole up into a salve, which may be preferred to all other whites.

Cold cream.

The article sold under this name is composed of white wax, almond oil, and rose-water, in the following proportions: Take of almond oil, four ounces, white wax, one ounce. To be gently melted, and well blended with four ounces of fresh rose-water, by stirring in a warm marble mortar. The rose-water should be added very gradually.

Curling the hair.

Curling is best effected in the usual way, by papering. Using hot irons is apt to injure the hair, and the curling fluids so confidently advertised, have but a very temporary effect, and are injurious. The use of pomatums, and hair-oils, will assist in curling some kinds of hair, but in other cases will be disadvantageous.

If the hair be soft and very fine, instead of washing and oiling it in the way usually directed, it will be better to clean it with a brush slightly dipped in spirits of hartshorn, or to dress it with the following composition, which will give it both a fine gloss and strength to remain in the curl:—

Cut into small pieces about two pounds of good common soap, and put it into three pints of spirits of wine or brandy, with eight ounces of potash, and melt the whole in a hot-water bath, stirring it continually with a wooden spoon. After it is properly melted, leave it to settle, pour off the liquor clear, and perfume it with any fragrant essence you prefer. This will be found to be as good, if not superior to any of the articles sold under the name of curling-fluids, and one-half cheaper.

Hair oil to prevent baldness.

Boil half-a-pound of green southernwood in one pint and-a-half of sweet oil, add half a pint of port wine. When boiled, strain it through a fine linen

Figure 17

bag three times, each time adding fresh southernwood; then add two ounces of bear's oil, and replace it near the fire, in a covered vessel, until the ingredients are thoroughly incorporated. Bottle it closely.

Emily Thornwell,
The Lady's Guide to Perfect Gentility
(New York, 1856), 26–30, 37–38, 42

Toilet Recipes

How to Darken Faded False Hair

The switches, curls and frizzes which fashion demands should be worn, will fade in course of time; and though they matched the natural hair perfectly at first, they will finally present a lighter tint. If the hair is brown this can be remedied. Obtain a yard of dark brown calico. Boil it until the color has well come out into the water. Then into this water dip the hair, and take it out and dry it. Repeat the operation until it shall be of the required depth of shade.

John H. Young,
Our Deportment
(Detroit, 1879), 385–86

Beware of "making up" in hot weather. An eyebrow gently trickling down the cheek, veins on the temple that run, lips that gradually expand into laughable proportions, present a sorry spectacle. In fact, it is better to avoid making up at all.

Louise Fiske Bryson,
Every-Day Etiquette, a Manual of Good Manners
(New York, 1890), 46

General Maxims for Health

Rise early. Eat simple food. Take plenty of exercise. Never fear a little fatigue. Let not children be dressed in tight clothes; it is necessary their limbs and muscles should have full play, if you wish for either health or beauty.

Avoid the necessity of a physician, if you can,

Figure 18

by careful attention to your diet. Eat what best agrees with your system, and resolutely abstain from what hurts you, however well you may like it. A few days' abstinence, and cold water for a beverage, has driven off many an approaching disease.

If you find yourself really ill, send for a good physician. Have nothing to do with quacks; and do not tamper with quack medicines. You do not know what they are; and what security have you that they know what they are?

Wear shoes that are large enough. It not only produces corns, but makes the feet misshapen, to cramp them.

Let those who love to be invalids drink strong green tea, eat pickles, preserves, and rich pastry. As far as possible, eat and sleep at regular hours.

Wash the eyes thoroughly in cold water every morning. Do not read or sew at twilight, or by too dazzling a light. If farsighted, read with rather less light, and with the book somewhat nearer to the eye, than you desire. If near-sighted, read with a book as far off as possible. Both these imperfections may be diminished in this way.

Have your bed-chamber well aired; and have fresh bed linen every week. Never have the wind blowing directly upon you from open windows during the night. It is not healthy to sleep in heated rooms.

Let children have their bread and milk before they have been long up. Cold water and a run in the fresh air before breakfast.

Mrs. Child,
The American Frugal Housewife
(Boston, 1832), 87–88

Beauty without grace is the hook without the bait.

Ralph Waldo Emerson, *The Conduct of Life*

Although her dress, her coiffure, and all the preparations for the ball had cost Kitty great trouble and consideration, at this moment she walked into the ballroom in her elaborate tulle dress over a pink slip as easily and naturally as though all the rosettes and lace, all the minute details of her attire, had not cost her or her family a moment's attention, as though she had been born in that tulle and lace, with her hair done up high on her head and a rose and two leaves on the top of it.

Leo Tolstoy, *Anna Karenina*

The Body: Composed and Harmonious

Part 1: Deportment, Grace of Carriage, and the Shrug

In order to dance well, the body should be firm and steady; it should particularly be motionless, and free from wavering, while the legs are in exertion, for when the body follows the action of the feet, it displays as many ungraceful motions as the legs execute different steps, the performance is then robbed of its ease, uniformity, harmony, exactness, firmness, perpendicularity, equilibrium, in a word, of all those beauties and graces which are so essential to make dancing give pleasure and delight.

The pleasing effect of moving the hand is seen, when presenting a card, letter or fan, gracefully, or genteelly to a lady, both in the hand moving forward and in its return. The hand must be waved in a Serpentine line, but care must be taken that the line of movement be but gentle, and not too S-like and twirling, which excess would be affected and ridiculous. Daily practising these movements with the hands, and at the same time, a gentle inflexion of the body, will in a short time render the person graceful and easy.

James P. Cassidy,
A Treatise on the Theory and Practice of Dancing
(Dublin, 1810), 54, 72–73

A dancer, holding his body perpendicular and firm upon his hips, will display his breast enlarged by the throwing of the shoulders backwards; the head must also be held a little in that way, the chin somewhat lower than the jaw-bone. The mouth must not be shut up with apparent force, the teeth must not press hard upon each other nor the eyes forcibly opened, because situations of this description give an expression of extreme harshness to the features and cause painful sensations to the beholders.

Elements . . . of the Art of Dancing,
by V. G.
(Philadelphia, 1817), 10–11

The thumb should rest upon the forefinger, keeping the other fingers loose, the body upright, and the shoulders well drawn back, with the head turned to the right, in order to see the person who is dancing with you.

F. J. Lambert,
Treatise on Dancing
(Norwich, Eng., 1820), 31

It is hardly possible to enumerate the disadvantages that arise from an awkward deportment of the person. It is therefore of the utmost consequence to commence by forming a genteel and elegant carriage or deportment of the body. Although the sole of the foot is undoubtedly the base upon which the weight of the body rests, yet it is the proper disposition of the waist, that really gives that *a-plomb,*—that steadiness and facility of execution, requisite in a good dancer. Without being firmly seated on the haunches, it is quite impossible to support one's self in a perpendicular position, and one runs the risk, at every movement, of losing the centre of gravity.

To be well seated on the reins, or haunches, one must advance or thrust forward the chest or sternum, by drawing back the tops of the shoulders, taking care to keep them down; and at the same time holding the arms a little forward, so that the hands may be in a line with the foreside of the thighs.

The head is to be held back in a becoming manner, but without stiffness; and the chin kept down, but not so as to give the figure an air of constraint.

Manner of Holding the Arms

The graceful display of the arms depends greatly on the manner in which the elbows and wrists are turned. The arms should be held in a rounded form, so that the elbows and wrists may make the least appearance possible; the elbows turned forward in a small degree, and the wrists held in contrast with them; the hands gently rounded, and the thumbs placed on the point, or rather over the first joint of the fore-finger, and turned towards the sides. In this position, the arms have a much more delicate appearance, than when the backs of the hands are held foremost.

Gentlemen should hold their arms near them in this manner, and Ladies should hold their robe lightly between the fore-finger and thumb, taking hold of it at the length of their arms, so as not in the least to confine the arms.

Those who are tall and slender, should hold the arms a little more forward, and farther apart, in order to give their bodies a just proportion.

When the manner of the dance requires an arm to be raised, the arm should be kept near the body, the hand brought gently before it, the elbow kept forward, and, without raising the shoulder, the arm is to be raised to the height of the breast, allowing the elbow to fold a little, in order to bring the hand before the breast, always taking care to hold the arm in a rounded form.

In lowering the arm, unfold the elbow a little, and let the arm descend gently to its place.

When the arms are to be raised alternately, at the first movement which the one arm makes to descend, the other must begin to rise, and should arrive at the proper height, just at the time when the other shall have descended to its place.

To raise both the arms at once, observe the same rule as in raising one of them, taking care to keep them rounded. To lower them, begin with the hands, and let the arms descend gently to their proper place.

It should always be remembered, that it is only by maintaining a proper deportment of the body, that one can exhibit that agreeable ease which constitutes the principal charm in dancing, especially in the execution of the steps, and the contrast of the head and shoulders regulated by a just taste.

Alexander Strathy,
Elements of the Art of Dancing
(Edinburgh: F. Fillans, 1822), 13–16, 19

To sit down and rise up gracefully is of the first importance in the accomplishments of persons *dans la bonne société.* It always gives me pain, when I see persons bending forward while quitting their seats, and indeed, it is not only ungraceful to rise by making a sudden motion forward of the body, but renders the person so doing liable to accidents; I once saw a very unfortunate disaster happen to a lady while rising in this way, by the assistance of the weight of a body being brought forward, she was accidentally pushed down by a gentleman who had been sitting by her side, who on perceiving her companion (a lady sitting on the other side of her) drop her fan, rose and bent forward hastily in order to pick it up, by doing which, he and the first mentioned lady (who was rising at the time) unfortunately came in contact with each other, which was the cause of the accident alluded to.

The proper way to sit down is, after the style of the courtsey, by bending on the foot that is before, then returning on that behind, and in this manner gain the seat: to quit it, the person should rise by the assistance of the foot that is behind, without inclining the body forward. The lady, while taking her seat, should hold her robe with one or both hands, at the same time slightly advancing her arms without raising them, this will prevent her tumbling or creasing her robe, and will cause it to fall gracefully by her side; she should likewise be careful not to turn her feet too much out, nor sit in an uneasy or awkward position, but advance one foot a little more than the other, and either cross the hands or arms, play with her fan, or do any other movement with the arms, that can be effected with quiet gracefullness, and without affectation.

E. A. Theléur,
Letters on Dancing
(London, 1831), 102–3

The steps cannot be learned without professional aid. But still we think, that while too much attention cannot be given to the learning of the steps, too little may be, and often is, bestowed upon the carriage of the figure.

The Ball Room Annual
(London, ca. 1844), 27

You desire to be a person of "good standing" in society. How *do* you stand? We refer now to the artistic or esthetic point of view. If you are awkward, you are more likely to manifest your awkwardness in standing than in walking. Do you know where to put your feet and what to do with your hands? In the absence of any better rule or example, try to forget your limbs, and let them take care of themselves. But observe the attitudes which sculptors give to their statues; and study also those of children, which are almost always graceful, because natural. Avoid, on the one hand, the stiffness of the soldier, and, on the other, the ape-like suppleness of the dancing-master; and let there be no straining, no fidgeting, no uneasy shifting of position. . . .

Hand-Books for Home Improvement
(New York, ca. 1856), 44

It is essential that every lady should understand that the most beautiful and well dressed woman will fail to be *charming* unless all her other attractions are set off with a graceful and fascinating deportment.

Madame Lola Montez,
The Arts of Beauty
(New York, ca. 1858), 70

In regard to the physical carriage of women, the grace of an upright form, of elegant and gentle movements, and of the desirable medium between stiffness and lounging, are desirable both for married and single [ladies]. . . . Her face should wear a smile, she should not rush in head-foremost; a graceful bearing, a light step, an elegant head to common acquaintance, a cordial pressure, *not shaking*, of the hand extended to her, are all requisite to a lady. . . . Let her sink gently into a chair. . . . Her feet should scarcely be shown and not crossed.

The Habits of Good Society
(New York, 1860), 309–10

Gesture

Composure is good form. Tranquility is self-mastery, and therefore a part of culture or breeding. An active use of the hands while talking is unpleasant to everyone but the speaker, who as a rule appears to find much gratification in an exercise that belongs by approval to the orator or the actor.

In the days of political intolerance in France, where the opinions of men and women were in danger of leading them to the guillotine, gesticulation was used to take the place of speech, or rather to conceal an utterance. No one could testify in court to the meaning of a gesture, although its significance was seldom misunderstood. Of the remnants of this mode of communication, the shrug, the most offensive of gestures, remains in use by thoughtless, or vicious persons. It is, however, in the worst possible form. It may be made to signify or to suggest anything.

A shrug is not unlike an anonymous letter of detraction, or accusation, which the author is too cowardly to father openly. The shrug may mean contempt, open contradiction, or anything and everything that is unpleasant and likely to be unjust, but in any event so uncandid an accusation must be looked upon with suspicion. No one shrugs his shoulders to convey a good impression.

Shrugs have no place among refined personal habits or elegant social customs. Nor can we welcome it among the many charming French usages that have been added to our social customs and personal graces.

Abby Buchanan Longstreet,
Manners, Good and Bad
(New York, 1890), 40–41

Part 2: Walking

We know that if we only chance to be standing in a group at a window, regarding the passers by, scarcely one escapes without exciting some observation; as—"How ridiculously that man wears his hat!"—"How affectedly that lady walks!" "There is another I should take for a gentlewoman if she did not swing her arm so violently, &c. &c." Can any thing be more inelegant than swinging the arm in such a manner, as actually to give one the idea, that the person is rowing themselves on with the unfortunate limb, exercised so unmercifully? Yet there is nothing more common than this most awkward action, which may very easily be got the better of, by at first compelling the active member to retain steady hold of a parasol, train or gown, or any other expedient that may prevent it from so far sympathizing in the action of the feet, as to appear to be vying with them in furthering our progress. But stiffness should be avoided; we would not have a lady appear like a recruit under the hands of a dull ser[g]eant, or as if her thumbs were sewed to her petticoats; and rather than she should betray one particle of affectation, we should prefer her rowing with all her might even with *both* arms, so she would have quite as much pretension to real gracefulness, as when distorted by an obvious attempt to *appear* elegant.

The ladies of the present day walk particularly

ill, and that chiefly from their anxiety to perform well. One advances with a start, another with a stamp, a third with a mincing irregular trip; while if they did not *think* about it they might get on very well without attracting notice either way; but *that is the very last thing they desire,* and the contrary design actuates every movement. . . . The body should partake as little as possible in the motion of the limbs; calm, easy, and unobtrusive, a female should advance, as if thinking of any thing rather than the effect her own appearance may create. We should always endeavor to divest ourselves of the idea that any eyes are fixed upon our persons, and move exactly the same as we do when we are alone; a direct contrary rule, this, to what should be pursued in regard to our *minds,* which we should do well to consider as open to the inspection of the whole world, as we know they are to Providence, and govern them so that they might be revealed without a blush.

Emma Parker,
Important Trifles
(London, 1817), 69–73

Walking fast in the streets is a mark of vulgarity, implying hurry of business. It may appear well in a mechanic or tradesman, but suits ill with the character of a gentleman or man of fashion.

The American Chesterfield,
By a Member of the Philadelphia Bar
(Philadelphia, 1827), 176

The employment of soldiers to teach young ladies how to walk, which, we are sorry to say, is a practice adopted by many parents and heads of seminaries, is much to be deprecated. The stiffness acquired under regimental tuition, is adverse to all the principles of grace, and annihilates that buoyant lightness which is so conducive to ease and elegance in the young.

The Young Lady's Book
(Boston, 1830), 418

They [ladies] do not walk well, nor, in fact, do they even appear to advantage when in movement. I know not why this should be, for they have abundance of French dancing-masters among them, but somehow or other it is the fact. I fancied I could often trace a mixture of affectation and of shyness in their little mincing unsteady step, and the ever-changing position of the hands.

I never saw an American male walk or stand well: notwithstanding their frequent militia drillings, they are nearly all hollow-chested and round-shouldered: perhaps this is occasioned by no officer daring to say to a brother free born "hold up your head:" whatever the cause, the effect is very remarkable to a stranger.

Mrs. Trollope,
Domestic Manners of the Americans
(London and New York, 1832), 241–42

Toward the close of the day, a young lady would conduct herself in an unbecoming manner if she should walk alone; and if she passes the evening with any one, she ought to take care that a domestic comes to accompany her; if not, to request the person whom she is visiting to allow some one to do so. . . .

If the master of the house wishes to accompany you himself, you must excuse yourself politely, from giving him so much trouble; but finish, however, by accepting. On arriving at your house, you should offer him your thanks.

In order to avoid these two inconveniences, it will be well to request your husband, or some one of your relations, to come and wait upon you; you will in this way avoid still another inconvenience.

E. C. de Calabrella,
The Ladies' Science of Etiquette
(New York, 1844), 20

A Gentleman's Behavior in the Street

Every man ought to know how to walk, and it is well to practice and acquire a proper gait. Don't walk with a strut like a turkey-cock, nor stiffly as if you had a poker down your back, nor, on the other hand, swing from side to side, nor push on head first, dragging your limbs after you. Don't swing your arms like a windmill, nor carry them stuck to your side like a trussed fowl. Wear your hat upright on your head, neither set back, nor drawn over the eyes, nor carried jauntily on one side. Keep your hands out of your pockets, and carry them easily as nature intended. A proper stick or cane of moderate size gives employment to one of them, and may be of advantage.

A Lady's Behavior in the Street

Should be modest, and dignified, yet pleasant and engaging. Nothing indicates the character more than the walk. Of all things, never stare—never giggle—never walk with a wiggle, or swing from side to side. Fast walking cannot be graceful; never run in the street.

The Art of Good Behaviour
(New York, ca. 1845), 17, 19

Gait and carriage.

A lady ought to adopt a modest and measured gait; too great hurry injures the grace which ought to characterize her. She should not turn her head on one side and on the other, especially in large towns or cities, where this bad habit seems to be an invitation to the impertinent. A lady should not present herself alone in a library, or a museum, unless she goes there to study, or work as an artist.

Attentions to others.

When you are passing in the street, and see coming towards you a person of your acquaintance, whether a lady or an elderly person, you should offer them the wall, that is to say, the side next the houses. If a carriage should happen to stop, in such a manner as to leave only a narrow passage between it and the houses, beware of elbowing and rudely crowding the passengers, with a view to get by more expeditiously; wait your turn, and if any one of the persons before mentioned comes up, you should edge up to the wall, in order to give them the place. They also, as they pass, should bow politely to you.

If stormy weather has made it necessary to lay a plank across the gutters, which have become suddenly filled with water, it is not proper to crowd before another, in order to pass over the frail bridge.

Further—a young man of good breeding should promptly offer his hand to ladies, even if they are not acquaintances, when they pass such a place.

If, while walking up and down a public promenade, you should meet friends or acquaintances whom you do not intend to join, it is only necessary to salute them the first time of passing; to bow, or to nod to them every round would be tiresome, and, therefore, improper; do not think they will consider you odd or unfriendly, as, if they have any sense at all, they will appreciate your reasons. If you have anything to say to them, join them at once.

Raising the dress.

When tripping over the pavement, a lady should gracefully raise her dress a little above her ankle. With the right hand, she should hold together the folds of her gown, and draw them towards the right side. To raise the dress on both sides, and with both hands, is vulgar. This ungraceful practice can only be tolerated for a moment, when the mud is very deep.

Emily Thornwell,
The Lady's Guide to Perfect Gentility
(New York, 1856), 78–80

In standing, the legs [of the gentleman] ought to be straight or one of them bent a little, but not set wide apart. In walking, they should be moved gently but firmly from the hips, so that the upper part of the body may remain in the same position. . . . The feet must be turned outwards very little indeed; the arms should be carried easily and very slightly bent at the sides, and in walking should be moved a little, without swinging them; and the shoulders should never be shrugged up. Avoid stiffness on the one hand, lounging on the other.

In walking the feet should be moderately turned out, the steps should be equal, firm and light. A lady may be known by her walk. The short, rapid steps, the shaking the body from side to side, or the *very* slow gait which many ladies consider genteel, are equally to be deprecated.

The Habits of Good Society
(New York, 1860), 282–83, 309–10

Part 3: Bows and Curtseys

Address of the Gentleman

In the simple mechanic movements of address, the foot takes the second position, the other the third, then the body gently falls forward, keeping the head in a direct line with the body. The bend is made by a motion at the union of the inferior

Figure 19

limbs with the body, and a little flexing at the limbs. Time, place, and other circumstances, must determine the quantity of bends as well as its quickness. In this manner, the gentleman, on his first entering company, must make an easy salutation. When in an assembly or ball room, he opens the chorus, politeness requires him in the same manner to salute his partner with that soft respect, which the fair sex require, nor not to omit the same at conclusion. By this complimentary salutation, is meant to be expressed the respect due to the person addressed; and when a person suffers his head to drop down, and his body to be bent almost into the shape of an ox-bow, he seems more to reverence the earth, than the object of his esteem. Whoever may have inculcated this form of address in familiar life, has never considered the idea, which this compliment is supposed to convey; the eyes, are the index of the mind, and convey with their glances its image to us.

The bend of the body must never be made so low, as to hide the eyes from the person saluted; for what looks worse, when respect is meant to be conveyed, than to present the hair of the head, instead of expressing with cheerfulness that sweet respect, which can only be expressed by presenting the body, as has been mentioned and the features to the person, to whom difference is required to be made.

Address of the Lady

The lady, in making her address, moves her foot to the second position, the other into the fifth forward, then sinks directly down, which is performed by making a middle bend of the lower limbs, at the same time keeping the body and head exactly perpendicular, then raising straight up again. She is required to salute her partner in like manner, when she joins the chorus or dance.

How to Enter & Behave In a Ball-Room

When a gentleman requests of a young lady the favor of dancing with her, he should, at the time of addressing her, make his bow, and also by the approbation of the elderly persons who may have the charge of her. On obtaining the requested favor, he will present his right hand to receive the lady's left hand, and hold up his own as we before described. The gentleman will, in that manner lead the lady to the stand on which they intend to dance, placing himself at her left side. When the cotillion is formed, every person will reciprocally salute each other, then, each couple, facing each other, will again make a bow and courtsey.

Dancing being an amusement practised in good company, it should, of course, be attended with civility of manners. When a dance is ended, each person should salute the other, and every gentleman, receiving his partner's left hand in his right hand, will lead her back to the seat and then bow to her. The lady will also make her courtsey.

Saltator,
A Treatise on Dancing
(Boston, 1802), 69–71, 90–91

The performance of the curtsey in a proper manner, proves a matter of difficulty to some young ladies; but it will be found very easy, after a little practice, to curtsey with grace, if proper directions be given and attended to. The following is the usual mode: The front foot is first brought into the second position; the other is then drawn into the third behind, and passed immediately into the fourth behind, the whole weight of the body being thrown on the front foot; the front knee is then bent, the body gently sinks, the whole weight is transferred to the foot behind while rising, and the front foot is gradually brought into the fourth position. The arms should be gracefully bent, and the hands occupied in lightly holding out the dress. The first step in walking, after the curtsey, is made with the foot which happens to be forward at its completion. The perfect curtsey is rarely performed in society, as the general salutation is between a curtsey and a bow.

The Young Lady's Book
(Boston, 1830), 417

(S)alutations, used in every-day life, and among all classes of the community, are among the most important rudiments of the Terpsichorian art. A proper knowledge of them is indispensible to both sexes. There is no movement so awkward as a stiff bow or courtesy, and their proper execution can only be accomplished by that combination of ease and grace which are acquired by attention and long continued practice.

Edward Ferrero,
The Art of Dancing
(New York, 1859), 118–19

To courtesy to her partner [in a quadrille] the lady steps off with the right foot, carrying nearly all her weight upon it, at the same time raising the heel of the left foot, thus placing herself in 2d position, facing her partner, counting *one,* she then glides the left foot backward and across till the toe of the left foot is directly behind the right heel, the feet about one half of the length of the foot apart. This glide commences on the ball of the left foot, and terminates with both feet flat upon the floor, and the transfer of the weight to the backward foot. The bending of the knees and the casting of the eyes downward begin with the commencement of the glide with the left foot, and the genuflexion is steadily continued until the left foot reaches the position described, counting *two;* then, without changing the weight from the backward foot, she gradually rises, at the same time raising the forward heel, and lifting the eyes until she recovers her full height, counting *three*; and finally transfers the weight to the forward foot, counting *four.*

To turn and courtesy to the gentleman now behind her, the lady will step with the left foot (placing her weight upon it) across and in front of the right, turning the toe of the left foot inward, at the same time pivoting upon the ball of the right foot, to turn the feet outward in 2d position, and face the other gentleman, counting *one*; she then glides the right foot behind the left and bends the knees, counting *two*; then rises, counting *three*; then throws the weight upon the forward foot, and draws the right foot to 3d position behind, and places the weight upon both feet, counting *four.*

The movement of the feet and the undulation of the body should be unbroken.

It devolves upon the lady to rid her method of every mechanical tendency; to cause the movements to flow together smoothly and uninterruptedly; to regulate the length of the steps and to so modify the entire action as to prevent the detection of a studied form.

William B. DeGarmo,
The Dance of Society
(New York, 1875), 63–64

Part 4: Conversation and Flirtation

Never use the term "*genteel.*" Do not speak of "*genteel people*;" it is a low estimate of good breeding, used only by vulgar persons. The fear of being vulgar often drives meritorious people, who have risen by their own exertions, into the opposite extreme, and causes them to be superlatively delicate. Such persons are shocked at the sound of "*breeches*," will substitute "inebriated" for "*very drunk*," and can not be brought to allow there are such animals as "*women*" in the world.

Etiquette, or, A Guide to the Usages of Society
(Boston, 1844), 35

When conversing with young and gay women, do not discourse of metaphysics, but chat about the last fashion, the new opera or play, the last concert or novel, etc. With single ladies past twenty-five, speak of literary matters, music, &c., and silently compliment them by a proper deference to their opinions. With married ladies, inquire about the health of their children, speak of their grace and beauty, &c.

True Politeness, A Hand-Book . . . for Gentlemen, By an American Gentleman
(New York, 1847), 24

Propriety of movement and general demeanor in company.—To look steadily at any one, especially if you are a lady and are speaking to a gentleman; to turn the head frequently on one side and the other during conversation; to balance yourself upon your chair; to bend forward; to strike your hands upon your knees; to hold one of your knees between your hands locked together; to cross your legs; to extend your feet on the andirons; to admire yourself with complacency in a glass; to adjust, in an affected manner, your cravat, hair, dress, or handkerchief; to remain without gloves; to fold carefully your shawl, instead of throwing it with graceful negligence upon a table; to fret about a hat which you have just left off; to laugh immoderately; to place your hand upon the person with whom you are conversing; to take him by the buttons, the collar of his cloak, the cuffs, the waist, etc.; to seize any person by the waist or arm, or to touch their person; to roll the eyes or to raise them with affectation; to take snuff from the box of your neighbor, or to offer it to strangers, especially to ladies; to play continually with your chain or fan; to beat time with the feet and hands; to whirl round a chair with your hand; to shake with your feet the chair of your neighbor; to rub your face or your hands; wink your eyes; shrug up your shoulders; stamp with your feet, &c.;—all these bad habits, of which we cannot speak to people, are in the highest degree displeasing.

Emily Thornwell,
The Lady's Guide to Perfect Gentility
(New York, 1856), 87–88

Young gentlemen are earnestly advised not to limit their conversation to remarks on the weather and the heat of the room. It is, to a certain extent, incumbent on them to do something more than dance when they invite a lady to join in a quadrille. If it be only upon the news of the day, a gentleman should be able to offer at least three or four observations to his partner in the course of a long half-hour.

Mixing in Society
(London and New York, 1860), 165

Handkerchief Flirtations

The handkerchief, among lovers, is used in a different manner than its legitimate purpose. The most delicate hints can be given without danger of misunderstanding, and in "flirtations" it becomes a very useful instrument. It is in fact superior to the deaf and dumb alphabet, as the notice of bystanders is not attracted. The following rules are the law on the subject:

Drawing it across the lips	*Desiring an acquaintance*
Drawing it across the cheek	*I love you*
Drawing it across the forehead	*Look, we are watched*
Drawing it through the hands	*I hate you*
Dropping it	*We will be friends*
Folding it	*I wish to speak with you*
Letting it rest on the right cheek	*Yes*
Letting it rest on the left cheek	*No*
Letting it remain on the eyes	*You are so cruel*
Opposite corners in both hands	*Do wait for me*
Over the shoulder	*Follow me*
Placing it over the right ear	*How you have changed*
Putting it in the pocket	*No more love at present*
Taking it by the centre	*You are most too willing*
Twisting it in the left hand	*I wish to be rid of you*
Twisting it in the right hand	*I love another*
Winding it around the forefinger	*I am engaged*
Winding it around the third finger	*I am married*

Glove Flirtations

Like the handkerchief, the glove at times takes an important part in flirtations. The following are the known rules on the subject:

Biting the tips	*I wish to be rid of you very soon*
Clenching them, rolled up in right hand	*No*
Drawing half way on left hand	*Indifference*
Dropping both of them	*I love you*
Dropping one of them	*Yes*
Folding up carefully	*Get rid of your company*
Holding the tips downward	*I wish to be acquainted*
Holding them loose in the right hand	*Be contented*
Holding them loose in the left hand	*I am satisfied*
Left hand with the naked thumb exposed	*Do you love me?*
Putting them away	*I am vexed*
Right hand with the naked thumb exposed	*Kiss me*
Smoothing them out gently	*I am displeased*
Striking them over the shoulder	*Follow me*
Tapping the chin	*I love another*
Tossing them up gently	*I am engaged*
Turning them inside out	*I hate you*

Twisting them around the fingers	*Be careful, we are watched*
Using them as a fan	*Introduce me to your company*

Fan Flirtations

The fan is also used for flirtations, and the following rules govern the subject:

Carrying in right hand	*You are too willing*
Carrying in right hand in front of face	*Follow me*
Carrying in left hand	*Desirous of an acquaintance*
Closing it	*I wish to speak with you*
Drawing across the forehead	*We are watched*
Drawing across the cheek	*I love you*
Drawing across the eyes	*I am sorry*
Drawing through the hand	*I hate you*
Dropping	*We will be friends*
Fanning fast	*I am engaged*
Fanning slow	*I am married*
Letting it rest on right cheek	*Yes*
Letting it rest on left cheek	*No*
Open and shut	*You are cruel*
Open wide	*Wait for me*
Shut	*I have changed*
Placing it on the right ear	*You have changed*
Twirling in left hand	*I love another*
With handle to lips	*Kiss me*

Parasol Flirtations

Like the Handkerchief, Glove and Fan, the "Parasol" has its important part to play in flirtations, and we give the following rules regulating the same.

Carrying it elevated in left hand	*Desiring acquaintance*
Carrying it elevated in right hand	*You are too willing*
Carrying it closed in left hand	*Meet on the first crossing*
Carrying it closed in right hand by the side	*Follow me*
Carrying it over the right shoulder	*You can speak to me*
Carrying it over the left shoulder	*You are too cruel*
Closing up	*I wish to speak to you*
Dropping it	*I love you*
End of tips to lips	*Do you love me?*
Folding it up	*Get rid of your company*
Letting it rest on the right cheek	*Yes*
Letting it rest on the left cheek	*No*
Striking it on the hand	*I am very displeased*
Swinging it to and fro by the handle on left side	*I am engaged*

Swinging it to and fro by the handle on the right side	*I am married*
Tapping the chin gently	*I am in love with another*
Twirling it around	*Be careful; we are watched*
Using it as a fan	*Introduce me to your company*
With handle to lips	*Kiss me*

Daniel R. Shafer,
Secrets of Life Unveiled
(Baltimore, 1877), 231–34

How charming Sonya Valakhina was as she danced the French quadrille opposite me with the awkward young prince! How sweetly she smiled when she gave me her hand in the chaîne!. . . . *I did my* chassé en avant, chassé en arrière *and* glissade *with aplomb, and as I approached her laughingly showed her the glove with the two fingers sticking out. She burst into a helpless laugh and tripped still more enchantingly over the parquet floor. . . .*

I knew that the pas de Basque *would be out of place, unsuitable, and might even put me to shame; but the familiar sounds of the mazurka acting upon my ears communicated a certain movement to my acoustic nerves which in turn passed it on to my feet; and these, quite involuntarily and to the surprise of all spectators, began to evolve the fatal circular gliding* pas *on the toes. . . . I got so confused that instead of dancing I stamped my feet up and down on one spot in the strangest manner, neither in time to the music nor in relation to anything else, and at last came to a dead standstill. Everybody was staring at me: some in surprise, some with curiosity, some derisively, others with sympathy: only grandmamma looked on with complete indifference.*

"Il ne fallait pas danser, si vous ne savez pas!' *said papa's angry voice just above my ear, and gently pushing me aside he took my partner's hand in his, danced a turn with her in the old-fashioned style and to the loud applause of the onlookers led her back to her seat. The mazurka was at an end.*

Leo Tolstoy, "Childhood," from *Childhood, Boyhood, Youth*

Grace and Folly in the Ballroom

Part 1: Hazards and Blunders of Ballroom Etiquette

Another gross species of Rudeness which frequently occurs in the Ball room, and though it properly belongs to the Etiquette, must nevertheless be noticed here: and that is, many Persons, after standing up in the Dance, on finding the Figure too difficult for them, with a View of concealing their Inability to perform it, take the Liberty of altering it to one more suitable to their shallow Capacities, without ever consulting the lady who called the *Dance.* This is always considered a certain Affront; as no Figure can be altered, or any Part of it, *without* consulting the lady who *called* it: therefore, if any Person should find a Figure too difficult for them to perform, they must withdraw from the Set, as it is not only the Disrespect shewn to the lady, but it is calculated to throw a whole Company into contention and confusion; by so misleading many Persons, with a Variety of different Figures, and thereby preventing their knowing which is the right one to Dance to.

Thomas Wilson,
A Companion to the Ball Room
(London, 1816), 197

We are not obliged to go exactly at the appointed hour; it is even fashionable to go an hour later. Married ladies are accompanied by their husbands, unmarried ones, by their mother or by a *chaperone.* These last ladies place themselves behind the dancers; the master of the house then goes before one and another, procures seats for them, and mingles again among the gentlemen who are standing, and who form groups or walk about the room.

The toilet of all the assembly should be made with great care. A gentleman who should appear in a riding coat and boots would pass for a person of bad *ton.*

When you are sure of a place in the dance, you go up to a lady, and ask her if she will *do you the honor* to dance with you. If she answers that she is engaged, invite her for the next dance, but take care not to address yourself afterwards to any ladies next to her, for these not being able to refuse you, would feel hurt at being invited after another. Never wait until the signal is given to take a partner, for nothing is more impolite than to invite a lady hastily, and when the dancers are already in their places; it can be allowed only when the set is incomplete. A lady cannot refuse the invitation of a gentleman to dance, unless she has already accepted that of another, for she would be guilty of an incivility which might occasion trouble; she would moreover seem to show contempt for him who she refused, and would expose herself to receive an ill compliment from him.

The master of the house should see that all the ladies dance; he should take notice particularly of those who seem to serve as drapery to the walls of the ball-room (or *wall-flowers*, as the familiar expression is), and should see that they are invited to dance. But he must do this wholly unperceived, in order not to wound the self-esteem of the unfortunate ladies.

When an unpractised dancer makes a mistake, we may apprise him of his error; but it would be very impolite to have the air of giving him a lesson.

Dance with grace and modesty; neither affect to make a parade of your knowledge; refrain from great leaps and ridiculous jumps which would attract the attention of all towards you.

Mme. Celnart,
The Gentleman and Lady's Book
(Boston, 1833), 183–86

Invitations to a ball should be issued at least ten days in advance, in order to give an opportunity to the men to clear away engagements; and to women, time to prepare the artillery of their toilet. Cards of invitation should be sent—not notes.

Upon the entrance of ladies, or persons entitled to deference, the master of the house precedes them across the room: he addresses compliments to them, and will lose his life to procure them seats.

While dancing with a lady whom you have never seen before, you should not talk to her much.

The master of the ceremonies must take care that every lady dances, and press into service for that purpose those young men who are hanging round the room like fossils. If desired by him to dance with a particular lady you should refuse on no account.

If you have no ear, that is, a false one, never dance.

To usurp the seat of a person who is dancing is the height of incivility.

The Laws of Etiquette,
By a Gentleman
(Philadelphia, 1836), 113–14

No gentleman should venture to enter a ballroom who has not *learnt* to dance, and in all other respects so to conduct himself as to impress the idea of feeling himself perfectly at home. Nothing is more preposterous than for a man whose station in society gives him a right of entry among the polished and the gay, venturing to claim the privilege without having duly qualified himself, by a due attention to those rules, to which he is expected to conform.

The Ball Room Annual
(London, ca. 1844), 14

No man should attempt to dance without being well acquainted with the figures; for his blunders place the woman who does him the honour to dance with him, in an embarrassing situation, and he will make quite a different figure from what he intends. But they are learned without any difficulty, being very simple and generally unvarying. As to the *steps*, that is quite another affair. Unless a man has a very graceful figure and can use it with great elegance, it is better for him to *walk* through the quadrilles, or invent some gliding movement for the occasion. To see an awkward or a grave man going with pious scrupulosity through the "one, two, three, and four" of a balancez, and shaking a vast frame in a manner to fill the bystanders with reasonable dread lest it should fall to pieces, is ludicrous enough.

When a woman is standing in a quadrille, though not engaged in dancing, a man not acquainted with her partner, should not converse with her. As this prevents the other from talking to her himself, it is extremely indelicate, and obliges the other to feel unpleasantly; and such a one would not be censurable, if he were to interrupt the conversation, if it were long continued, and to turn his back upon the intruder. Where this third person is known to both parties, to join for a short time in colloquy with both is obvious to no objection.

Etiquette for Gentlemen,
By a Gentleman
(Philadelphia, 1844), 176–77

The rule is, never to introduce one person to another without knowing that it is agreeable to both. Ladies are always to be consulted beforehand. Gentlemen are introduced *to* ladies, not ladies to gentlemen. In other cases, the younger to the elder. Where persons are equal, we "introduce" them. Where there is much difference in age or station, we "present."

The Art of Good Behaviour
(New York, ca. 1845), 22

If a gentleman presumes to ask you to dance without an introduction, you will of course refuse. It is hardly necessary to supply the fair reader with words to repel such a rudeness; a man must have more than ordinary impertinence if he was not satisfied by your saying, "I must decline, sir, not having the honor of your acquaintance;" and recollect that his previous rudeness ought to be punished by your refusing to be introduced.

True Politeness, A Hand-Book . . . for Ladies,
By an American Lady
(New York, 184–), 38–39

If a lady should excuse herself from dancing when you have asked her, and you should immediately afterwards see her dancing with another, do not take any unpleasant notice of it; the probability is, that she preferred and expected to dance with someone better known and more highly favored, and not that she had any objection to you.

If a lady waltz with you, beware not to press her waist; lightly touch it with the open palm of your hand, lest you leave a disagreeable impression not only on her *ceinture*, but on her mind.

True Politeness, A Hand-Book . . . for Gentlemen,
By an American Gentleman
(New York, 1847), 37

I would ask those who so abuse [dancing], what enjoyment can there be in rushing up and down a room, to the danger of yourself and all you meet with? What elegance can there be in being tightly clasped in a gentleman's arms, the lady's chin projecting over his shoulder? What pleasure in being pushed backwards and swung round until a palpating heart and a fevered frame compel you to sink exhausted to your seat?

Mrs. Alfred Webster,
Dancing as a Means of Physical Education
(London, 1851), 25–26

Even the most humane man, whatever may be the kindness of his head, would rather not exhibit himself on the floor with a partner *ni jeune ni jolie*, who is ill-drest, looks badly, moves ungracefully, can neither keep time to the music nor understand the figure, and in fact has "no dancing in her soul." If, with all the rest, she is dull and stupid, it is cruel for any kind friend to inflict her on a gentleman as a partner. . . .

A deformed woman dancing is "a sorry sight." She should never consent to any such exhibition of her unhappy figure. She will only be asked out of mere compassion, or from some interested and unworthy motive. We are asked—"Why should not such a lady dance, if it gives her pleasure?" We answer—"It should *not* give her pleasure."

Now as a deformed lady may render herself very agreeable as a good conversationalist, we repeat that she has no occasion to exhibit the defects of her person by treading the mazes of a cotillion, or above all, in going down a country dance, should those "never-ending, still beginning" performances come again into fashion. Young men say that an ugly, misshapen female who waltzes, or joins in a polka, or redowa, or mazurka, deserves the penitentiary.

Miss Leslie,
The Behaviour Book
(Philadelphia, 1853), 319–21

On the finish of the dance, lead your partner to her seat; and as the lady seats herself, gracefully bow to her, tendering your services to her slightest desires that may subserve her comforts. All this can be effected without any over officious bustle of attention. It is the manner and not the *maximum* of ceremony that marks the true gentleman. When you take your position in the Quadrille, bow to your partner first, and then to the lady on your left corner, during the time of the introductory music; a slight salutation to the entire Quadrille would not be unbecoming.

Dancing and etiquette are inseparable; they must go hand in hand to impart pleasure and to secure a just moral result,— therefore it is wiser to invest the embellishments of the art with the graces of refined manners (which indeed are the ornaments of it). Thus will dancing become a rational, and necessarily an innocent amusement, worthy of a place among the other elegant arts.

Charles Durang,
The Dancer's Own Book
(Philadelphia, 1855), 171, 179

In the quadrille, and most dances, ladies take their positions and make their forward and side movements with the right foot in advance, as we have illustrated; but in all such cases the gentleman dances with the left foot in advance, which corresponding to the lady's right, makes up the symmetry of the figure, and when required, brings them facing each other. In the gallope, the sliding balance, now mostly used in the quadrille, in the polka and schottisch, this is an evident necessity; but some teachers of dancing have made the curious blunder of teaching both sexes to dance with the same movement in the quadrille, destroying much of the symmetry of this most beautiful and graceful of all dances. Gentlemen accustomed to military exercises will naturally move with the "left foot forward."

In the dancing of the parlor and ball room, the feet are scarcely ever raised an inch from the floor, but carried with the toes depressed with deliberate gentle gliding movement. Perhaps the only exception to this is the polka, which consists in a series of little bounds, or gentle springs, but without any extravagant effort.

The Illustrated Manners Book
(New York, 1855), 389

If gentlemen go to balls, they should dance. It is a great breach of etiquette to stand idling and sauntering while ladies are waiting for an invitation to dance.

In the present day, it is as requisite to dance well as it ever was; but elaborate steps are no longer in fashion. Be sure you know the figures of all the dances you stand up to perform your part in, whether the first of quadrilles, the Lancers, the Caledonians, the Mazurka, the Polkas, the Schottische, the Varsoviana, or the *valse à trois temps, à deux temps,* or *à un temps.*

Not only be certain of the figure, but of the tune, in order to keep in time. Partners who dance out of time are carefully avoided.

Jumping and *cutting capers* are not in accordance with modern taste.

Lead the lady through the quadrilles; do not drag her.

If you are obliged to withdraw from the ballroom earlier than the other guests, do so as quietly as possible, lest your departure should tend to break up the party.

The Hand-Book of Etiquette
(London, 1860), 42–43

Bear in mind that all *casino* habits are to be scrupulously avoided in a private ball-room. It is an affront to a highly-bred lady to hold her hand behind you, or on your hip, when dancing a round dance.

A thoughtful hostess will never introduce a bad dancer to a good one, because she has no right to punish one friend in order to oblige another.

Lastly, a gentleman should not go to a ball unless he has previously made up his mind to be agreeable: that is, to dance with the plainest as well as with the most beautiful; to take down an elderly chaperone to supper, instead of her lovely charge, with a good grace; to enter into the spirit of the dance, instead of hanging about the doorway; to abstain from immoderate eating, drinking, or talking; to submit to trifling annoyances with cheerfulness; in fact, to forget himself, and contribute as much as possible to the amusement of others.

Mixing in Society
(London and New York, 1860), 164–66

Do not be the last to leave the ball room. It is more elegant to leave early, as staying too late gives others the impression that you do not often have an invitation to a ball, and must "make the most of it."

Cecil B. Hartley,
The Gentlemen's Book
(Boston, ca. 1860), 97

On entering a ball-room, all thought of self should be dismissed. The petty ambition of endeavoring to create a sensation by either dress, loud talking, or unusual behavior, is to be condemned; also the effort to monopolize a certain part of the room during the evening, or of forming exclusive circles when unanimity and good feeling should prevail, are, to say the least, exceptionable.

Thomas Hillgrove,
A Complete Practical Guide to the Art of Dancing
(New York, 1863), 24

Once having procured a partner, [a gentleman] cannot be sufficiently careful of her. He must never leave her until he restores her to her chaperone. He must be careful to guard her against any collisions whilst dancing, and give her his arm directly the dance is finished. It would not be etiquette to walk up and down the ball-room at the conclusion of the dance. One turn around the room would be sufficient, and then the dancers would seek some cooler retreat. The gentleman should ask his partner if she would take any refreshment, and if she reply in the affirmative, he must see she is comfortably seated, and provided with all she needs. He must stay with her all the time she is in the refreshment room, and escort her to her chaperone and bow before leaving her. A gentleman should be up to time in keeping his engagements, as it looks very ungracious to keep a lady waiting after the music has begun. If the dance is a "square," he should be expeditious in providing a *vis-à-vis*; as it is very disagreeable to the lady to be left out in the cold.

Etiquette is rather hard upon girls in the matter of dances. They must not refuse one partner in order to dance with another. If they refuse they must say that they are not dancing at this time. Choice is not allowed to a girl, she must wait until somebody asks her. Yet if he is the very worst dancer in the room she must either accept him or sit out the dance. For the prevention of this catastrophe, programmes have been invented, and a girl is able to account for a mistake by saying that her programme had got into such a state of confusion that she thought she was engaged when she was not.

The Ball-Room Guide, a Handy Manual
(London and New York, 186–), 27–30

The length to which the ordinary dancing party or ball is prolonged is a serious evil. In our working community there are but few who, if they dance all night, can sleep all day, for most of the gay cavaliers of the evening are the busy drudges of the morning. Our youthful damsels, it is true, by the mistaken indulgence of their parents, can, if their excited nerves will let them, sleep away as many of the twenty-four hours as they please, but their partners cannot, for they are wanted, for the most part, at the shop and counting-house. The mere loss of sleep, the recuperative influence of which is so necessary, must be a serious damage to the health of the young gallants who strive to comply with the requirements both of fashion and business. We would advise our friends to be always among the earliest to leave a fashionable party. There is, moreover, no rule of politeness which exacts a very prolonged stay.

Robert Tomes,
The Bazar Book of Decorum
(New York, 1870), 229

Especially is it necessary, now that ladies are wearing drawing-room and dinner dresses at balls, that he should understand the engineering of "trains" in all their most extravagant curves, lengths, and contortions.

Always apologize when you step on a lady's train. . . .

C. H. Cleveland, Jr.,
Dancing at Home and Abroad
(Boston, 1878), 30, 35

Introductions take place in a ball-room in order to provide ladies with partners, or between persons residing in different cities. In all other cases, permission is generally asked before giving introductions. But where a hostess is sufficiently discriminating in the selection of her guests, not attempting to fuse circles which are entirely distinct of assimilation as oil and water, those assembled under her roof should remember that they are, in a certain sense, made known to one another, and ought, therefore, to be able to converse freely without introductions.

Ladies in American cities have much more license than in European society, nor is this license often abused. They are at liberty to walk about with their partners after a dance; while there, they must return to the care of their chaperones, or retire to the room appropriated for their use in the pauses of the cotillion.

Young ladies ought not to accept invitations for every dance. The fatigue is too wearing, and the heated faces that it induces too unbecoming. But they must be careful how they refuse to dance; for unless a good reason is given, a man is apt to take it as an evidence of personal dislike. After refusing, the gentleman should not urge her to dance, nor should the lady accept another invitation for the same dance.

Mrs. H. O. Ward,
Sensible Etiquette of the Best Society
(Philadelphia, 1878), 217, 223

It is usual for young ladies to return to their chaperones after each dance, or after they have partaken of refreshments or supper, but it is not considered good style for a lady to promenade up and down and around the ball-room leaning on the arm of her partner; to take one turn through the rooms with her partner being in better taste. It would be also bad style for a couple to stand arm-in-arm during the pauses in the figures of a quadrille, or while resting during a valse, or for a gentleman to turn his partner round at the conclusion of each figure of the quadrille, as the quadrille should be danced in the quietest possible manner, without any display of "steps" acquired from the dancing mistress.

A ball is usually opened either by the hostess herself or by one of her daughters. Opening a ball simply signifies dancing in the first quadrille at the top of the room with a gentleman of highest rank.

If a member of the Royal Family, or a foreign Prince, were expected, dancing would not commence until the arrival of the Royal guest; and if the guest were a lady, the host would open the ball with her, having his wife or daughter as vis-à-vis. If the royal guest were a Prince, the reverse would be the case.

When a Prince wishes to dance with any lady present, with whom he is unacquainted, his equerry informs her of the Prince's intention, and conducts her to the Prince, saying, as he does so, "Mrs. A—, Sir," or "Miss B—, Sir." The Prince would bow and offer her his arm; the lady would curtsey, and take it. She would not address him until addressed by him, it not being considered etiquette to do so. The same course is followed by a Princess; strangers would not on any account indiscriminately ask a Princess to dance, but the host would have the privilege of doing so.

Manners and Tone of Good Society,
By a Member of the Aristocracy
(London, ca. 1879), 124–25, 129.

It is not binding upon any gentleman to remain one moment longer than he desires with any lady. By constantly moving from one to another, when he feels so inclined, he gives an opportunity to others to circulate as freely; and this custom, generally introduced in our society, would go a long way toward contributing to the enjoyment of all. The false notion generally entertained that a gentleman is expected to remain standing by the side of a lady, like a sentinel on duty, until relieved by some other person, is absurd, and deters many who would gladly give a few passing moments to lady acquaintances, could they but know that they would be free to leave at any instant that conversation flagged, or that they desired to join another. In a society where it is not considered a rudeness to leave after a few sentences with one, to exchange some words with another, there is a constant interchange of civilities, and the men circulate through the room with that charming freedom which insures the enjoyment of all.

John H. Young,
Our Deportment
(Detroit, 1879), 138–39

Never take your place upon the floor unless you are a thorough master of the step. If it is a square dance a single person unfamiliar with the changes will interrupt the whole set and not only embarrass himself but spoil the pleasure of the others in the set. To attempt a round dance which you are unfamiliar with is ridiculous on its face.

Hudson K. Lyverthey,
Our Etiquette and Social Observances
(Grand Rapids, Mich., 1881), 61

I have said nothing about dancing, because that is a subject for professional teachers. For my own part, I do not like to see a gentleman dance *too well*; he does not want to be taken for a dancing-master. It is enough if he dance *like a gentleman*, without that constraint, that *gene*, which most Englishmen seem to experience, so that they look as if they were performing a task, or as if they felt they were making fools of themselves. For Heaven's sake don't dance out of time! That would show you have no ear for music, and, moreover, 'twould embarrass your partner. And don't go through your steps with the prim and deliberate air of a board-school prodigy repeating the names of the rivers in Mesopotamia. Use your hands and feet as if they belonged to you, and not as if you had hired them for the occasion, and were afraid of wearing them out. Do not assume the grave air of Lord-justice X. when he is engaged in solving some abstruse legal problem; but, on the other hand, avoid that vacant, silly stereotyped smile which the ladies of the ballet seem to think is *de rigueur* to display. Unless you are entirely self-possessed, have a good figure, and know what you are about, you should confine your efforts to the modest quadrille, and not venture upon the prancing polka or the bounding valse. Remember that no spectacle under heaven provokes more laughter than a bad dancer floundering round a ball-room, exposed to the sharp criticisms of pitiless bright eyes and relentless rosy lips. A man can never recover from the shame in which such an exposure involves him.

Our young men have an odious and selfish habit of not dancing if they cannot secure just the partners they want, and of standing, a black-coated and dismal group, like so many crows, around the doorway.

"Social Etiquette and Home Culture,"
in Franklin Square Library,
By the Lounger in Society
(New York, 1881), 7, 140

[I]n the ball-room the P.G. [Perfect Gentleman] must sink his individuality and conform. He is there by courtesy of his hostess and his own free will, not so much to enjoy himself in the dancing as to play the part of "dancing man."

The P.G. feels that the ball-room is not the place to let off epigrams, discuss agnosticism or exercise one's art as a "raconteur." He is there with business in hand, to wit: to dance with the partners whom his hostess may provide for him, to aid her with all his strength of body and mind in preventing the growth of that genus of plant, yelept [*sic*: yclept] "wall flower."

The P.G. at a ball should not be too heavy in his conversation, nor yet too light and trivial.

Therefore, should the P.G. follow the safe middle course marked by Apollo for his presumptuous son. The freshest novel; the last play; the opera, if in season; the latest efforts of theatrical amateurs; one's favorite periodicals; wholesome criticism of prominent women and notable men present at the ball; art in general or as represented at any of the exhibitions; noted social gatherings of the season; any of the amusing "fads," or weaknesses of the day, provided there be nothing personal or indelicate about them; these are some of the topics with which the P.G. may endeavor to draw his partner into pleasant conversation.

One great injustice, of which young Americans—of both sexes—are guilty, is the unceremonious and needless manner in which they crowd the "old folks" from the ball-room. In continental Europe, it is not an uncommon sight to see three generations represented in a waltz. This is as it should be.

Ingersoll Lockwood,
The P.G. or Perfect Gentleman
(New York, 1887), 33, 35, 41–42

It Is the Correct Thing—For a gentleman when he asks a young lady to dance with him, to do so in a definite and polite way.

It Is Not the Correct Thing—For a gentleman to say to a lady, "Are you engaged for the polka?" This is a very impolite form of invitation.

The Correct Thing in Good Society
(Boston, ca. 1888), 118–19

Part 2: Arrangements for the Ball

The ball-room especially should be that which has the lightest paper; and if there be dark curtains, particularly red ones, they must be taken down and replaced by light ones. The best color for a ball-room is very pale yellow. The light should come from the walls, heightened by strong reflectors. Chandeliers are dangerous, and throw a downward shadow; at any rate, wax should always be replaced by globe lamps.

English people have as great a horror of taking up their carpets as Frenchmen are supposed to have of washing their necks. Probably the amount of dust which would meet their gaze is too appalling to think of. Then, again, English boards are of a wood which it is not easy to polish. Commend me to the old oak-floors, which, with a little bees' wax, come out as dark as ebony, and help the unskilled foot to glide. However, a polished floor, whatever the wood, is always the best thing to dance on, and, if you want to give a ball, and not only a crush, you should hire a man who, with a brush under one foot and a slipper on the other, will dance over the floor for four or five hours, till you can almost see your face in it. Above all, take care that there is not bees' wax enough to blacken the ladies' shoes.

The Habits of Good Society
(New York, 1860), 384–85

A room which is nearly square, yet a little longer than it is broad, will be found the most favourable for a ball. It admits of two quadrille parties, or two round dances, at the same time. In a perfectly square room this arrangement is not so practical or pleasant. A very long and narrow room is obviously of the worst shape for dancing, and is fit only for quadrilles and country dances.

The top of the ballroom is the part nearest the orchestra. In a private room, the top is where it would be if the room were a dining-room. It is generally at the farthest point from the door. Dancers should be careful to ascertain the top of the room before taking their places, as the top couples always lead the dances.

Mixing in Society
(London and New York, 1860), 158

The ball-room should be light and well-ventilated. A square room is better than one which is long and narrow, but a medium between these extremes is best. Wax candles furnish the most becoming light to the complexion, but care should be taken that they are provided with *bobèches* so that the grease does not drip over the dresses of the guests.

A good floor is one of the first essentials at a ball, and care should be taken that the boards present no irregularity of surface. The best way to prepare a floor for dancing is to scrub the boards with very hot water, and then pour a quantity of milk over them before they are perfectly dry. A parquet floor is perfection for dancing on and gives a pretty appearance to a ball-room.

Dance cards may be of any fanciful design selected by the hostess; but modern taste is inclined to favour plain and chaste designs rather than florid. The old dance programmes were made with two pages, the one containing the dances and the other the space for engagements. The two leaves, however, showed such a decided disposition to part company before the evening was over that a new kind of card has been introduced, a simple square made of the strongest, mill-board, with a hole bored at the left-hand side for the purpose of attaching the pencil. No reliable method has yet been discovered of inducing the pencil to cleave the cord, so that it is safer for gentlemen to be provided with a pencil of their own, in case of accidents.

The name of the house where the ball is given is usually printed on the cover of the programme, also the date on which the entertainment takes place. Twenty-one dances is a convenient number to arrange for. Supper causes a convenient break after the twelfth dance, and extra dances (the happy refuge of the young lady who has made up her programme in haste to repent at leisure) are played by the band during the progress of supper, often rather a lengthy period in a house where only a very small detachment of the guests can go in at a time.

The Ball-Room Guide, a Handy Manual
(London and New York, 186–), 18–21

Invitations are sent from 10 days to two weeks previously, and should be answered immediately, as has been already stated. The requisites for a successful ball are good music and plenty of dancing men.

Mrs. H. O. Ward,
Sensible Etiquette of the Best Society
(Philadelphia, 1878), 200–201

Several fashionable ball-givers are beginning to perceive the folly of crowding of from between two hundred to three hundred people together into rooms not properly ventilated, and have discovered that the only way in which to render the temperature of a London ball comparatively cool, is to remove the windows, and to substitute lace draperies in lieu of bunting, with the addition of large blocks of ice placed in every convenient spot.

Ball-goers appreciate these alterations as only those who have experienced night after night the close, stifling, vitiated atmosphere of an over-crowded ball-room can do, and as half the London ball-rooms are only average-sized drawing-rooms, and by no means spacious reception-rooms, the absurdity of excluding air from the ball-room with yards and yards of thick canvas, cannot be too severely criticised.

Manners and Tone of Good Society,
By a Member of the Aristocracy
(London, ca. 1879), 133–34

Persons giving balls or dancing parties should be careful not to invite more than their rooms will accommodate, so as to avoid a crush. Invitations to crowded balls are not hospitalities, but inflictions. A hostess is usually safe, however, in inviting one-fourth more than her rooms will hold, as that proportion of regrets are apt to be received. People who do not dance will not, as a rule, expect to be invited to a ball or dancing party.

John H. Young,
Our Deportment
(Detroit, 1879), 137–38

The best floors for dancing are the parquet floors that are now so fashionable. Where a house does not boast of these, the next best thing is to take up the carpets and have the floors smoothed and planed by a carpenter, so that there shall be no danger of splinters getting into the feet of the dancers. Formerly, carpets were covered with crash, which was nailed down over them smoothly, and made quite a pleasant surface to dance upon; but the fine lint which arose from it was found to have a very bad effect on the lungs of dancers and musicians. A favorite player of dance music in New York died a few years ago of consumption, caused by constantly inhaling this lint; and the use of crash has now been abandoned in a great measure because it has proved so unwholesome.

Florence Howe Hall,
Social Customs
(Boston, 1881), 132

Part 3: The Ballroom: Public and Private

Rules for Public Balls

Any lady refusing to dance with a Gentleman, if disengaged, will be under the penalty of not joining the two next Dances.

To commit the following is considered a great breach of good manners:

Objecting to stand up when a dance is called.
Clapping of hands when a Dance is finished.
Holding the hands of another too fast.
Introducing Hornpipe or beating steps.

G. M. S. Chivers,
A Pocket Companion to French and English Dancing
(London, 1821), 36, 39

The etiquette of the ball-room differs slightly in the country, and in different cities in the union. In country ball-rooms generally, a gentleman may ask any lady to dance with him, and after an introduction, may enter into conversation or promenade with her through the room, without being considered guilty of the least presumption in so doing; but, in the city, a regular introduction must take place before the gentleman can be entitled to offer himself as a partner; and, though he may be intimately acquainted with a lady, it is generally considered proper for him to ask the consent of the person accompanying her, as well as the lady herself, before engaging her for a set.

The Ball-Room Instructor
(New York, 1841), [9]

In private parties, introductions are not considered necessary. The fact of your being invited is a voucher for your respectability, as well as that of all persons present; but at a public ball, you must not only have an introduction by the manager of the ball, or a mutual acquaintance, to the lady with whom you mean to dance, but the permission of the gentleman who attends her as well as her own.

The Art of Good Behaviour
(New York, ca. 1845), 25

At the ordinary public balls, it is desirable to make up a party sufficiently large to render you independent of the introductions of the master of the ceremonies, as, in spite of his best efforts, objectionable individuals will gain access to such. When such a party is formed, you can easily and without rudeness refuse to be introduced to any gentleman, by stating that you are engaged; as of course you would be to your friends for that evening.

True Politeness. A Hand-Book . . . for Ladies, By an American Lady
(New York, 184–), 38

Formerly, it was not considered improper or derogatory for ladies and gentlemen to attend public balls, and share in their performance; but as the population augmented and the ball-room *habitués* degenerated into a mixed assemblage, the more refined portion of the community avoided them. Dancing, therefore, among the most cultivated and *élite*, is confined to parlors and private assembly rooms. If any proof were required of the high favor in which it is held, when conducted upon approved principles, it would be found in the fact that, at a private entertainment, given at the Academy of Music, in New York, by the writer, for his pupils and their friends, upward of four thousand persons were present, a large portion of whom shared in the entertainment.

Edward Ferrero,
The Art of Dancing
(New York, 1859), 74

Public balls are not much frequented by people of good society, except in water-places and country towns. Even there a young lady should not be seen at more than two or three in the year. Country-balls, race-balls, and hunt-balls, are generally better than common subscription-balls. Charity balls are an abominable anomaly.

The Habits of Good Society
(New York, 1860), 396

Balls are of two kinds—public and private. Those called public take different forms. There is the charity ball, military ball, race ball and country ball, and what may be called the public or subscription ball. The latter is generally given in public assembly rooms and admission is obtained by a ticket obtained before hand from the committee. Much care must be taken to secure the selectness of these assemblies, or they can never be successful.

Private Balls.—It is the lady of the house who gives the ball. The invitations should be in her name, and the replies addressed to her.

The Ball-Room Guide, a Handy Manual
(London and New York, 186–), 11, 14

"Invitation Balls" are those balls which are given by society at large, in town and country, as well as Military and Naval balls, Hunt balls, and Bachelors' Balls, &c.; while "Public Balls" are balls for which a ticket of admission can be purchased, and include the "Country balls," those held in aid of local charities, "Subscription balls," held at watering places, cathedral cities, &c.

In London, public balls are but little patronized by society, save with a few exceptions, in favor of such balls as the "Caledonian ball," the "Yorkshire," "Wiltshire," and Somersetshire Societies balls, which are attended principally by those ladies and gentlemen who are interested more or less locally in the various charities they support, and for which purpose these balls are annually held.

The "Country ball" season generally commences in "November" and lasts until the commencement of Lent, and every town, in almost every country, can boast of its annual ball, which is attended more or less by the aristocracy and gentry of the neighbourhood, and by the professional classes of the town itself. The stewards of these balls are, as a rule, the representatives of the various classes by whom they are attended; the members of the aristocracy residing in the country heading the list of stewards, and the members of the professional classes usually closing it. Thus, the stewards are able to make a ball pleasant to all their individual friends.

The office of "Master of the Ceremonies" has long since become obsolete, and has not been revived under any other title, and introductions at balls are therefore made *only* by persons themselves acquainted with those whom they introduce to each other. Stewards of a ball do not make introductions, even if solicited to do so by strangers attending it.

When a friend or an acquaintance desires to make an introduction, it is usual to ascertain the wishes of the lady, or the inclinations of the gentleman before doing so, unless aware that a lady is in want of a partner, or that a gentleman is anxious to dance with someone, and is indifferent as to whom she might be.

Manners and Tone of Good Society,
By a Member of the Aristocracy
(London, ca. 1879), 122–23

State Balls.—There are two of these given every season. They are given at Buckingham Palace, and are very grand affairs. But they are so bound and tied up by etiquette, and are generally such stupendous crushes, that little amusement and pleasure, such as one is accustomed to expect at a ball, can be had. Only those who have been presented are invited, and not many of them. The Prince and Princess of Wales always (in these days) represent the Queen, and enter the ball-room about 10.15 o'clock in formal procession. There is no dancing till then. A "state quadrille" is formed, the Prince and Princess dancing *vis-à-vis* with "swell" partners, the sides being other princes and princesses, and so the ball is opened. After that the Prince dances with whomsoever he likes. The "form" is for him to send one of his equerries to a lady to inform her that he wishes to dance such a dance with her. Of course, she *must* accept. It would be execrably bad form to refuse. All other engagements must give way. The Princess of Wales askes her partners to dance. No one may ask her.

Balls.—Private balls in England are, in the main, very similar to those in America—I speak, of course, of the best classes of "society" in both countries—so that it will not be necessary to enter into a lengthy description of them. There are, however a few customs to be considered whose observance or non-observance would be a display of good or bad form, which are different from American usages. There are balls in town and balls in the country. Balls in town first. They begin from 11 to 12 o'clock, but it is not "good form" to go to a ball before 11.30 at the earliest. Of course, a good deal depends on the number of balls one has to go to on one night—two, three, and even four being not uncommon during the season's height. And perhaps there is a dinner-party or the opera first. In the case of several balls on hand the hour of arrival at the first might be a trifle earlier than 11, while that at the last—even though you stay as short a time at the preceding balls as "good form" will permit, say half an hour to an hour—must be what under different circumstances would be so late as to be considered "bad form." If you had but one ball to go to, and went to it at one o'clock, it could not be called "good form," as it would be rude to the giver. But, as people who have many balls to go to are supposed to choose what they consider the best ball for the last, an arrival, no matter how late, is regarded as a compliment. Late comers have come to stay, and not hurry away, as they had been obliged to do at the other and less favored houses. There are no "dressing-rooms" at an English ball—in town, at all events. People are supposed to come ready to go into the ball-room immediately upon the removal of "wraps," without change of shoes, brushing of hair, pinning of flowers or ribbons, or anything of that sort. They simply leave their "wraps" in the "cloak-room," an apartment at the foot of the stairs or the back hall.

"Good Form" in England,
By an American Resident in the United Kingdom
(New York, 1888), 155–56, 158–60

Music must take rank as the highest of the fine arts—as the one which, more than any other, ministers to human welfare.

Herbert Spencer, "On the Origin and Function of Music"
from *Essays on Education*

It is sweet to dance to violins
When Love and Life are fair;
To dance to flutes, to dance to lutes
Is delicate and rare:
But it is not sweet with nimble feet
To dance upon the air!

Oscar Wilde, *The Ballad of Reading Gaol*

Music is the universal language of mankind,—poetry their universal pastime and delight.

H. W. Longfellow, *Outre-Mer*

It is music which most completely realises this artistic ideal, this perfect identification of matter and form. . . . In music, then, rather than in poetry, is to be found the true type or measure of perfected art.

Walter Pater, *The Renaissance*

Music and Musicians

Part 1: Singing and Other Diversions

There are many young women, who when they sit down to the piano or the harp, or to sing, twist themselves into so many contortions, and writhe their bodies and faces about into such actions and grimaces, as would almost incline one to believe that they are suffering under the torture of the toothache or the gout. Their bosoms heave, their shoulders shrug, their heads swing to the right and left, their lips quiver, their eyes roll; they sigh, they pant, they seem ready to expire! And what is all this about? They are merely playing a favourite concerto, or singing a new Italian song.

What they call *expression in singing*, at the rate they would show it, is only fit to be exhibited on the stage, when the character of the song intends to portray the utmost ecstasy of passion to a sighing swain. In short, such an echo to the words and music of a love ditty is very improper in any young woman who would wish to be thought as pure in heart as in person.

Let their attitude at the piano, or the harp, be easy and graceful. I strongly exhort them to avoid a stiff, awkward, elbowing position at either; but they must observe an elegant flow of figure at both. The latter certainly admits of most grace, as the shape of the instrument is calculated, in every respect to show a fine figure to advantage. The contour of the whole form, the turn and polish of a beautiful hand and arm, the richly-slippered and well-made foot on the pedal stops, the gentle motion of a lovely neck, and, above all, the sweetly-tempered expression of an intelligent countenance; these are shown at one glance, when the fair performer is seated unaffectedly, yet gracefully, at the harp.

Similar beauty of position may be seen in a lady's management of a lute, or guitar, a mandolin, or a lyre. The attitude at a pianoforte, or at a harpsichord, is not so happily adapted to grace. From the shape of the instrument, the performer must sit directly in front of a straight line of keys; and her own posture being correspondingly erect and square, it is hardly possible that it should not appear rather inelegant. But if it attain not the *ne plus ultra* of grace, at least she may prevent an air of stiffness; she may move her hands easily on the keys, and bear her head with that elegance of carriage which cannot fail to impart its own character to the whole of her figure.

The Mirror of the Graces,
By a Lady of Distinction
(New York, 1813), 182, 184–86

Never exhibit any particular anxiety to sing or play. You may have a fine voice, have a brilliant instrumental execution; but your friends may by possibility neither admire nor appreciate either.

Do not sing songs descriptive of masculine passion or sentiment; there is an abundance of superior songs for both sexes.

True Politeness, a Hand-Book . . . for Ladies,
By an American Lady
(New York, 184–), 43

After a little time allotted to conversation, music is generally introduced by one of the ladies of the family, if she plays well; otherwise, she invites a competent friend to commence. A lady who can do nothing "without her notes," or who cannot read music, and play at sight, is scarcely enough of a musician to perform in a large company—for this incapacity is an evidence that she has not a good ear, or rather a good memory for melody—or that her musical talent wants more cultivation.

Miss Leslie,
The Behaviour Book
(Philadelphia, 1853), 312–13

Accomplishments of Men

We Americans are too grave a people; we laugh too little; we amuse ourselves too little; we make business the "be-all and end-all" of life. Work is both better done, and more thoroughly done, when varied and intermingled with recreation. There are many amusements and accomplishments which should form part of the training of every young man. This is far better understood across the water than with us, and we should be glad to see the games of the universities of Oxford and Cambridge introduced amongst us.

Boxing, fencing, boating, riding, and dancing are all both useful and desirable amusements, which should be cultivated, as tending to muscular development and personal health; and, to those who are aware how much mental effort is aided and stimulated by a sound condition of body, nothing which can produce such condition will seem of slight importance.

Thus for the amusements; for the accomplishments, we would place first a knowledge of music, which, by some strange freak of fashion or custom, has, until lately, been considered more for women, and beneath the dignity of men.

Music is the medicine of the soul: it soothes the wrinkles of a hard life of business, and lifts us from thoughts of money, intrigue, enterprises, hatred, and disgust, to a calmer, more heavenly frame of mind.

Accomplishments of Women

There is certainly no lack of amusements or accomplishments for women and girls; but, in these days of ours, we have come to consider it as a bait to lure a lover. The lover being lured, the bait is detached from the hook, and looked upon as useless for the rest of existence.

This is oftener the fault of the trainer than the trained.

Let the mother or teacher insist into the young girl's mind that she is learning not merely a showy accomplishment, useful only in society as a means to gain an end, but what may and should be used, to the end of her life, as a means of brightening and enlivening her home,—let her be taught this, and we shall cease to find music and matrimony so fatally opposed as they appear to be at present.

When asked to sing, if you do not intend to do so, refuse so decidedly that you cannot be compelled; but, the more decided the refusal, the gentler should the manner be. There is a style of saying "No" that never offends.

Mrs. Hale,
Manners; or Happy Homes and Good Society
(Boston, 1867), 170, 176–77, 181

The happiness of home will be promoted by a due attention to recreation. The heads of a family should see that its younger members are provided with wholesome amusements; and the cultivation of music or drawing, the reading aloud of good books, the introduction of a dance or a round game, will help wonderfully to facilitate the smooth passage of the hours. Man cannot live by bread alone; his mind must be cheered, his heart lightened, by the supply of refining pastimes.

To pause in the day's occupations, and play a sonata of Beethoven, or one of Mendelssohn's *lieder*, or a bit of Mozart or Bach, or to sing some manly English ballad, or some tender air of Bellini or Gounod, or take part in a good glee, is to the mind like a bath to the tired body—it refreshes and invigorates. The nervous system is happily composed; the imagination gains a fresh activity; the judgement grows clearer; we put on the new man.

There is ample choice of instruments. For men, if they have the requisite musical faculty, I know of none more fit than the violin, but it is not to be mastered except by the most resolute perseverance. Certain sins, it is said, can be conquered only by fasting and prayer—the same may be said of the violin. Gardini, I think, asserted that to become a good violinist you must play twelve hours a day for twenty years; but you may well be content with a shorter probation and a less complete absorption of your time. Two hours a day of good, steadfast, intelligent practice will, in three or four years, enable you to get a glimpse of what can and should be done by the violin. He who scrapes at its chords to produce a jerking polka or a commonplace waltz knows as little of its real capabilities as a child who has just learned the alphabet knows of the capacities of written speech. He may be a tolerable fiddler, but he is nothing of a violinist. Do not, my dear sir, on the strength of your rendering of certain polka airs, presume to inflict yourself and your instrument on your friends and acquaintances. You must not make their drawing-rooms your place of practice. They don't want your oddities, your imperfections; they can wait, and so can you. The annals of the Inquisition record nothing equal to the tortures which are every day inflicted upon innocent people by barbarous amateurs—young men who have been "learning" the violin for three or six months, and then presume to harass Society with their catgut exasperations. . . . But stop! There is one thing worse—a cornet—a badly-played *Cornet-à-piston.* You know what it is in the hands of a fine musician. But you don't know, perhaps, what it is in the hands of an audacious youth engaged in brutally murdering "Casta Diva!" I think that even the bagpipe can convey no greater agony to the soul. . . . The cornet is not for ladies, happily. Minerva, we know, was partial to the flute until she discovered that in playing it she distorted her countenance *most unlovelily*; but the disfigurement caused by the mild "tooting" of the flute is as nothing compared to the hideous expansion of the cheeks induced by the action of the cornet. A lady with a cornet would be a *monstrum horrendum.*

Few ladies adopt the violin, though some, as everybody knows, have obtained a wonderful command of it, and I do not see why it should not become a lady's instrument. It does not exact more time for practice than the piano, nor does it entail greater labor, and it is by no means ungraceful when properly managed. I have seen a lady play it without an ungraceful attitude, or any of those facial contortions by which some players apparently hope to impose themselves upon you for inspired sibyls. But, now that the harp has fallen out of favor, there is probably no instrument so popular among ladies of all ages as the piano. Unfortunately, popular as it is, and many as are the hours devoted to its practice, one seldom hears it well played by amateurs. The school of musical pyrotechny has still too many followers; and when a young lady sits down to the piano, as a rule, we may expect an immediate display of digital fireworks. And if it be rare to meet with good players—players possessing a thorough sympathy with the instrument, imbued with the spirit of the great masters—it is rarer still to meet with graceful players. I could almost believe some ladies consider it essential to the success of their drawing-room performances that the listeners (or spectators) shall be startled into contemplation of their engaging attitudes. Some "wobble" upon their tripod as if it were a reproduction of the Laurentian gridiron; others throw themselves alternately to right and left, as if preparing for the trapeze; others sit bolt-upright, like a grenadier on parade. Some there are who bring their hands down upon the unoffending instrument with a crash like that of a pavior's hammer; others there are who fling them up into the air at every pause, as if supplicating pardon from St. Cecilia. Note also your nervous player, who drops her handkerchief half a dozen times, is unable to seat herself comfortably upon her stool, upsets the music-book just as she begins to play, and, after stammering through broken chords and lame arpeggios, suddenly breaks down with the pitiful declaration that her memory is, "Oh, really—yes—so bad, you know!" And hurries to hide her blushes in the obscurest corner. On the other hand, you sometimes meet with the serenely-audacious player. Opened full before her is the well-wrought composition of a great master: for the nonce it is hers, to work her wicked will with it. Away she fires, "through brush, through briars," through exquisite undulations, up complex crescendos, along cunning cantabiles, always with the same breathless velocity and always with the same heartlessness; omitting a bar here, dropping a chord there, striking half a dozen erroneous notes in every page—blurring, confusing, disorganizing the composer's fair ideas—and, at the conclusion of the massacre, rising with a smiling face as if to demand the applause of her despairing auditors!

"Social Etiquette and Home Culture,"
in Franklin Square Library,
By the Lounger in Society
(New York, 1881), 5–7

Part 2: Music at the Ball

The Musicians are particularly requested, that when they play a Dance from this Book, to observe, whether the Strains, or any part of them, should be repeated, and to play them accordingly; otherwise the various Figures set to them will not answer the Music, and the Blame will certainly fall on the Composer of the Figures though in Reality it is caused through the neglect or oversight of the Musicians.

The author has availed himself of this opportunity of saying something respecting Ball Room Musicians, on the opinion in which they are held, and their general treatment by the public, that they are a useful class of persons will not be doubted; for whatever opinion has been, or may be hereafter formed of them, there is one thing certain, that there is no Dancing without them, as the Music must always guide the Dancer. From the number of the Author's own Public Balls and Assemblies, and a multitude of others both public and private, at which he has been present, has given him good and frequent opportunities of observing the manner in which Musicians are in general treated by their Employers and by the Company, which is too generally in a contemptuous manner, their being considered as obliged to play for hire for their Employers Amusement, they are to be treated worse than their servents, and never, or seldom spoken too, but in imperious haughty manner, generally addressing them, and, speaking of them, by the names of fiddlers, endeavoring thereby to shew a superior consequence in themselves, and the dependence of the Musicians: or otherwise, adopt the other extreme, and become very familiar and ply them with Liquor, in order to make them drunk, being with those persons a common opinion and saying, that nothing is so amusing as a drunken fiddler, the whole of the Musicians coming under this title whatever instrument they play. This is a base and pitiful advantage, and reflects no credit on those who practice it. That these persons should occasionally drink is no wonder from the Dust arising from the Room, and great Exertions in playing long Dances; but more should not be forced on them than is needful. Another thing that requires remark is, that Musicians are seldom payed for their playing, without their Employers complaining of the high price of their labour; yet these Employers never think, that the Musicians cannot find employment for more than five or six months in the Year, and that generally in the winter Season, when the weather is bad, and their employment being principally at night, and from leaving warm rooms and being exposed afterwards to the bad effects of night air, and consequently severe colds, together with the want of rest, in a few years their constitutions, are destroyed or ruined, and they rendered totally unfit for business. It is true, that there may be found amongst them, whose talent will not entitle them to name of Musician, although they carry a card to that effect; yet, notwithstanding the majority are Men of Talent, amongst which will be found a number belonging to our national Theatres, Men of unquestionable ability, and of the greatest respectability, both in manners and appearance.

Thomas Wilson,
A Companion to the Ball Room
(London, 1816), xx, 214–16

The musicians ought to be instructed (as the necessity for it frequently occurs) to play the waltzes tenderly and distinctly, laying the emphasis on the first note of each bar, which more clearly marks the time for the dancers, and enables them, in performing the several movements, to keep a regular pace with the music; without such attention, the beauty and effect altogether will be completely destroyed, and the dancers be disappointed of the enjoyment of that pleasure otherwise to be derived.

Thomas Wilson,
A Description of the Correct Method of Waltzing
(London, 1816), lvi

Fashion and custom usually determines the kinds of instruments to be used for dancing, but what is fashionable is not always the best.

Brass instruments and most of those which go to make up a military band would be highly improper in a small parlour or drawing-room. If but one instrument is used for dancing, the Violin is unquestionably the best, if two are used for dancing, a Violin and a Clarionette, which should play the second. The third instrument if in a small or medium sized room should be another Violin, Harp or Flute; if in a large hall it should be a Cornet, Sax-horn, Post-horn or E*b*, Bugle.

If a fourth is added some Bass instruments would be proper, which is not the case for any less number of instruments when used for dancing. The Bass instrument used should be a Violoncello, which is best, or some rich toned Brass instrument.

If five instruments are used in a large hall, a Violin, Clarionette, Cornet (Sax-horn or Post-horn), Harp and Violoncello will produce the best music for dancing. For a sixth instrument, add another Violin, and for any larger number add any of the instruments used in military Bands.

The Piano-Forte well played will alone produce good music for dancing, the Violin, Clarionette, Flute or Harp for a second instrument would be most proper, for a third add one of the Brass instruments named above. If the room is large and well-filled, the instruments should be played with full force and vigour, but if the room is small or a large one not well-filled, the music should be soft and mellow.

The musicians should not be elevated too much, especially if the ceiling of the room is low, as the heat and unwholesome air that arises from a crowded room, is not only injurious to the musicians, but it has a very bad effect on the instruments. The prompter or caller should however, be elevated enough to be able to see all parts of the ball-room.

Howe's Complete Ball-Room Hand Book
(Boston, ca. 1858), 16–17

The hostess should secure the attendance of a professional pianist, because the guests ought not to be left to the mercy of chance players, while it often happens that those who oblige out of courtesy would prefer taking part in the dance.

The Ball-Room Guide, a Handy Manual
(London and New York, 186–), 19

Good music is even more important than a good floor. The piano is a good instrument for dancing but not as played by ordinary players. Dancing music is a branch of music in itself and few who do not prepare themselves particularly for it can give that sharp accent and keep the precise time which is indispensable. The violin is a good instrument for dancing, but should only be used in connection with other instruments.

Hudson K. Lyverthey,
Our Etiquette and Social Observances
(Grand Rapids, Mich., 1881), 60

Plenty of good music is a great desideratum for a ball. Where a band of four or five or more players is employed, it is usual to place them in a small room adjoining those used for dancing, or at the end of the hall, a screen of vines and flowers concealing the usually prosaic forms of the hired musicians.

What a pity it is that we cannot hire Apollo to play for dancing-parties! Then we should not mind looking at him; and he, being a god, would not get so desperately tired as do the poor human musicians, who begin to wail out the dance music in rather lugubrious fashion toward three or four in the morning. How utterly inconsiderate and thoughtless, not to say selfish, are very young people! To them the fatigue of a fat, elderly German musician is incomprehensible; indeed, they cannot understand that he should even want to stop playing long enough to eat his supper.

Florence Howe Hall,
Social Customs
(Boston, 1881), 132–33

Modern dancing is injuriously affected by the incompetency of many who make the playing of dance music an occupation. Some of these are persons who cannot occupy situations where a considerable measure of talent is required. Others have recourse to this branch of their art, influenced by the same reasons that govern an artist in painting when he produces what are known as "Pot-boilers." Neither of these two classes will care to give themselves much trouble to learn the necessary details of their work; to them playing the notes begins, and receiving their pay ends, all their anxieties.

Accustomed as many of these persons may be to the playing of dance music in public gardens and dance-houses, they are unable or unwilling to abandon the habits of playing formed in such places when in the better atmosphere of the drawing-room.

The dance player of the present suffers from past prejudices. The dance music of to-day is so far in advance of the old, that when we look at the compositions of only a hundred years ago they seem childish in the extreme, requiring very little executive ability. A dance player of those times was what is expressed in the word "fiddler." But to-day musicians have compositions to deal with of high order, containing all that science and genius can produce, and requiring for their proper interpretation performers of decided ability.

Conductors not infrequently treat a waltz as if speed were the only excellence. A scherzo, in a symphony, which may be a movement extremely trivial in character, will be given with all the perfection that careful training can produce, but a waltz, with its beautiful melody, rich harmonies, instrumentation full of science and genius, and with unbounded possibilities for light and shade, is, as it is said, "left to play itself." Is there not a little musical pedantry in this? Light and shade seem to be thought of as unnecessary in this music, yet nowhere can these effects be used to greater advantage.

Pianists complain of being compelled to repeat compositions so many times, feeling themselves musical martyrs in so doing, but this is an unfortunate admission; for if interested in their art and occupation, true artists find constant sources of amusement in the ever-varying expression which may be given to the same work.

Soloists repeat their specialities thousands of times. Lecturers repeat their ideas for years, giving new interest to the same courses of thought by different modes of expression. So should it be with one who plays dance music—monotony of expression makes a parched desert of sound.

Allen Dodworth,
Dancing and Its Relations to . . . Social Life
(New York, 1885), 140–43

Part 3: The Manner of Playing the Tunes

The various terms of Allegro, Allegretto, Moderato, Andante, etc. are absolutely necessary, according to the present System, to distinguish the proper Time in which every *Dance* should *be played*. Formerly, before the introduction of steps, it was customary to play every *Air*, whatever might be its Character, in one time: namely, with the *utmost Rapidity*, because the Dancers were at a loss what to do, either with their feet or themselves, if they were not in *perpetual Motion*. But, since Dancing has become a science, various *Steps* have been introduced, with a view to display the Skill of the Dancer; and as these require more *Time to perform them* with Elegance it follows of course, that the Time in which they ought to be played will be considerably slower than before their Invention. Strathspeys, from the nature of their Steps, will be uniformly *Andante*; Reels will be quicker; and consequently *Allegro*; and Airs in 6/8, having similar steps to *common Time*, will naturally be slower, or Moderato, owing to their having but six Quavers in a Bar, instead of 8; 9/8 has One Quaver more, and is consequently *Allegro*.

Thomas Wilson,
A Companion to the Ball Room
(London, 1816), xviii-xix

On the Manner of Playing Cottilion Tunes

When a tune is not properly played, it is absolutely impossible to dance correctly, or with any grace. Hence, it is necessary to establish a rule, from which the musician must not deviate.

Movement 2/4 or 6/8—These movements should be played at forty bars in one minute. When the music is either too fast or too slow, it impedes or embarrasses the performance of steps and destroys the elastic motion of dancing. . . . It is a great defect in a musician not to dwell on the dotted note, which sometimes ends a trait, a length of time according to its value. That neglect causes the dancer to appear faulty when he really is not so. Musicians, who do not understand dancing, imagine that the dancer is to finish his step at the very moment they beat time at the beginning of the last bar of the trait they are playing. In this they are mistaken. . . . A musician, who wishes to learn how to play a cottilion, and make himself sure of its true movement, may comprehend it without being a dancer. To attain this, when beating time, he has only to double the strokes. . . . This number agrees, perfectly with the number of movements of the dancer, as we have before shown. By doubling again the beating of the time, the musician will produce a movement similar to that of the execution of double or beaten (battus) steps, and may then form an idea of the difficulties created by playing too fast.

Elements . . . of the Art of Dancing, by V. G.
(Philadelphia, 1817), 74–76

Quadrilles are variously composed in 6/8, 2/4, and Common Time. These Tunes generally consist of two, three, four, and some will even extend to five strains; but this last number seldom, if ever occurs, as the Dances are generally short, and may be considered as Rondos, each Tune finishing with the first Strain.

In Playing the Quadrilles, the first eight Bars are always lost to the Dancer; and, if the first Strain be not repeated, then the Dance commences with the second Strain, as in *Le Pantelon, L'Eté*, &c. As these Dances are composed as Rondos, they should always finish with the first Strain: they should neither be played very quick, or very slow: if very slow, they would appear heavy and tiresome; and, if very quick, would prevent the Dancer from applying the Steps with ease and effect.

Thomas Wilson,
The Quadrille and Cotillion Panorama
(London, ca. 1818), 4

Of the Time

The music for the Quadrille, marked 2/4 or 6/8, should be played about the time 88 or 92 of Maelzel's Metronome beating two crotchets in a bar; that is, about forty bars in a minute. If the music be too quick, or too slow, it will be impossible to preserve the true elastic movement in dancing.

In each bar of music the dancer performs two of the simple steps, and each of these is accompanied by a bend and rise; consequently, in a figure of four bars, there are sixteen movements, and even more in steps where the movements are doubled; for, as these must be reduced to the same value, that is to say, performed in the same time, the music should not be played too quickly.

As two of the simple steps are performed to each bar, it is therefore improper to observe rests of longer duration than the time of a quaver, in the airs for the Quadrille, unless they are filled up by accompaniments.

Alexander Strathy,
Elements of the Art of Dancing
(Edinburgh, 1822), 81–82

The movements of the waltzes, polkas, and all the dances described in this volume have been indicated by M. Maxine Alkan.

Polka	104, ♩
Valse à Trois temps	66, ♩
Deux Temps	88, 𝅗𝅥

Valse à Cinq Temps	152, ♪
Mazurka	176, ♪
Mazurka-Waltze	208, ♪

Henri Cellarius,
Fashionable Dancing
(London, 184–), 23, 27, 34, 48, 53, 76

We are also disposed to call attention to another matter wherein the dancing public are often times seriously inconvenienced and annoyed (if not outraged); to wit, the uneven *tempo* of the different orchestras. This fault we are disposed to attribute largely to the fact that prompters of orchestras that play for dancing are virtually directors or managers of the same, and who as a class are generally very inferior musicians, and frequently without the slightest knowledge of the dance. It is not to be presumed, therefore, that they are competent to entertain correct ideas respecting proper time. It is desirable that something should be done to remedy this evil, as very rapid movements on the part of the dancer are tiresome and exhaustive. We therefore offer the following suggestions as to time, and commend them to musicians employed to play for dancing parties.

Measures of Music Per Minute

For Society Waltz, 3/4	70
For Waltz Galop, 2/4	65
For Glide Waltz, 3/4	60
For Polka, 2/4	55
For Polka Redowa, 3/4	50
For Schottisch, 2/4	50
For Newport, 3/4	45
For Quadrilles, 2/4 or 6/8	60

E. Woodward Masters,
The Standard Dance Album
(Boston, 1883), 37–38

The letters found at the beginning of each dance, M.M. ♩ = 36, refer to Maelzel's time-indicator or metronome, by which the exact speed of all music is determined.

M.M. means Maelzel's metronome, the notes 𝅝 𝅗𝅥 ♩ ♪ indicate the length of note to be taken at each beat of the pendulum.

The figures are those at which the index upon the pendulum should be placed. A simple substitute can be made by attaching an ounce weight (a bullet of lead is best) to a piece of thread. Allowing this to swing, and varying the length of the thread according to the following scale, it will be found sufficiently accurate for the purposes here required.

	Metronome.		String. Ins.	
Waltz	𝅗𝅥	72	23	One beat to a bar
Galop	𝅗𝅥	76	22	" " " " "
Polka	𝅗𝅥	104	11	Two beats " " "
Polka Redowa		60	36	" " " "
Schottische	𝅗𝅥	76	21	" " " "
Knickerbocker Polka		76	21	" " " "
Mazurka	𝅗𝅥	56	43	One beat " " "
Five Step	♩	144	5	Five beats " " " "
Quadrille	♩	104	11	Two beats " " " "
Lancers	♩	104	11	" " " " "
Varsovianna	𝅗𝅥	54	49	One beat " " " "
Court Quadrille	𝅗𝅥	76	21	Two beats " " "

Allen Dodworth,
Dancing and Its Relations to . . . Social Life
(New York, 1885), 42–43

Hostesses who entertain much must make up their parties as ministers make up their cabinets, on grounds other than personal liking.

George Eliot, *Daniel Deronda*

In her self-guided search for self-improvement, the elder sister went to many church lectures on a vast variety of secular subjects, and usually came home with a comic account of them, and that made more matter of talk for the whole family. She could make fun of nearly everything; Irene complained that she scared away the young men whom they got acquainted with at the dancing-school sociables. They were perhaps, not the wisest young men.

The girls had learned to dance at Papanti's; but they had not belonged to the private classes. They did not even know of them, and a great gulf divided them from those who did.

William D. Howells, *The Rise of Silas Lapham*

The adjutant-stewart, a master of his art, grasped his partner firmly, and with confident deliberation and smoothness broke with her into the first gallop round the edge of the circle, then at the corner of the ballroom caught his partner's left hand, turned her; and through the quickening strains of the music nothing could be heard but the regular jingle of the spurs on the adjutant's rapid, practiced feet, and at every third beat the swish of his partner's flying velvet skirt as she whirled around.

Leo Tolstoy, *War and Peace*

Dances and Party Games

Part 1: The Minuet and Diverse Group Dances

A. The Minuet

My chief aim is, to give my sentiments on the advantages arising to youth, from their being well instructed in the *Minuet*; a dance essentially necessary for them to learn, on account of its utility as a foundation for the superstructure of those graces which distinguish people of fashion, and good breeding, from others whose education has been neglected or their manners perverted by bad teachers. . . .

It is, indeed, with regret, I have observed that, for many years past, the Minuet has, almost, totally fallen into disuse in our public assemblies; a circumstance I cannot otherwise account for, than by supposing it, in a great measure, owing to the gentlemen not keeping pace with the ladies, in the fashionable improvements of this dance.

I know not if I may be thought singular in my opinion, but I certainly have remarked, that since the *pas-grave* has been so generally adopted in the Minuet, elegance and grace, instead of adding to, has on the contrary, impaired its practice. Here, again, some blame may be attached to the gentlemen, who seldom pay the smallest attention to it after they leave school, perhaps at the early period of thirteen to fourteen years of age; while the ladies, on the contrary, continue to improve till they are sixteen or seventeen, when they are introduced into the assemblies of fashion from the hands of their teachers. How mortifying, then, must it be to them, when, after so much attention and practice, they find but few opportunities of displaying those captivating acquirements in a Duet, formerly so popular, that it was always adopted as a *prelude* to the more sprightly dance! Whether these observations be just or not, it is not for me to say; but in this everyone must agree, that there is a fluctuation in the *tide* of fashion, as well as in all other changes in the *ocean* of life, which can seldom be accounted for, or counteracted, and must, therefore, be complied with. A striking proof of this observation is seen in the rage which, for sometime past, has prevailed in England, and elsewhere, for a very different mode of Dancing: what I allude to, are the national dances of the Scotch, especially their Reel. This dance, indeed, admits of so great a variety of natural and brilliant steps, as seldom fail to please.

Francis Peacock,
Sketches Relative to . . . Dancing
(Aberdeen, 1805), 73–74, 82–83

The minuet is allowed, by every professor of the art, to be the perfection of all dancing, but the difficulty of acquiring a knowledge of the true beauties of it, has discouraged many from attempting it.

James P. Cassidy,
A Treatise on the Theory and Practice of Dancing
(Dublin, 1810), 66

I cannot finish my observations on the deportment of the person, without strongly recommending the study of the Minuet, as one of the surest means of acquiring and preserving the most noble and graceful deportment. In the study of the Minuet, one acquires that perpendicularity, and command of balancing, so requisite in good dancing, and without which one can never arrive at any degree of perfection,—but to excell requires a particular talent.

The airs for the minuet should be played about the time 72 of Maelzel's metronome beating three crotchets in a bar, which will be about twenty-four bars in a minute.

Alexander Strathy,
Elements of the Art of Dancing
(Edinburgh, 1822), 17, 81–82

(F)or instance, a dance which has not been executed in France for many years, but which still finds partisans in other countries,—the minuet de la cour.

This dance is much too foreign to our manners for us ever to expect to see it reappear. But, as a study it offers very great advantages; it impresses on the form positions both noble and graceful.

Henri Cellarius,
Fashionable Dancing
(London, 184–), 12–14

This dance [minuet] has a traditional reputation for grace, which it is supposed to possess in an inexplicable degree. Its beneficial influence upon manner and motion is often mentioned, with accompanying lamentations for the loss of this to the present generation. These lamentations are, however, wasted upon a secondary fact, the primary truth not being recognized, that this dance in the time of its glory was confined exclusively to the cultivated classes, with whom the dancing-lesson was an important part of education.

It may be that the exaggeration of motion which was formerly common would be condemned at the present day, and justly so; yet the same movements, when not so exaggerated are identical with those required in all social intercourse.

Allen Dodworth,
Dancing and Its Relations to . . . Social Life
(New York, 1885), 125–126

B. The Reel

Those who have acquired a little knowledge of Music, and are acquainted with Reel and Strathspey tunes, cannot but know that they are divided into two parts, each consisting of four bars, which severally contain four crotchets, or eight quavers and that, in the generality of Strathspeys, the notes are, alternately, a dotted quaver, and a semiquaver; the bar frequently terminating in a crotchet. This peculiar species of Music is, in many parts of the Highlands, preferred to the common Reel; on the contrary, the latter, by reason of its being the most lively tune of the two, is more generally made choice of in the dance.

I have further to remark, that for the purpose of distinguishing steps, many of which do not materially differ but in their number of motions, I make use of the previous terms *Minor, Single, and Double.* The first (Minor) is, when it requires two steps to one bar of the tune; the second (Single) is, when one step is equal to a bar; and the third (Double) is, when it requires two bars to one step.

Of the Steps

1. *Kemshóole,* or Forward Step.—This is the common step for the *promenade* or figure of the Reel. It is done by advancing the right foot forward, the left following it behind: in advancing the same foot a second time, you hop on it, and one step is finished. You do the same motions after advancing

the left foot, and so on alternately with each foot, during the first measure of the tune played twice over; but if you wish to vary the step, in repeating the measure, you may introduce a very lively one, by making a smart rise, or gentle spring, forward, upon the right foot, placing the left foot behind it: this you do four times, with this difference, that instead of going a fourth time behind with the left foot, you disengage it from the ground, adding a hop to the last spring. You finish the *promenade,* by doing the same step, beginning it with the left foot. To give the step its full effect, you should turn the body a little to the left, when you go forward with the right foot, and the contrary way when you advance the left.

2. Minor *Kemkóssy,* Setting or Footing Step.—This is an easy familiar step, much used by the English in their Country Dances. You have only to place the right foot behind the left, sink and hop upon it, then do the same with the left foot behind the right.

7. *Aisig-thrasd,* Cross Passes.—This is a favorite step in many parts of the Highlands. You spring a little to one side with the right foot, immediately passing the left across it; hop and cross it again, and one step is finished; you then spring a little to one side with the left foot, making the like passes with the right. This is a minor step; but it is often varied by passing the foot four times alternately behind and before, observing to make a hop previous to each pass, the first excepted, which must always be a spring, or bound: by these additional motions, it becomes a single step.

Francis Peacock,
Sketches Relative to . . . Dancing
(Aberdeen, 1805), 89–92, 95

The Scotch reel has steps appropriated to itself and in the dance can never be displaced for those of France, without an absurdity too ridiculous to even imagine without laughing. . . . Hence as the character of reels is merriment, they must be performed with much more *joyance* of manner than even the country-dance; and therefore they are better adapted (as society is now constituted) to the social private circle than to the public hall.

The Mirror of the Graces,
By a Lady of Distinction
(New York, 1813), 174

C. Country Dances

Country Dance is the most common of all Dances, now practiced. The taste for the country dance arises from the agreeable party, not from the elegance of the dance. It is so simple, that the most illiterate are in some measure able to perform it.

The very late fashion of performing music in the quickest time, requires the time to be beat in a different manner. The steps are performed altogether by springs, hops, or leaps, in the most sprightly manner. . . .

Definitions of the times used in describing the figures of country dances.

BRISÉ, is to cast round, or turn round another person, or by one's self.

DANCE ADDRESS, is to perform a set step, as the ballotte, or pas et basque.

OLEVETTES, is to interchassè, as in the common reel of three, with three persons on one side of the choir, and employ as much time in doing it, as in right and left.

MOULINET, is to cross right hands with contrary partners, and pass round half of a circle and cross left hands, and pass back again to your places.

Figures of Country Dances

CATCH FLEETING PLEASURES
First gentleman and second lady change places, first lady and second gentleman change places, all moulinet back to their places, first couple down the middle, up brisé, right and left atop.

TARTAN PLAID
Six olivettes, first couple down the middle, up cast off.

IRISH WASH WOMAN
First couple down the middle, up brissé, second couple down the middle, up brisé, then the second couple down the middle, up cast off, right and left atop.

Saltator,
A Treatise on Dancing
(Boston, 1802), 83–86, 88, 92, 94

When country Dancing has commenced, and the top couple have gone down three couples, the next couple must go off.

When every couple have gone down the dance, and the couple who called it have regained the top and gone down three couples, the dance is finished; for the next dance they stand at the bottom.

T. Wilson,
An Analysis of Country Dancing
(London, 1808), 135–136

So many causes for Complaint existing of the miserable state of our Ball Room Dancing, particularly English Country Dancing, which is our boasted national Dance, and which (if the present plan is pursued, will soon become a disgrace to the country) it is necessary for its Improvement, that its neglected state be shewn, and where and on whom ought to fall the Blame; and that a Remedy be pointed out, not only for the Direction of those who wish to improve, but also to answer the purpose of those who may be about to learn.

No person during a country dance should hiss, clap, or make any other noise, to interrupt the good order of the company.

Snapping the fingers, in country dancing and reels, and the sudden howl or yell too frequently practised, ought particularly to be avoided as partaking too much of the customs of barbarous nations; the character and effect by such means given to the Dance, being adapted only to the stage, and by no means suited to the Ball Room.

Thomas Wilson,
A Companion to the Ball Room
(London, 1816), 188, 225

In the country dance the attention should be given more to the management of the arms than to the feet, because the ear will naturally adapt easy movements suitable to the tune; the only attention that is necessary with respect to the feet is, to have them well turned out and pointed, that they may not incommode those who are dancing, and to move them exactly in time with the music. It is not the feet that are looked at, it is the whole carriage; persons are distinguished by this for their genteel and elegant style. The hands across, which is a single figure in itself, shews the management of the arms and head to great advantage. When you present the right hand, turn the head and look at the person to whom the hand is given, and observe the opposition of the arm to the head; the left arm is raised much higher than the right, and in giving the left hand raise the right in opposition to it. The effect of this is striking, but if the hand is carelessly given, without looking at the person, and the contrary arm hanging down, the figure has no expression or effect, and the dancing is inelegant.

F. J. Lambert,
Treatise on Dancing
(Norwich, Eng., 1820), 38–39

Country-Dances are the most popular, the oldest, and as capable of almost unlimited variety the best style of Dancing that the English Ball-Room presents; they are considered to be of English origin, and as according in a remarkable degree with the genius of "merrie England" we are inclined to that opinion, and till better reasons are exhibited we shall continue to consider them as national.

Analysis of the London Ball-Room
(London, 1825), 67

D. The Early Cotillion, Quadrille, and Mazurka Quadrille

The Figures of Cotillions, consist of two parts, the one is termed the change, the other the figure. There are ten changes, which are the same in all regular cotillions, but every cotillion has a different figure, which is performed between every change, and once after the last change. In every cotillion, its figure is performed ten times. In learning cotillions, it is necessary to walk over the changes, four or five times, until the choir, or set understand them perfectly; then the figure in the same manner.

A description of the ten changes, used in all regular cotillions, requisite to be first known, follows:

Change 1st. All eight address partners, in the time of chassè, then the ballette. All eight circinate to the left hand round, balance, circinate back to their places.

Change 2nd. All dance address to partners, promenade them round with the right hand, dance address, promenade round with the left hand.

Change 3rd. All dance, address to partners, circinate them round on the right, dance address, circinate quite round on the left.

Change 4th. All dance address to partners, allemand them quite round to the right, dance address, allemand quite round on the left.

Change 5th. The four ladies centre balance, moulinet half round brissé, center balance, back again.

Change 6th. All four gentlemen centre balance, moulinet half round brisé, centre balance, moulinet back again to their places.

Change 7th. All the ladies centre balance, circinate half round, centre balance back.

Change 8th. All the gentlemen centre balance, circinate half round, centre balance, back.

Change 9th. All eight right and left quite round to their places.

Change 10th. All eight circinate quite round, then back again in a circle.

Marshal Cotillion

After the first change the following figure is performed.

Figure—Two opposite Ladies change places, there [*sic*] partners at the same pass ronnd [*sic*] them on the right, to each others places; then the two other ladies change places, their partners in the same manner as the others change places; then the two first ladies and their partners pass back to their places; after that, the other couple pass back. This figure must be performed between all the changes. The tune for this cotillion consists of two parts eight bars each part being played over twice. Every change requires as much music, as right and left in country dances. It is plain, that the tunes of cotillions must be played over ten times.

Saltator,
A Treatise on Dancing
(Boston, 1802), 79–81

The Quadrille

This fashionable species of Dancing is entirely of French origin, and only differs from the well-known Dance, the Cotillion, by leaving out the changes; being much shorter, and frequently composed of Figures that require but four Persons to their performance; as may be seen by the first set of French Quadrilles that were publically danced in this country, viz. "Le Pantalon," "L'Eté," "La Poule," and "La Trenise" neither of which require more than four persons in their performance.

STEPS USED IN QUADRILLES*

Sissonne baloté	Chassé
Coupe baloté	Jetté
Balancez	Assemblé
Rigadoon	Glissadé
Emboittés	Pas de basqué

Thomas Wilson,
The Quadrille and Cotillion Panorama
(London, ca. 1818), 5

To use steps fitted for the English country dance or Scotch reel to French music, would be as incompatible as speaking the French language with the Scotch or English accent.

It is no uncommon thing for teachers of dancing to boast of the proficiency of their scholars, by

*Although professed dancers, for the sake of variety, frequently introduce other steps than the above-named, yet they are sufficient for the correct performance of any quadrille; nor should any other be attempted before these can be executed with ease and effect.

Figure 20

telling, that a certain set can *pirouette*, or whirl round upon one foot, like a whipt top, and finish *en attitude*; that some can *cut*, or twirl their legs in the air several times; and that others could have danced an immense variety of steps before they had finished their third or fourth set of lessons! But I have remarked, with surprise, that few teachers of dancing ever told me how well any of their pupils *presented themselves before company, walked,* and *sat*; or *how easily* and *gracefully they managed their heads, and disposed of their arms* in the dance.

Barclay Dun,
A Translation of . . . Fashionable Quadrilles
(Edinburgh, 1818), v, 6–7

PRINCIPAL FIGURES IN THE QUADRILLE

Chaine Anglaise, or Right and Left—This figure is performed by making the *Temps Levé*, and three *Chassés* connected by the *Temps Levé*, as already described: then the *Jeté* and *Assemblé.*

Two Gentlemen opposite, with their Ladies, commence with the right foot, make the *Temps Levé* and *Chassé*, and at the same time raise the right arm, in the manner directed for the arms, in order to receive the right hand of the opposite person; in making the second *Chassé*, with the left foot before, they turn a little to the right, quit the right hand of the Ladies, and give the left to their partners, turning a little to the left side, make the third *Chassé* with the right foot before, then the *Jeté* and *Assemblé*, placing themselves on the left of their Ladies, who at the same time perform the same steps. The two couples will now have exchanged places; this is called *Demi Chaine Anglaise.*

To complete the figure, they perform the same over again to their original places.

This figure requires eight bars of music.

For Balancer, or to Set to your Partner—Make a *Glissade Dessous* to the right, and *Jeté* before with the right foot; a *Glissade Dessous* to the left, and *Jeté* before with the left foot; the same again to the right, then an *Assemblé* before with the left foot, and *Changement de Jambe.*

This *enchainement* requires four bars of music.

Tour de Main, to Turn your Partner with both Hands—A Gentleman and his lady, facing each other, join hands, raising the arms in the manner already directed, and at the same time make the *Temps Levé* with the right foot before; then three *Chassés* connected by the *Temps Levé*, as already described, the Gentleman turning towards the right of the Lady, and the Lady towards the right of the Gentleman. At the commencement of the third *Chassé*, the Gentleman quits the right hand of the Lady with this left, and both finish in their respective places with the *Jeté* and *Assemblé*, facing the centre of the dance.

This figure is performed to four bars of music.

Chaine des Dames, or Ladies' Chain—This figure is performed by two opposite couples, with the same steps as for *Chaine Anglaise*; viz. three *Chassés*, connected by the *Temps Levé*, and terminated by a *Jeté* and an *Assemblé.*

Two Ladies cross over, giving the right hand to each other as they pass; they then give the left to the opposite Gentleman, who commences at the same time with the Ladies, by making a *Chassé* to the right, in order to place himself in a situation proper to receive in his left hand the left hand of the Lady; both make a turn to their left, into their respective places.

The Ladies repeat the same figure and steps to their original places, while the Gentlemen make another circular turn to the left, receiving with the left hand the left hand of their Ladies as they advance, and, turning into their places, finish, facing the manner of the dance.

This figure requires eight bars of music.

Demi Promenade—This figure is performed by two opposite couples.

The Gentlemen receive in their right hand the right hand of their Ladies, and in their left the left hand, raising the arms a little, and holding them rounded, as already directed; the couples change places, passing each other on the left, and performing three *Chassés, Jeté,* and *Assemblé.* In doing this, the Gentlemen lead their Ladies a little forward on their right, that they may arrive at their proper places on the right of their partners, where they quit hands, facing the centre of the dance.

This figure is performed to four bars of music.

Figures of the Favourite Quadrille, in French and English.

NO. I.—LE PANTALON

No.		Bars.
1.	Chaine Anglaise,	8
2.	Balancez à vos Dames,	4
3.	Un Tour de Mains,	4
4.	Chaine des Dames,	8
5.	Demi Promenade,	4
6.	Demi Chaine Anglais,	4
	Contre partie pour les quatre autres.	
1.	Right and left, by the first and third couples,	8
2.	Set to partners,	4
3.	Turn Partners round,	4
4.	Ladies' chain,	8
5.	Half promenade,	4
6.	Half right and left,	4
—	The other four repeat the same figures.	

Alexander Strathy,
Elements of the Art of Dancing
(Edinburgh, 1822), 65–69, 89

Quadrilles

An inconvenience, arising from its French origin, occurs in the Anglo-French terms which are used, and renders a knowledge of them necessary, they are easily acquired, but as we consider our own language fully capable of expressing them, we have preferred its use, so far as was consistent with perfect intelligibility.

Analysis of the London Ball-Room
(London, 1825), 93

Cotillon Figure La Belle Flamand

Four half right and left, the other four the same, half promenade, all eight to your places and turn your partners round, ladies chain by those who began the dance, balancez eight and turn your partners. The same again the other four.

Cotillon Figure La Caprice de Vauxhall

The four ladies balancez to the gentlemen on their right and tour de mains, the lady at the top couple and the opposite gentleman advance and retire, dos-à-dos, half promenade, and half right and left. Grand round. Four times over until the ladies come back to their places.

E. H. Conway,
Le Maître de Danse, *2d ed.*
(New York, 1827), 39

La Danse de Société Française, according to my idea of it, should be composed of easy, flowing, graceful steps, such as the *glissades,** the *chasses,* the *assemblées,* the *brisés,* the *fouettés,* the *pas de basques* forward and in turning around, the *pirouettes* on the points of the toes, the *jétés,* and a number of others of the same class, varying them continually, choosing those steps which unite with each other well and without difficulty, introducing occasionally a few steps in which vigour is required for their execution, such as the little *pas de bourrees,* the little *battemens,* the *emboités,* the *tems de cuisse,* the *sissones,* and sometimes, but very rarely the *en-*

*Care should be taken, while performing this or any other step wherein the sliding movement is introduced, to glide the heel lightly on the ground; nothing is more ridiculous than to see the heel elevated while executing this movement.

trechat four, the whole to be done in an easy, quiet manner, the motions of the arms, head and body corresponding with the actions of the legs; in fact room-dancing is nothing more or less than that which is used for the stage, but executed in a more quiet style, avoiding all extravagances, or large steps. . . .

E. A. Theléur,
Letters on Dancing
(London, 1831), 100–101

The Mazurka, As Danced at the Duke of Devonshire's Grand Balls

The figures of the Mazurka are generally danced by four couples: they may be varied according to the fancy of the first gentleman who begins them, and is afterwards imitated by the others; always commencing and ending by that which the Poles call *Kolo,* or hands round.

Figure 21

Mazurka Figure, No. 3

Begin with the tune.

1. Right and left all around. (16.)
2. Gentleman, No. 1, leads his partner all round, and kneels at the end of this promenade. (8.)
3. Holding his Lady by the left hand, he makes her pass round him, and rises quickly at the eighth bar. (8.)
4. Set, in turning. (8.)
   The other Gentlemen do the same. (72.)
5. Finish by *Kolo,* or hands round to the right. (8.)

Hommage à Taglioni
(Philadelphia, 1836), 35–36, 40

[Quadrilles and Cotillons] have completely taken the place of all former dances which have enlivened our ancestors, and are at present the most popular figures among fashionable classes of society in this country and Europe. The difference between *cotillons* and *quadrilles* is that the former are single figures, as *right and left, forward two,* &c., while the latter are more complicated and consist of a number of figures, varying according to the fancy of different teachers, or as the leader of the orchestra may choose to call them.

Quadrilles differ materially in figures, but generally are set to particular pieces of music, or the music arranged to suit them, in which case they are always danced the same; and different sets as known by different titles, as the Postillion, La Bayadere, Diavalo, and others; but when a person becomes acquainted with the different figures, he need pay no attention to the set named as the one to be danced, only observing what figures are called by the leader of the orchestra.

The Ball-Room Instructor
(New York, 1841), 11

Quadrilles

LANCERS. FIRST SET

First Figure—Lady and opposite gentleman chassez right and left, then swing quite round with right hands to places; the top couple lead between the couple opposite, and return leading outside; the gentlemen join their left hands in this case, and give their right to their partners; ladies join both hands, forming a cage; the ladies dance round to the left, and the gentlemen lead round outside to the right, and turn partners to place.

The Ball Room Annual
(London, ca. 1844), 35

The *Cotillon*, that once universal favorite in the ball-room has now also, in a great measure, been superseded, at least in name; but "even in its ashes live its wonted fires," for its figures have been cut up to form new quadrilles. The difference between *Quadrilles* and *Cotillons*, at present, may be said to be, that the latter are the single dances, as *Le Pantalon, L'Eté, &c.*, while the former are more complicated, with regulated steps, but now all are styled *Quadrilles*.

The fashionable *Galop*, the *Quadrille*, and the *Waltz*, at present reign paramount in the ball-room.

The Mazourka or Russian Cotillon

This well-known Polish dance was introduced into this country by the Duke of Devonshire, on his return from Russia, after his residence there as British ambassador. It resembles the quadrille, from being danced by sets of eight persons in couples, the lady in each couple taking the place to the right of the gentleman; and the first and second couple and the third and fourth couple face each other.

The Ball-Room Preceptor
(London, 1846), 13, 67–68

The Quadrille

FIGURE ONE

Le Pantalon—Top and bottom couples cross over (traversez,) eight walking steps—re-crosss (re-traversez,) the same. This crossing and re-crossing is called *Chaine Anglaise*. It is also called right and left, and occupies eight bars. The gentleman in crossing and re-crossing, always keeps to the right of his *Vis-à-vis* lady, keeping her inside the figure; in other words, he moves first towards his own left hand, and then towards his right, thus describing an arc, or part of a circle—set to partners, that is, *chassé* (move) four steps to the right and four to the left, turn partners (Tour de mains)—ladies' chain—half promenade; *i.e.*, couples crossing over to each other's places, hands joined. (Four bars, or eight walking steps)—return apart to places (Four bars.) Side couples do the same *if standing as in the old method.*

Charles Durang,
The Fashionable Dancer's Casket
(Boston, 1856), 31

Rules for Calling the Changes to Cotillons, and Contra Dances

There seems to be a general fault with most callers, owing in a great measure to negligence in the beginning, and that combined to carelessness, causes the player to call out of time with his music, which is very unpleasant to the dancers, as it keeps them all the while before or behind the time. The place for calling is generally about one measure ahead of the music where the figure is to commence. Some figures require the caller to speak twice, in such as, forward and back, back to back, half right and left, half promenade, &c., the first takes place at the commencement of the fourth measure, and the last at the eighth. Endeavor always to finish calling, both in the middle and the end of a strain, by the time you commence the music where the figure is to begin; if you do not, the dancers will be left one or two measures behind the time.

In calling, let the voice be natural and easy, speaking just loud enough to be distinctly heard throughout the room. When there are a number of instruments playing, and especially if the room is larger, the caller will have to speak from the top of his voice in order to be heard. He should take, at such times, the most prominent place in the orchestra; standing up is the best position; if sitting down, it should be on a high seat above the rest of the players.

Howe's Complete Ball-Room Hand Book
(Boston, 1858), 18–19

The Quadrille is one of the oldest dances that retains its position in the ball-room, or among the lovers and patrons of the art. It has, however, been so materially and essentially altered, that those who practised it even fifteen years ago, would be compelled to learn it anew; still, it retains its distinctive type of a quadrille.

As we have already hinted, in our history of the dance, the quadrille of former times was adopted as a medium for the display of agility, and the indulgence of violent exercise; as, however, the art of dancing, considered with reference to the execution of difficult steps, vaults and pirouettes, required a long and tedious pupilage, combined with perfect gracefulness of bearing, if not symmetry of form, and could be attained only by years of devoted study and unwearied zeal, it was but natural that few succeeded in not making themselves ridiculous, and that it needed revision and alteration to render it acceptable.

Consequently the quadrille now in use, in which performers walk or slide gracefully through the dance, may be executed without any special knowledge of the art of dancing, a familiarity with the figures being all that is essential.

Formation of the Quadrille

Previous to each figure there are eight bars of music to be played, during which performance it is customary for the gentleman to bow, first to his partner, and then to the lady on his left, the lady, at the same time, courtesying to her partner, and afterward to the gentleman on her right.

Basket Quadrille

Forward two .... 16 *bars*
Balance .... 8 *bars*
Four ladies, hands-round to the center .... 8 *bars*
turning to the left, 4 bars; and reverse, 4 bars; keeping hold of hands, and standing in the center in a circle
Four gentlemen, hands-round on the outside .... 8 *bars*
to the left, 4 bars; and reverse 4 bars; finishing so as to stand on the left of their partners, raising their hands, joined, so as to allow the ladies to pass backward and rise on the outside, forming a basket.
All forward and back, ... 4 *bars*
twice in same position (taking one step forward and one back).
Turn partners, ... 4 *bars*
by giving both hands and turning completely round to place.

Repeated by the first and second couple and by the third and the fourth couple.

The last time, the gentlemen with hands-round are in the centre and ladies outside.

Edward Ferrero,
The Art of Dancing
(New York, 1859), 120–22, 125

The author of a recent work on etiquette, published in England, gives the following hints for those who do go to balls: He says—"I do not attempt to deny that the quadrille, as now walked, is ridiculous; the figures, which might be graceful, if performed in a lively manner, have entirely lost their spirit, and are become a burlesque of dancing; but, at the same time, it is a most valuable dance. Old and young, short and thin, good dancers and bad, lazy and active, stupid and clever, married and single, can all join in it, and have not only an excuse and opportunity for tête-à-tête conversation, which is decidedly the easiest, but find encouragement in the music, and in some cases convenient breaks in the necessity of dancing. A person of few ideas has time to collect them while the partner is performing, and one of many can bring them out with double effect. Lastly, if you wish to be polite or friendly to an acquaintance who dances atrociously, you can select a quadrille for him or her, as the case may be."

Cecil B. Hartley,
The Gentlemen's Book
(Boston, 1860), 97, 108–9

26
Javotte-Quadrille
nach Motiven der gleichnamigen Operette von
Emil Jonas.
Eduard Strauss, Op. 94.
Pantalon.
1.
Fine.
Dal Segno al Fine.
Été.
2.
Fine.
24106

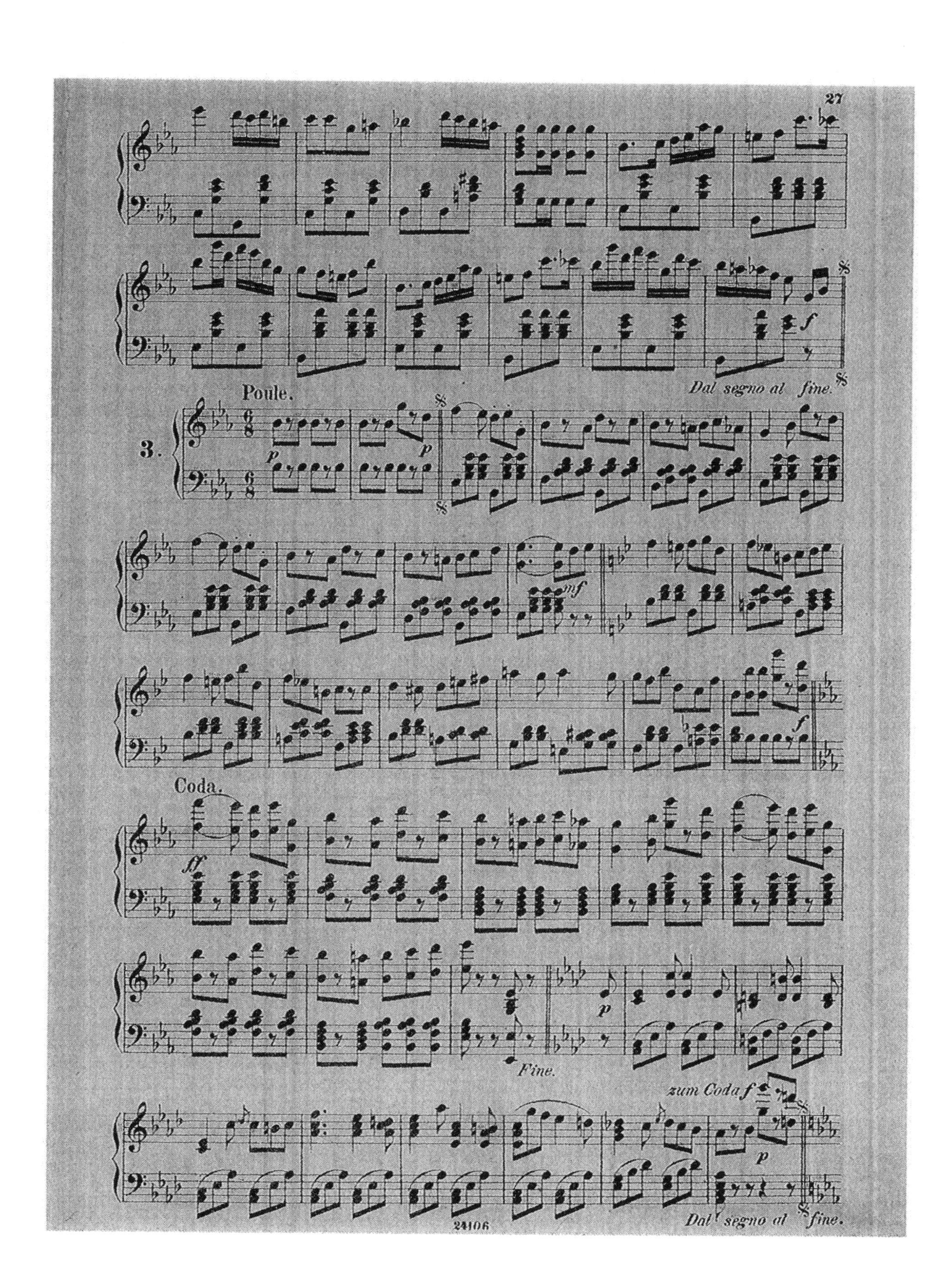
27
Dal segno al fine.
Poule.
3.
Coda.
Fine.
zum Coda
Dal segno al fine.
24106

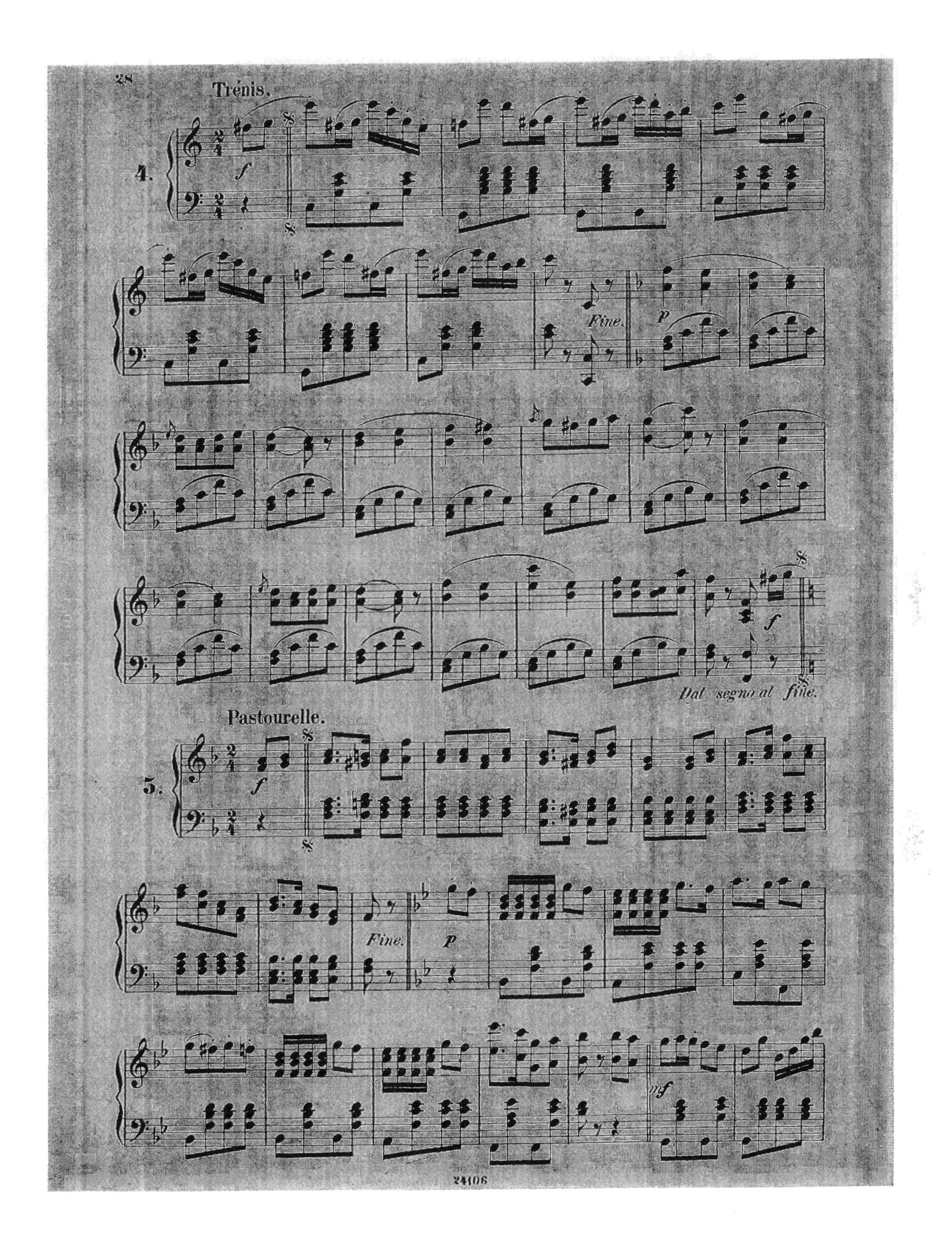
28
Trénis.
4.
f
Fine.
p
Dal segno al fine.
Pastourelle.
5.
f
Fine.
p
mf
24106

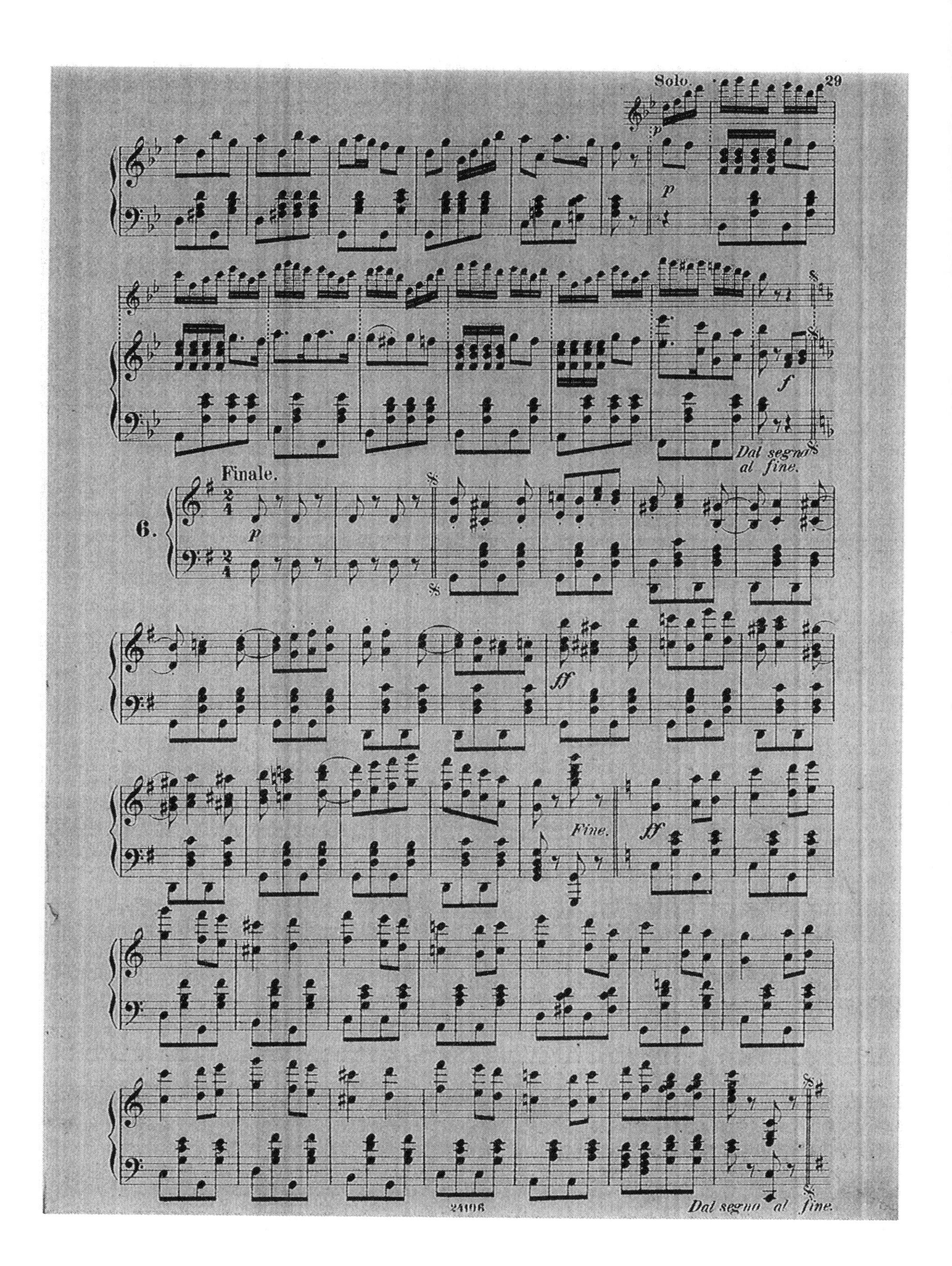
Solo.
29
p
p
f
Dal segno
al fine.
Finale.
6.
p
ff
Fine.
ff
24106
Dal segno al fine.

Motions

All the figures may be executed by aid of three motions.

1. *Walk (Pas Marché).*—No explanation is necessary, except that it is better to push the feet about, not raising them from the floor.

2. *Slide (Chassé)* . . .

3. *Balancé.*—The English word balancing might be used, as somewhat descriptive of the motion.

Balancé, Forward

1. Step forward on the right, balancing on that foot.

2. Extend the left, to second position.

Balancé, Backward

1. Step backward on the left, balancing on that foot.

2. Extend the right to second position.

This is also executed twice forward, with alternate feet, and the same backward.

The Polo Quadrille

Four couples, formed as for the ordinary quadrille or Lancers. Each number twice. Eight bars are played before the commencement of each figure.

No. 1.
All Promenade Half Round 4 bars.
Head Couples Forward and Back 4 bars.
When head couples are going back, the sides forward, and go back as the others forward again for next movement.
Head Couples Half Right and Left to Places 4 bars.
Sides Same 4 bars.
Double Ladies' Chain. Ladies crossing hands in center. 8 bars.
Same for Gentlemen. 8 bars.

Caledonian Quadrille
First Figure (Twice)
First and second couples cross hands round with right hands 4 bars
Same couples cross hands back to places with left hands 4 bars
Same balancé to, and turn, partners 8 bars
Ladies' chain 8 bars
Half promenade 4 bars
Half right and left 4 bars

Allen Dodworth,
Dancing and Its Relations to . . . Social Life
(New York, 1885), 81–82, 96, 98

E. The March

Opening March—The Ball is always inaugurated by a march. To make it a complete and assured success, no gentleman should enter the line of march with two ladies, as the different figures require the marching to be done in couples. The leader should regulate his pace to circumstances, endeavoring to keep the line unbroken and the couples at a proper distance one from the other, being careful to march in time with the music, so as to preserve harmony between sound and motion. The other couples should follow exactly those going before, and conform in every detail with the movements of the leader.

The Leader may at his choice and as his fancy dictates, introduce any number of figures, being careful not to prolong the march until it becomes wearisome and monotonous and loses its peculiarly, pleasing characteristics.

The march should be led by a gentleman and lady who are initiated in the details and cognizant of the various evolutions, and if necessary the floor committee should render every assistance within their power in order to insure its uniformity of action and appearance.

The marching must be done in straight lines, following the direction of the walls of the Salon, the changes being accomplished at the corners. One or two turns round the room are sufficient to enable all the couples, who wish to participate in this feature of the ball, to fall in line.

The March in Line—As soon as all the arrangements are completed, the leader heads the line and marches up the centre of the room, on reaching the top, the couples separate, the ladies advancing to the right in single file, the gentlemen to the left. When they have regained the bottom of the room, the leader and his lady pass to the left of each other, followed by the rest, and again march to the top of the room in opposite directions. Having reached it they join and march in couples to the right.

In changing from one figure of the march to another, the leader should be careful to see that he executes sufficient plain marching, in order that the couples may all be in columns before commencing a new figure.

Prof. Baron's Complete Instructor
(New York, ca. 1880), 22–24

Part 2: About Waltzing and Other Round Dances

A. The Position

Prior to engaging in the dance, the gentleman places himself in front of his partner, a little to the right, encircles her waist with his right arm, supporting her firmly, yet gently, and holds her right hand with his left, extending it nearly to the height of her waist, slightly bent at the elbow.

The lady's left hand should rest lightly upon her partner's right shoulder, while the right arm should be extended nearly straight with the palm of her hand turned downward. The gentleman places the inner side of the fingers of his left hand against the inner side of the fingers of the lady's right hand.

The gentleman is at all times, responsible for the guidance of his partner, and should therefore use the greatest precaution against colliding with other couples. He should regulate the proper distance to be maintained between himself and his partner, neither holding her so close as to impede her freedom of action, nor so far aloof as to prevent him from rendering her sufficient and necessary support. The lady should allow herself to be entirely guided by her partner, without in any case endeavoring to follow her own impulse of action.

William B. DeGarmo,
The Dance of Society
(New York, 1875), 66

Figure 22

I am fully aware of the dangerous, the combustible constituents, that lie sleeping under the surface of the ground I am now surveying; but allegiance to my art will not permit me to pause, since I have fortified myself with the necessary courage to make the invasion. . . .

I refer to the manner in which ladies sometimes permit themselves to be supported by gentlemen in round dances. The attitude of both the lady and the gentleman should be erect and firm, without being rigid. It is neither necessary nor respectful for any part of the gentleman's person to touch the lady voluntarily, except his right forearm and hand, and his left hand, both placed firmly but gently in position,—the right hand on the lady's waist, below the shoulders, and as nearly central as the respective heights of the two will render easy and comfortable, while his left hand should hold the lady's right, or support her arm with the palm and fingers at the elbow, according to her preference. The author is compelled to say, that he has sometimes seen ladies and gentlemen waltzing to our furious music, in attitudes that more plainly illustrated the language of Melnotte in "The Lady of Lyons" than any acting he has ever seen on the stage:—

"Two souls with but a single thought,
Two hearts that beat as one."

I have introduced these remarks in the chapter devoted to ladies, for the reason that the remedy for the evil is in their own hands. No lady can be blamed for declining to dance with a gentleman, if his "style" or movement is not respectful; and a few sharp and timely rebukes, administered courageously, would soon produce a change.

C. H. Cleveland, Jr.,
Dancing at Home and Abroad
(Boston, 1878), 23–25

In round dances, it is customary to take frequent pauses, and not to race round and round until the music ceases; to do so would be considered vulgar.

A lady should be careful that her partner does not hold her right hand upright in the air when dancing, or hold it against his left side, or move it up and down in an ungainly fashion, neither should a lady permit her partner to assist her in holding up her dress when dancing.

Manners and Tone of Good Society,
By a Member of the Aristocracy
(London, ca. 1879), 124–25

When dancing a round dance, a gentleman should never hold a lady's hand behind him, or on his hip, or high in the air, moving her arm as though it were a pump handle, as seen in some of our western cities, but should hold it gracefully by his side.

John H. Young,
Our Deportment
(Detroit, 1879), 142

With the square dances, it does not matter if a few mistakes are made, but with round dances it requires an almost perfect knowledge to make them thoroughly enjoyable.

With careful practice one may be able to master any of the round dances in one or two nights.

Let the student retire to some spot where he or she will be secure from interruption; take the book in hand and follow each direction minutely, never passing from one point to another until understanding each point thoroughly. After going through the description given in this book (or whatever dance the student may select to study), lay down the book and practice from memory; after which they may practice with some friend of the opposite sex (who knows how to dance round dances) until the friend tells them that they are proficient to appear in public.

George E. Wilson,
Wilson's Ball-Room Guide and Call Book
(New York, 1884), 95

We often see those who consider themselves *au fait*, (and usually they are the only ones who entertain that opinion) making themselves conspicuous by distorting their bodies, stiffening their arms, and twisting their legs, until they have the appearance of being afflicted with some terrible deformity, from which they are suffering intense pain. They carve the air with their arms, they shuffle about with an unheard-of combination of movements, collide with everybody and everything within their reach and all the while labor under the delusion that they are being observed by admiring eyes.

M. B. Gilbert,
Round Dancing
(Portland, Maine, 1890), 33–34

B. Comments on the Waltz

But with regard to the lately-introduced German waltz, I cannot speak so favourable. I must agree with Goethe, when writing of the national dance of this country, "that none but husbands and wives can with any propriety be partners in the waltz."

There is something in the close approximation of persons, in the attitudes, and in the motion, which ill agrees with the delicacy of woman, should she be placed in such a situation with any other man than the most intimate connexion she can have in life. Indeed, I have often heard men of no very over-strained feeling say, "that there are very few women in the world with whom they could bear to dance the german waltz."

The Mirror of the Graces,
By a Lady of Distinction
(New York, 1813), 177

In short, Waltzing, notwithstanding all the opposition its more extensive practice has had to encounter, is now generally considered so *chaste*, in comparison with Country Dancing, Cotillions, or any other species of Dancing, that truth looses *not a jot* of its veracity when it is affirmed, that, in most parties, where Dancing is resorted to as an amusement, Waltzing is more frequently substituted for Country Dancing, than the *latter* is for the *former*.

Thomas Wilson,
A Description of the Correct Method of Waltzing
(London, 1816), xxxii–xxxiii

The waltz is a dance of quite too loose a character, and unmarried ladies should refrain from it altogether, both in public and private; very young married ladies, however, may be allowed to waltz in private balls, if it is very seldom, and with persons of their acquaintance. It is indispensable for them to acquit themselves with dignity and modesty.

Mme. Celnart,
The Gentleman and Lady's Book
(Boston, 1833), 187

Vertigo is one of the great inconveniences of the waltz; and the character of this dance, its rapid turnings, the clasping of the dancers, their exciting contact, and the too quick and too long continued succession of lively and agreeable emotions, produce sometimes, in women of a very irritable constitution, syncopes, spasms and other accidents which should induce them to renounce it.

Donald Walker,
Exercises for Ladies
(London, 1836), 148–49

True, there have been violent objections [to waltzing]; and those who believe that a woman should never come into any near personal contact with any gentleman but a near relation, or a probable or actual husband, must still object to this and all similar dances, but more especially to this; for in no other are the spheres of two persons so entwined with each other, and none exercises so great an influence over the personal magnetism, the senses and the emotions. Doubtless it should be engaged in with caution by all sensitive organizations. A woman, especially, ought to be very sure that the man she waltzes with is one worthy of so close an intimacy; and one who understands her nature and relations well, will not waltz with any other.

But the waltz, the polka, the schottish; the dances of couples, involving personal associations of too free a character for the public ball-room, strangers, or ball-room acquaintances, may yet be proper and agreeable, as the pleasant exercise of a morning or evening at home, where, in a family group, or a little party of select and intimate friends, the pianoforte is opened, and the dance occupies the pauses of conversation, and gives life and motion; a deeper respiration and a quicker circulation to those who so often grow languid and ill for want of it.

The Illustrated Manners Book
(New York, 1855), 397–99

It Is Not the Correct Thing—For a man or woman, but especially man, to endeavor to waltz in public unless he know the correct ball-room step.

It Is the Correct Thing—To remember that the waltz-step changes every few years, and that a blunder in dancing is very like a crime.

The Correct Thing in Good Society
(Boston, ca. 1888), 118–19

Reversing in the waltz (always put *valse* on the dance-cards) is not "good form." Why it should not be can only be accounted for by the fact that English men and women (whom candor compels me to say, after many years observation, are the worst dancers in the world) "can't" reverse themselves, and therefore, in the spirit of "sour grapes," excuse their awkwardness by stigmatizing what they only wish they could do as "bad form." They are able to reverse in the polka, if (as they term it) *going the wrong way* can be termed reversing—*ergo*, it is good form to reverse in the polka!

"Good Form" in England,
By an American Resident in the United Kingdom
(New York, 1888), 160–61

In my book "Dancing As It Should Be," I happened to make some allusion to American waltzes, which I was asked to explain by our cousins across the Atlantic, and I take this opportunity of stating that my remarks implied no reflection whatever on American dancing, which is generally speaking very good. I was really alluding to such movements as the "Rockaways" and Boston or "Dip Waltzes"—which latter I am informed on good authority is a "hybrid unknown in well regulated society." It is possible that the arm movement known as the "Berkley pump" is worthy to be compared with some of our own Kensingtonian monkeyisms to which I shall presently call attention; but dancing and foolery are different things, and, as I have said, legitimate dancing in America is good. I will not go so far as to say that the Americans waltz better than we, for when the English do waltz well, they waltz as well as any people in the world; but Americans are as a rule very good waltzers, and make a great feature of reversing.

Edward Scott,
Dancing and Dancers
(London, 1888), 87–88

[In waltzing] he presses [his partner] close to his breast and they glide over the floor together as if the two were but one.

When she raises her eyes, timidly at first, to

that handsome but deceitful face, now so close to her own, the look that is in his eyes as they meet hers, seems to burn into her very soul. A strange, sweet thrill shakes her very being and leaves her weak and powerless and obliged to depend for support upon the arm which is pressing her to himself in such a suggestive manner, but the sensation is a pleasant one and grows to be the very essence of her life.

She grows more bold, and from being able to return shy glances at first, is soon able to meet more daring ones until, with heart beating against heart, hand clasped in hand, and eyes looking burning words which lips dare not speak, the waltz becomes one long, sweet and purely sensual pleasure.

But let us turn our attention again to the dancers, at two o-clock the next morning. This is the favorite waltz, and the last and most furious of the night, as well as the most disgusting. Let us notice, as an example, our fair friend once more.

She is now in the vile embrace of the Apollo of the evening. Her head rests upon his shoulder, her face is upturned to his, her bare arm is almost around his neck, her partly nude swelling breast heaves tumultuously against his, face to face they whirl on, his limbs interwoven with hers, his strong right arm around her yielding form, he presses her to him until every curve in the contour of her body thrills with the amorous contact. Her eyes look into his, but she sees nothing; the soft music fills the room, but she hears it not; he bends her body to and fro, but she knows it not; his hot breath, tainted with strong drink, is on her hair and cheek, his lips almost touch her forehead, yet she does not shrink; his eyes, gleaming with a fierce, intolerable lust, gloat over her, yet she does not quail. She is filled with the rapture of sin in its intensity; her spirit is inflamed with passion and lust is gratified in thought. With a last low wail the music ceases, and the dance for the night is ended, but not the evil work of the night.

T. A. Faulkner,
From the Ballroom to Hell
(Chicago, 1892), 10–11, 14–16

C. A Canon for Mr. Polka

In the early winter, strange sounds, fleeting and indistinct, came over the Channel, of a new fascination having established itself in Paris, but little attention was paid to those rumours; it was well known, that a cameleopard or a regicide, a new fiddler or a new pattern, a singing mouse, or a dancing rhinoceros, or any thing of that sort, would speedily kick the Polka out of favour of the Parisians. If a new sin could be discovered, adieu Polka; but there was no reasonable chance of such a godsend, that field was pretty well exhausted by this time; so the Polka held undisputed sway for that winter, so much so, that a considerable fall took place in the prices of truffles, foie gras, bals masques, and blasphemous novels.

Such too is the mystic ubiquity of Polka, that not only it stirred the social system of Europe to its very foundations, not only was its sway acknowledged by the shorn royalty of the Bourbons, and the unshaven empire of the Romanoff's, but its mesmeric influence crossed the Atlantic, and a gentleman of whose very existence, nobody, excepting his butcher, baker, &c., &c., was aware, obtained the Presidential chair, by simply reading aright and rapidly what was written in the signs of the times, and assuming the name of Polk, for nobody believes that that is the worthy gentleman's real name. Of course he assumed it for the occasion, as the French Republicans did classical names, and he deserves great credit for the "smartness" he displayed.

The dance was nothing but a Parisiennised jig, a hornpipe in French; and indeed it is remarkable that to this day, any artist who wishes to represent an Irishman in a state of excitement, of whatever sort, invariably represents him in a Polka attitude, that is to say, standing upon one leg.

Every ballroom was like a whirlpool; dancing more resembled the driving home from Derby than anything else; the collisions rivalled in frequency and severity, those of the iron railways before the infants had learned how to behave themselves. The price of fans rose frightfully, partly from the pressing necessity for them, and partly from the enormous destruction of them in the melee. A mystical sign like that of the freemasons became established among the fraternity and sorority of the Polka, whereby they recognized one another, viz. the standing significantly upon one leg.

We may here be allowed to present to our readers, a most valuable code of rules, to be observed by all aspiring youths who wish to shine in Polka, a code which was kindly communicated to us by a gentleman of whom we are not at liberty, at present, to say more than that we are perfectly certain, that our readers will put implicit faith in the great authority that compiled.

The Canon of the Polka

I. At the concluding note of the bar before you begin, throw back your left foot. If there is such a thing as a pewter Mercury, or a plaster Cupid in any of the gardens in your neighbourhood, you may practise standing in the attitude the figure is in, the being able to stand like a goose on one leg, being an important, and indeed, essential facility to those who aspire to be rated, A.1. in Polka.

II. Take a good tight hold of your partner and keep it; it is the height of spooniness to let any thing slip through your fingers.

III. Remember, that in your step you stride, not straddle. If you cannot keep your own legs in their proper places, you may rely upon it, nobody else will do it for you.

IV. Be moderate in your kicks, as you ought to be in all your other pleasures, and do not forget that kicking, you lash, not prance.

V. Stop when you hear your partner sobbing very painfully, or when you observe her gown is coming off. Nothing marks a chivalrous mind, more than consideration for women; for which reason also, you will not fail to carry a small pincushion in your pocket to repair damages, for their dresses are everlastingly coming to pieces, and the 12 to 14 spare pins they generally carry, are seldom sufficient to keep them together for more than two, or at most, three Polkas.

VI. Recollect that utter disregard of time, common at present in Waltzing, is not safe in Polka, as it can be more easily detected. If you *cannot* dance in time, dance with nobody under nine or ten stone. At that weight, if she has any ear, she will probably keep you tolerably steady; if she has none, everyone will think it is her fault.

VII. If you *can* dance, impress upon your partner that she must trust herself implicitly and unresistingly to your guidance—Faith being the only virtue that saves in Polka.

VIII. Remember that the momentum of a body in motion is composed of its weight and its velocity; and where collisions are plenty, choose accordingly.

IX. Holding your left hand up in the air, like the figure of justice dangling the scales over a country court-house, seldom fails to excite admiration; walking (not dancing, but *walking*) backwards through the thickest of the crowd will impress the by-stander with a high opinion of your good taste, or you may stop in the middle of the room, and lift your feet alternately, like a turkey in deep mud; in short, the paths of fame are innumerable, if you have only tact enough to select that best suited to your own capacity.

X. If you have just been introduced to your partner, you may every now and then stop, as if you were astonished at something before you, and then make a hop or two backwards; she will of course take you for a shop boy, and then you may produce a considerable effect by talking familiarly of some great person. None but a blundering blockhead thinks he can go straight ahead into a woman's good graces. To lose a little on one tack, and to gain a great deal on another, is the way to get to windward of the terrestrial angels.

XI. If you have a taste for going round the room on the wrong side, against the stream, never mind the inconvenience it puts others to, but take care to push your partner *before* you. Everybody that can *must* get out of *her* way, though you yourself might find it otherwise. Whenever Irish mobs are taking liberties with regular troops, they always keep any woman they can catch in their front; and there is a good deal of discretion in the practice.

XII. In case of casualties, go on never minding,

the maxim will stand you in good stead in many things besides Mr. Polka; and now, if you cannot distinguish yourself in Polka and small tea parties, don't blame me.

Captain Knox,
The Spirit of the Polka
(London, 1845), 3–4, 13–14, 19, 35, 38–43

D. Directions for Performing the Waltz

The Slow Waltz

The *Slow Waltz Movements* . . . are commenced by the *Gentleman's left* foot being brought from the *fourth position* behind into the *second position* with a *turn* of the *body*. . . .

A *slow pirouette,* as technically so called, immediately follows; and is performed, by bringing the *right* foot from its Situation into the *fifth position behind* the *left; both feet raised* on the *toes,* the *knees* perfectly *straight,* and turning slowly round on the *points* of the toes of *both feet together,* preserving in the turning an easy equilibrium of the Body; and, in turning on the toes, *passing* the *heels* perfectly *close* and as much *raised* as may be.

The *right* Foot by this means becoming placed in *front* of the left . . . finishes the *pirouette,* and leaves the *right* foot prepared for the performance of *Three Movements forward* in the fourth position, technically named, *Pas de Bouree,* which next follow.

It is necessary however to *explain* the movements [of the Pas de Bouree], which are as follow:

The *right foot* is passed *forward* into the *fourth position* on the *toe* pointed, and the knee as straight as possible; the *left* foot being left in the *fourth position behind* and on the toe pointed, is brought forward into the *fourth position* in *front* of the *right* foot; the *right* foot being then in the *fourth position behind,* is *again* brought forward into the *fourth position* in *front* of the *left.*

Regard must be had in performing the *Pas de Bouree* (which must be on the toes, with the knees perfectly straight) that a *rising* and *sinking motion* of the *body* be *totally avoided.*

The *left* foot, after the performance of the *last* of the *three Pas de Bouree,* being situated in the *fourth position* behind, is *prepared* to pass into the *second position.* . . .

The *movements* in *this* department or class of Style in French Waltzing . . . though, as performed by the *Lady* and *Gentleman,* are *precisely the same;* yet the *same movements* are *not* performed by *both* at the *same time.*

This description given, commences with the *Gentleman's* part, and is *equally* adapted to the instruction of the *Lady,* observing this *difference,* that at the commencement of the waltz movements, as the *Gentleman* passes his *left* foot into the *second position,* the *Lady* commences with her *right* foot for the *first* movement of the *Pas de Bouree* and consequently, while the *Lady* is *performing* the three *Pas de Bouree,* the *Gentleman* passes the foot into the *second position,* and turns the *slow pirouette* . . . and as the *Gentleman* commences and performs *Pas de Bouree,* the *Lady* passes her foot into the *second position,* and turns the *slow pirouette;* after which she is again *prepared* for, and in *continuing* the Waltzing, performs the *Pas de Bouree,* whilst the *Gentleman* is *again* passing his foot into the *second position, &c. as* at the *commencement* of the Waltz Movements.

Thomas Wilson,
A Description of the Correct Method of Waltzing
(London, 1816), 65–71

[The waltz] is composed of two steps, each of three beats to a bar, which also contains three *tems,* according to musical principles. Each of these two steps performs the *demi-tour,* or half-turn of the waltz, which lasts during one bar; the two steps united form, therefore, the whole waltz, executed in two bars. These steps differ one from the other, yet so as to fit one into the other, if it may be so expressed, during their performance, and in such endangering those of the other; thus while the gentleman performs one step, the lady dances the other, so that both are executed with uninterrupted exactness, as will be clearly demonstrated.

In order to perform one of these waltz steps,

place your feet in the third position, the right foot forward, then advancing the right foot in the natural way, not turning it out, to place it in the fourth position (first time), then immediately bring forward the left foot, turning the toe inward, and placing it crossways before the other foot, to form the fourth position, that foot being raised immediately, and the body is, at the same time, turned half-round; in placing the foot for the fourth position (second time), that foot which you have raised, while placing the last mentioned, must then be placed before the other in the third position, and outwardly, resuming its ordinary posture, and to perform the third bar. The step being thus executed while turning half round, will bring the face where the back was.

In order to execute the second step, and to perform at the same time the other half-turn, *demi-tour*, which completes the waltz, turn out the side of your left foot, the toe being inward, and moving the body round at the same time, place it in the second position (first beat), put the right foot behind the left, always continuing to turn the body (second beat), then bring the left foot before you, turning the toe inwards, the body turning also, to come half-round, at the moment you are placing the left foot in the second position, to execute the third beat of the second step, and the second half-turn, which complete the waltz.

By this example, it may be seen that a waltz is composed of two steps, each of which contains three *tems*, or beats, making six for both, and for the entire figure of the waltz, which is performed during two bars; also, that when either of the two persons waltzing advances the right foot to begin the first step described above, the opposite person draws back the left foot at the same time to begin the other step, allowing his partner an opportunity of advancing her foot, both performing then the *demi-tour*; when one repeats the step the other has just executed in the second *demi-tour*, to complete the waltz. When the position for waltzing is taken, in order that the step may be properly commenced, and that both persons may be in unison, the lady being on the right of the gentleman, he must go off on the left foot, turning himself before his partner, as if that had been his first position; and with respect to the second step described before, it is always performed by that person who has his back towards the side on which the waltz begins, as the person who faces that side always executes the first step.

To waltz properly, all the beats, or *tems* should be clearly marked, being attentive not to turn upon *les pointes*, or toes, in the same beats, such a system not being convenient for the turning of two persons at once; every turn in a waltz should be clearly and fully performed, so that on finishing, the waltzers should come always opposite to the same side as they were on setting out; without which, the course of the waltzes cannot be followed, and the waltzer would, in consequence, fall upon those who are coming behind him, or who are in the middle of the room, which is very frequently the case.

The gentleman should hold the lady by the right hand, and above the waist, or by both hands, if waltzing be difficult to her; or otherwise, it would be better for the gentleman to support the right hand of the lady by his left. The arms should be kept in a rounded position, which is the most graceful, preserving them without motion; and in this position one person should keep as far from the other as the arms will permit, so that neither may be incommoded.

C. Blasis,
The Code of Terpsichore
(London, 1828), 503–5

The Step of the Waltz

Standing in the third position, right foot in front:

Place the right foot forward (count one); then the left forward, slightly turning it inward (count two); draw up the right foot in front of the left, in third position (count three); place the left foot out (count four) draw the right foot so that the toe be behind the hollow of the left foot (count five); then turn on the toes, so as to bring the right foot in front of the left, in the third position (count six).

The above is intended for the lady; the gentleman executes the same, but commences with the 4,

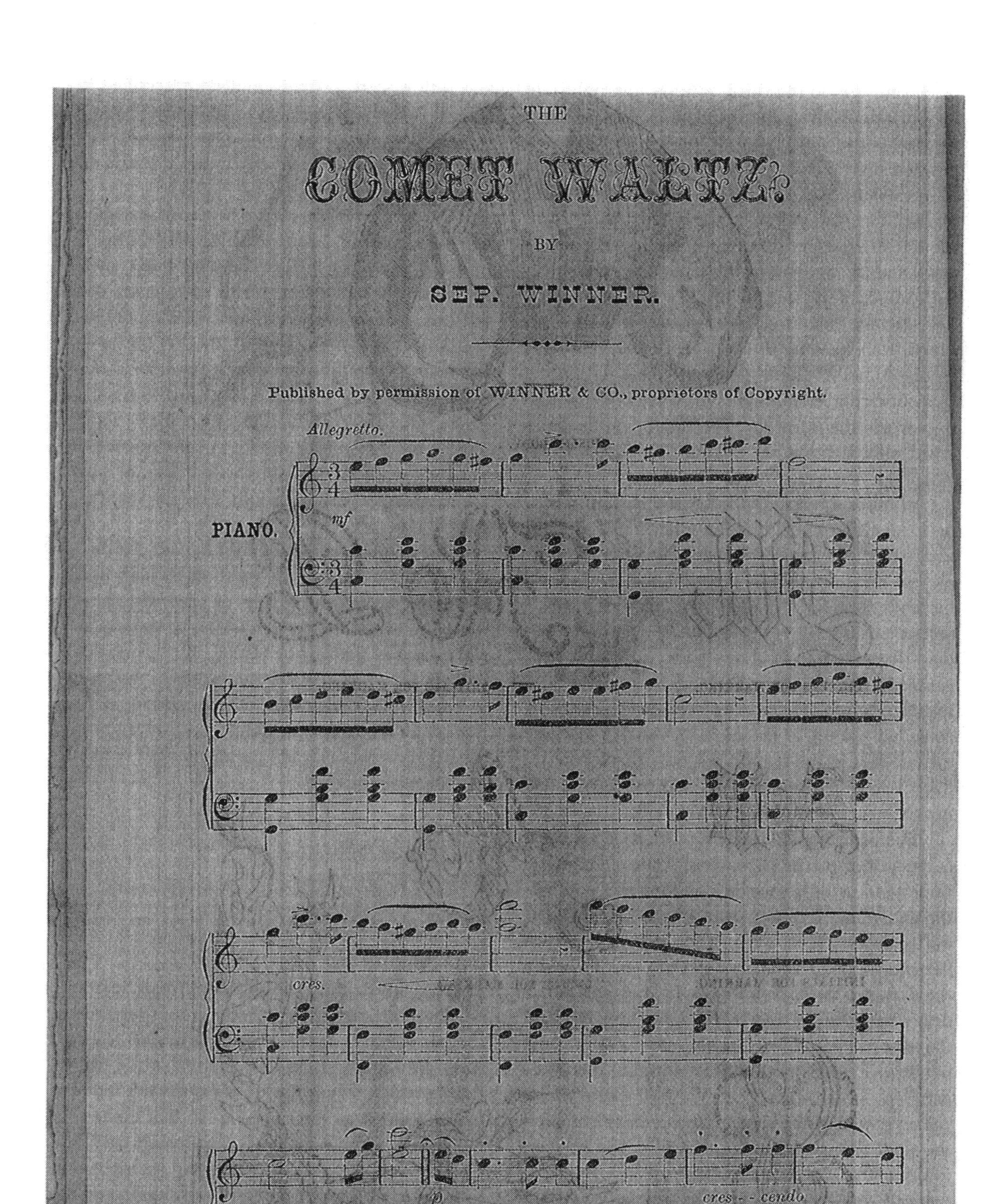
THE
COMET WALTZ.
BY
SEP. WINNER.
Published by permission of WINNER & CO., proprietors of Copyright.
Allegretto.
PIANO.
mf
cres.
fp
cres - - cendo

THE COMET WALTZ.
cres - - cen - - do
f
8va.
D.C.
D.C.
Trio.
Dolce
p
mf
f
cres.
ff
D.C.
D.C.

5, 6 while the lady executes the 1, 2, 3; turning half round with three, and the other half with three, making six steps in all.

Edward Ferrero,
The Art of Dancing
(New York, 1859), 143

The Glide Waltz

Music in 3–4 time.—This waltz particularly commends itself on account of its easy and graceful movement, and its entire freedom from all apparent physical effort. With the exception of the bending motion it is identical with the plain waltz, which has outlived all attempts to improve upon it.

GENTLEMEN

1. Glide backward with the left foot, one step, bending both knees; *count one.*

2. Draw the right foot back about six inches beyond the left, at the same time straightening the knees, by lightly rising on the toes, and turn nearly half round to the right (the way of the clock), by throwing the right shoulder back; *count two.*

3. Complete the half turn by bringing the left heel up to the right, settling down on both; *count three.*

4. Glide the right foot directly forward, bending both knees: *count four.*

5. Advance the left foot directly in front of the right (fourth position), and straighten both knees by slightly rising on the toes; at the same time turn half round; *count five.*

6. Complete the half turn by bringing the right heel up to the left, and settling down on both.

LADY

The lady commences at No. 4 right foot forward, continuing thus: 4, 5, 6, 1, 2, 3 and so on, all through the waltz.

The Boston Dip

This waltz is an exaggeration of the Glide Waltz each glide being accompanied by a considerable bend of the knee, which causes the whole body to sink down or dip at constantly recurring intervals. In appearance this movement is not only ungraceful, but frequently ungainly. . . .

The Ball-Room Guide and Call Book
(New York, 186–), 59

Waltz.—Turning to Right
[Directions for the Woman]
Two bars of music are required for each revolution. One bar may be termed the progressive, the other the pivot.
1st Movement: Leap forward upon right [foot].
2nd Movement: Slide left.

In making this slide, turn to the right, so that the slide will follow the same direct line forward as the leap.

3rd Movement: Change to right.

At this change, complete the half turn with left foot raised behind.

4th Movement: Leap backward upon left [foot].
5th Movement: Slide backward with right.

At this slide continue the turning to the right, keeping upon the same line.

6th Movement: Change to left.

Complete the second half turn, resting upon left with right in front, ready to recommence the series of motions.

Allen Dodworth,
Dancing and Its Relations to . . . Social Life
(New York, 1885), 66–67

Waltz Variations

The Step of the Polka Redowa

Music in 3–4 Time—Slide the left foot forward; bring the right behind in the third position; spring out on the left foot, bringing the right foot up close; recommence the same with the right foot.

This dance is composed of the same step as the polka, with the exception that you slide the first step instead of springing, and omit the pause, as in this dance you count three both for the music and dance.

The dance admits of various changes of direction.

5
Tausend und eine Nacht.
Walzer.
INTRODUTION.
Andante.
Johann Strauss, Op. 346.
p
p
pp
poco cresc.
p
rit.
Tempo di Valse.
pp
cre
scen
do
f
24106.

6
Walzer.
1.
p
cresc.
f
pp
cresc.
ff
1.
pp
2.
mf
Schluss.
Fine.
Trio.
mf
p
mf
p
mf
24106

7
mf
p
mf
p
mf
No 1 dal segno al fine.
Eingang.
Walzer.
2.
f
p
mf
ff
pp
24106

8
f
p
tr
cresc.
f
p
dol.
mf
ff
pp
f
24106

9
1.
Schluss.
p
Eingang.
Walzer.
3.
f
p
cresc.
1.
2.
p
p
cresc.
1.
f
2.
p
f
24106

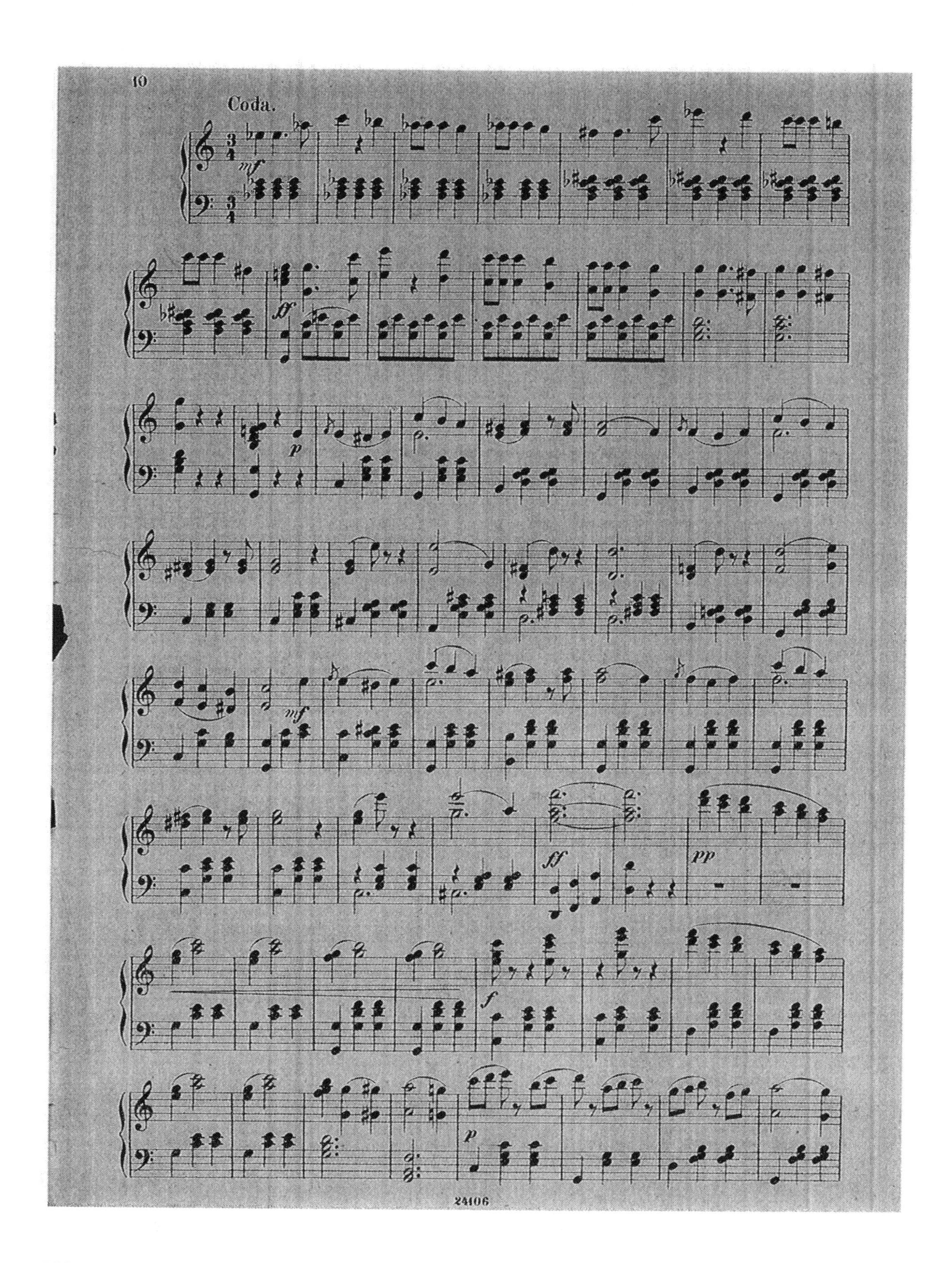
10
Coda.
mf
ff
p
mf
ff
pp
f
p
24106

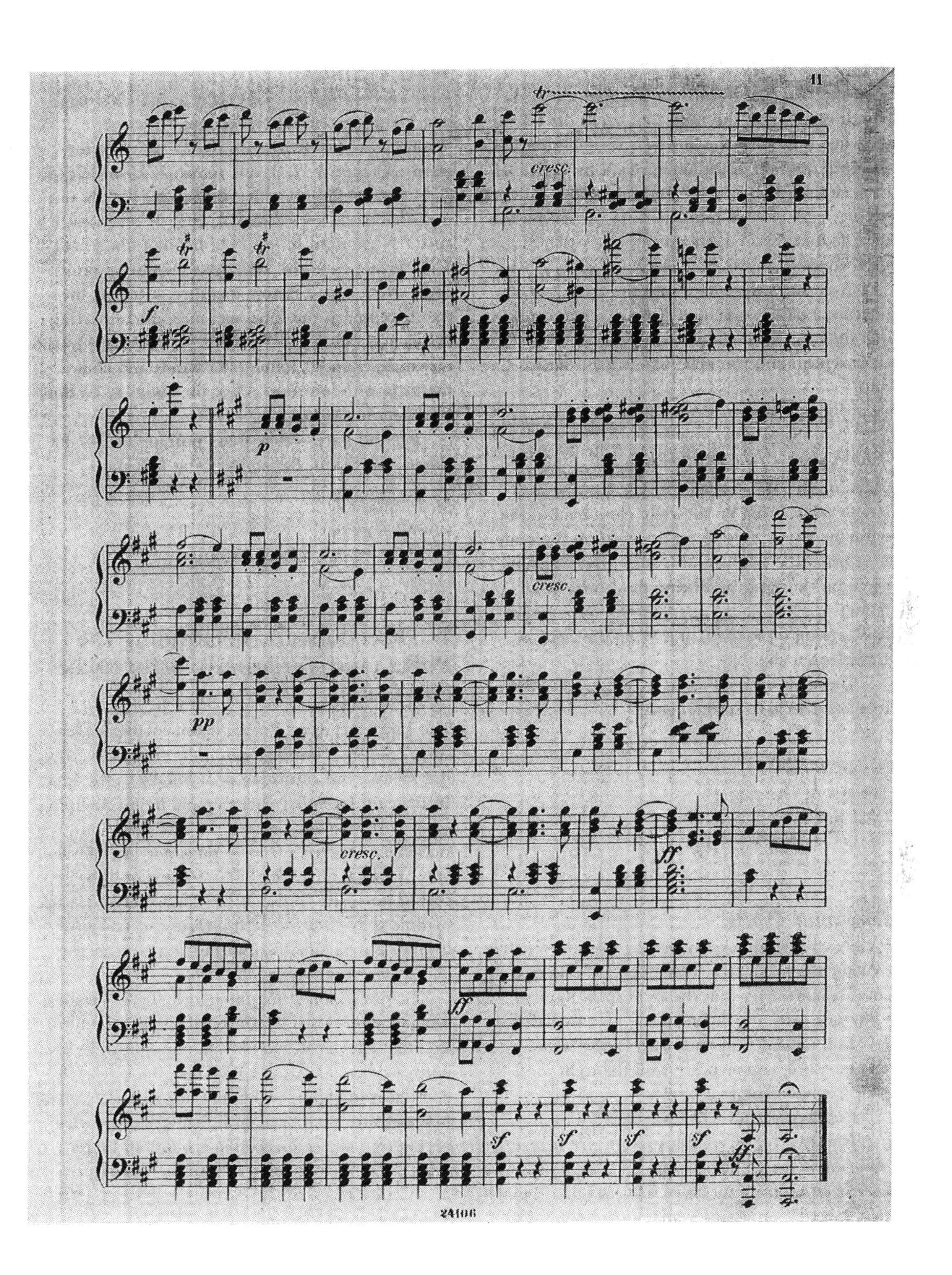
11
tr
cresc.
f
tr
tr
p
cresc.
pp
cresc.
ff
ff
sf
sf
sf
sf
ff
24106

The Step of the Polka Mazourka

Music in 3–4 Time—Slide the left foot forward (count one); bring the right foot up to the left; at the same time raise the left foot, extending it, pointing the foot down (count two); bring the left back close to the right; at the same time springing on the right foot without touching the left on the floor (count three); then execute the polka redowa step (count 3).

Commence the whole with the right foot; the mazourka part is executed forward without turning; then turn half round with the polka redowa step; repeat, and you make the whole round.

The Step of the Zingerilla

Music in 3–4 Time—Slide the left foot forward (count one). Bring up the right close behind the left (count two). Spring on the right; at the same time bring the left behind (count three). Spring again on the right, and bring the left in front (count four). Slide the left forward again (count five). spring on the left, and bring the right in front (count six).

The same with the right foot, changing the feet alternately to recommence.

Edward Ferrero,
The Art of Dancing
(New York, 1859), 146, 148–49, 153

Diagonal Waltz

Waltz one measure, commencing with the left foot, making a quarter turn. Waltz forward one measure, commencing with the right foot. Reverse waltz one measure, commencing with the left foot forward, making a quarter turn. Waltz backward one measure, commencing with the right foot. Repeat, commencing as at first.

Counterpart for lady.

It will be observed that no full turn is made; *le changement de tour* being made on every third measure, causing the dancers to move around the hall in a diagonal or zig-zag course.

Waltz Minuet

First Part:—Position; join right hands with partner, facing in opposite direction.

Both commencing with right foot, slide forward one step, 1, 2, 3; one measure. Draw left to right (3d behind), bending the knees, 1, 2, 3; one measure. Slide left backward, 1, 2, 3; one measure.* Draw right to left (3d), bending the knees, 1, 2, 3; one measure. Walk (par marche) around each other, one step to a measure, bringing the feet together at the third measure, disconnecting hands and saluting partner during third and fourth measures. Repeat, joining left hands and commencing with left foot. All of the above to be done in sixteen measures.

Second Part:—Take waltz position and Waltz sixteen measures. Recommence at first part.

M. B. Gilbert,
Round Dancing
(Portland, Maine, 1890), 98, 102

E. Directions for Performing the Polka (and Variations), Schottische, and Galop

The Polka is a *danse à deux*, commencing at pleasure, couples following each other adopting any of the figures, but returning occasionally to the first. In dancing La Polka, there should be no stamping of the heels or toe; this may be tolerated at a Bohemian *auberge*, but is inadmissible into the *salons* of London or Paris. The Polka should be played not quite so fast as the Galop. The measure or time is 2–4, divide each measure or bar into four parts: viz. one, two, three, four, the accent being placed on the second.

Before commencing the figure, there is a short introduction, consisting of four bars, danced thus: leading your partner to her place in the circle, placing yourself *vis-à-vis*, you then take the lady's left hand in your right, making the first step four times; first forward, then backward, forward again, then backward, taking care to gain ground in the forward steps, then commence with the first figure.

*Pas minuet.

The Polka must be danced quietly, gracefully and without any awkward gestures, such as lifting up the leg too high, or starting off in an abrupt manner.

There are only two *pas* in the Polka. The first consists of the previously mentioned jump and glissade; the second is performed by touching the ground lightly with the foot, on each measure: viz. with the heel when the leg is forward, and with the toe when backward. All other *pas* belong either to the Mazourka or Crakovien.

All sorts of chasses must be carefully avoided, as bringing the Polka too near the mere Quadrille, and taking away all the characteristic features of the dance.

Those who have seen the Polka danced in Paris know that the gentleman has alone the right of forming or changing the figures, leading his partner as he pleases either backward or forward.

The Ball Room Annual
(London, ca. 1844), 70–72

The Polka Taught Without the Aid of a Master

For the following clear and explicit key to the intricacies of this elegant and fashionable dance, we are indebted to one of the most distinguished professors, and by attending to the annexed admirable exposition, in conjunction with our plate, the subscribers of the "Lady's Book" will be enabled to accomplish with ease and grace this exquisite dance without the aid of a master.

Description of the Step

The Polka step being the same in all the figures, we will here describe it once for the entire.

It is executed in four parts or movements:—

1st. You raise the part of the left foot behind the ankle, to the commencement of the calf of the right leg, and then let it glide before you to the point of the heel, at the same time bounding on the point of the right foot.

2d. You are then to draw back the right foot behind the left foot.

Figure 23

3d. You again advance the left foot, giving a slight bit with the heel, so as to mark the measure more strongly.

4th. Finally, raise the right leg, throwing back the foot behind the left leg to about the height of the calf.

This last movement is joined to the first part of the next step, which is executed in the same manner as the first, commencing this time with the right foot, and so on.

The lady goes through exactly the same step, but commences with the right foot, so as to continue always on the foot opposite to that of her partner.

The Figures—The National Polka is composed of the ten following figures, of which the first five only are performed in the saloons.

1st. The promenade.
2d. The waltz.
3d. The *valse à rebours*, or reversed waltz.
4th. The *valse tortillée*, or shuffling waltz.
5th. The *pas Bohemien*, or Bohemian step.
6th. The changing arms.
7th. The Bohemian step, with changing of arms and waltzing.
8th. The hand-mill, or *Moulinet d'une main.*
9th. The *Moulinet*, with following and returning his partner.
10th. The double figures.

The Promenade.—The gentleman takes, with his right hand, the left hand of his partner, holding it as high as the breast. In executing the first movement, he lowers his hand gently, turning it a little towards the left; but in the fourth part he turns it in a contrary direction towards the lady, and the hands then again meet in the raised position as before.

They thus proceed sometimes about the saloon, and when the see-saw movement is well executed, it is full of gracefulness and coquetry.

The Revolving or Shuffling Waltz.—The gentleman places himself in front of his partner, holding her as for waltzing. In executing this step he always puts forth the left foot; at the same time impressing on the lady a semi-circular movement from right to left and from left to right, now advancing towards her, and now retiring from her.

Sometimes the cavalier holds the *danseuse* as in the plate, taking her right hand in his right hand, and frequently changing hands.

The Pas Bohemien.—The gentleman executes the figure holding his partner as in waltzing; but, in the fourth movement, instead of resting the right foot on the floor, as in the ordinary step, he extends the leg, resting the heel, the part of the foot being raised, then on the toes, the heel being raised—at the same time gliding the foot forward, and recommencing the same step.

This step is executed in the same manner in retiring, and also to the right and to the left, so as to trace a cross.

This terminates the figures executed in the Polka of the ball rooms; but we shall proceed to describe the other figures, that are not so complicated but that they may be learned in the same manner.

The Changing Arms.—The Cavalier sets out as in the *promenade*, holding his *danseuse* by the waist. At the given signal he withdraws his right arm, and quickly darts his left arm around the lady to receive her—and reciprocally.

In performing this movement he continues to mark the step, and the lady should always fall away at the proper time.

This figure possesses something aerial and poetic, which cannot be well imagined. What blind and tender confidence must she not have in her cavalier, to thus cast herself so dangerously into his arms! But, also, with what ardent and devoted anxiety does her partner receive her, fearful lest he should allow her to drop on the floor! What confidence on her part—what solicitation on his! What affection is required between both! It is a figure that we would, therefore, not recommend to have introduced into our ball rooms.

The Pas Bohemien, with Change of Arms and Waltzing.—This figure, as the name indicates, is a threefold combination of the *Pas Bohemien*, the Waltz, and the preceding step, and it is, therefore, mingled still more emphatically—grace, poetry, and love. It is a figure which we would not wish to see introduced in our saloons.

The Moulinet d'une Main.—This is a charming figure, and one easily executed. The cavalier holds his partner, and revolves after her, marking the

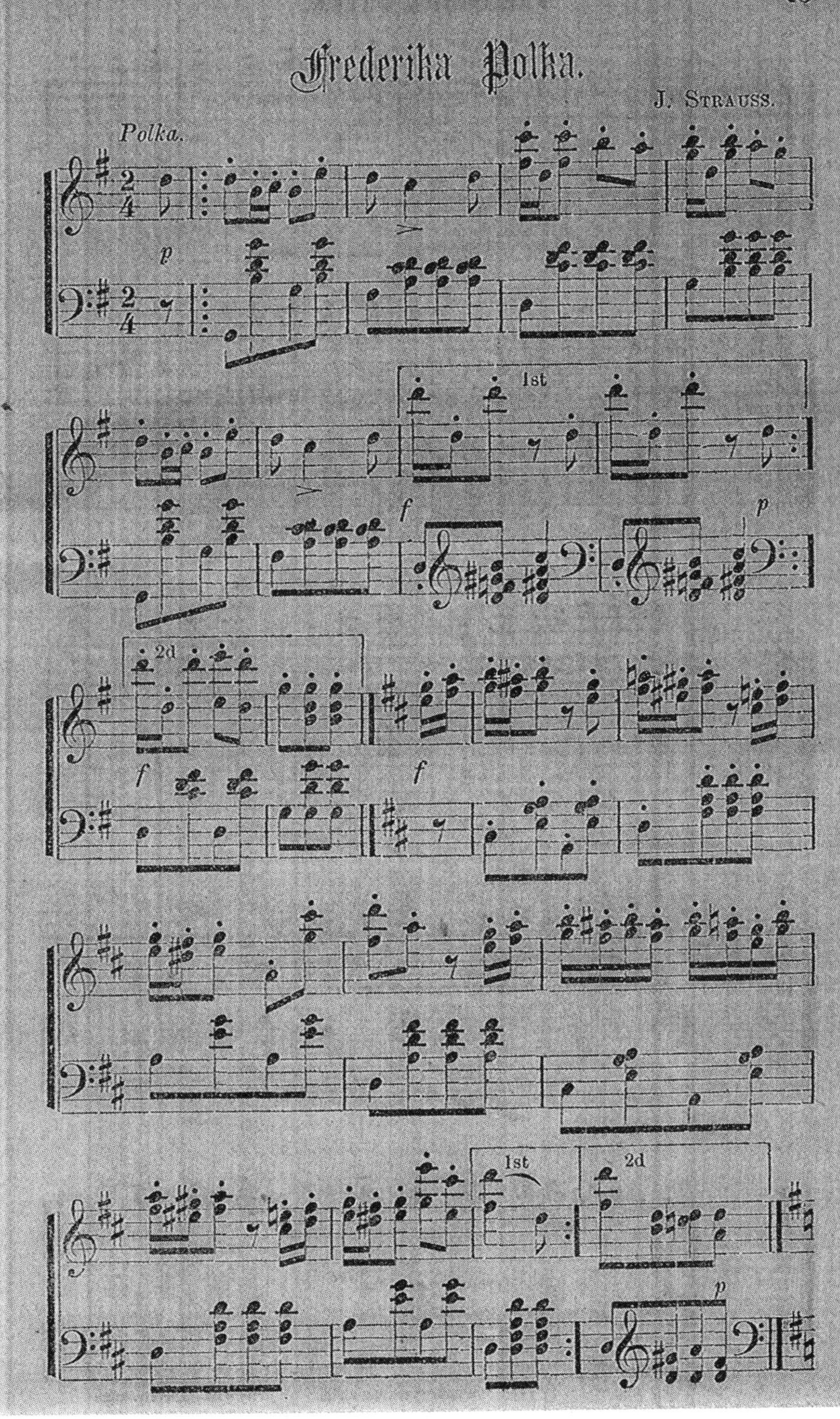
43
Frederika Polka.
J. Strauss.
Polka.
p
1st
f
p
2d
f
f
1st
2d
p

44
FREDERIKA POLKA.
Trio.
p
f

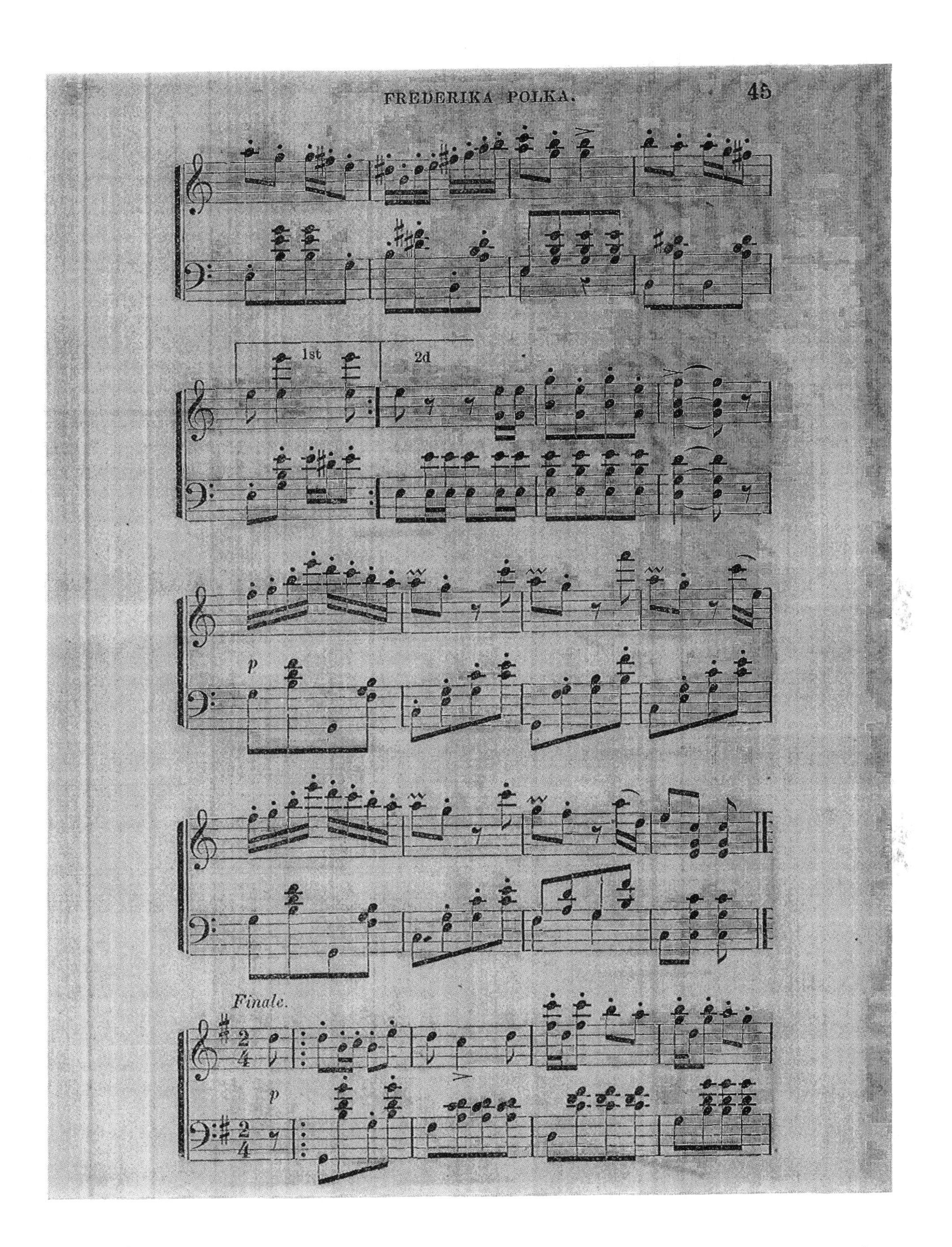
FREDERIKA POLKA.
45
1st
2d
p
p
Finale.

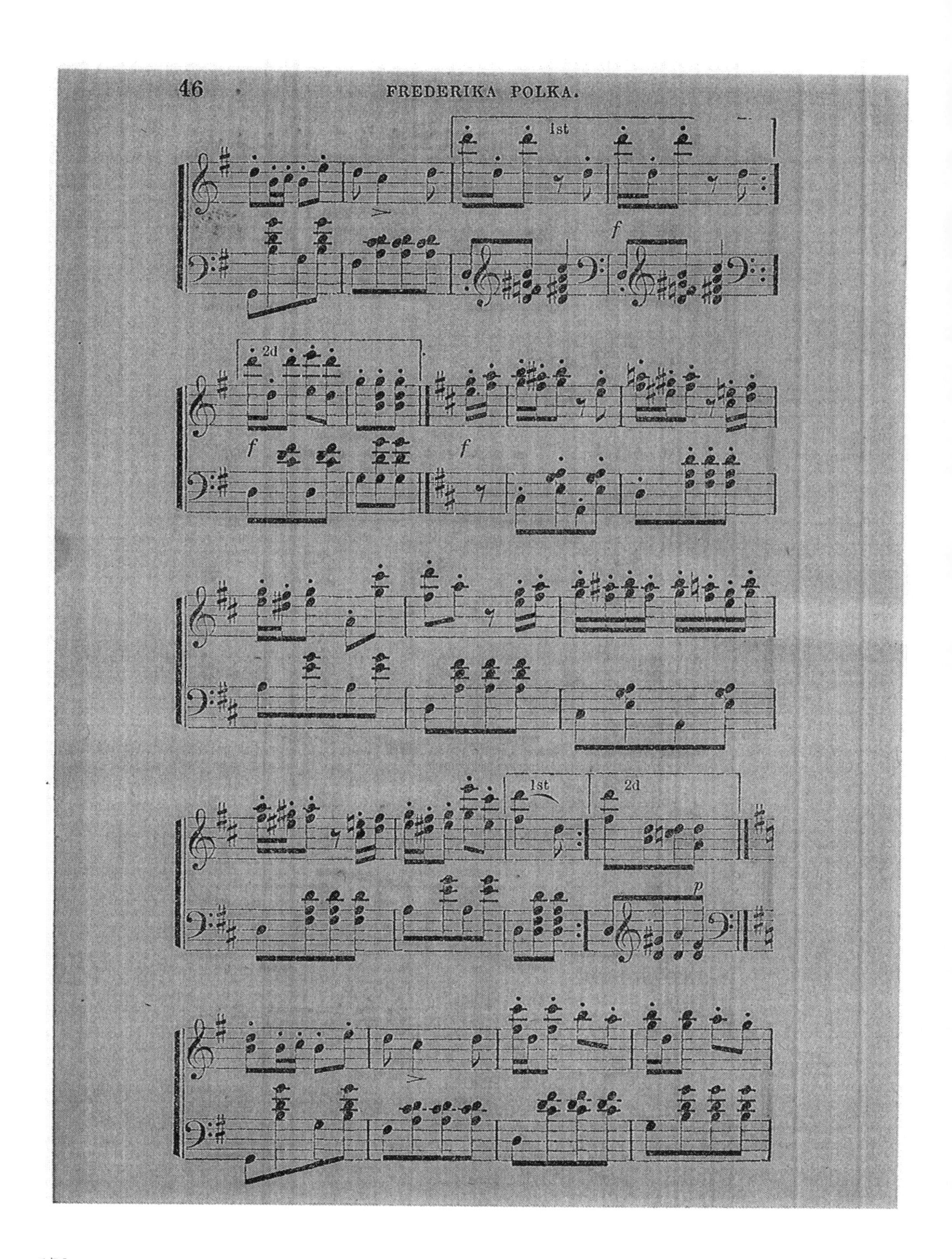
46
FREDERIKA POLKA.
1st
f
2d
f
f
1st
2d
p

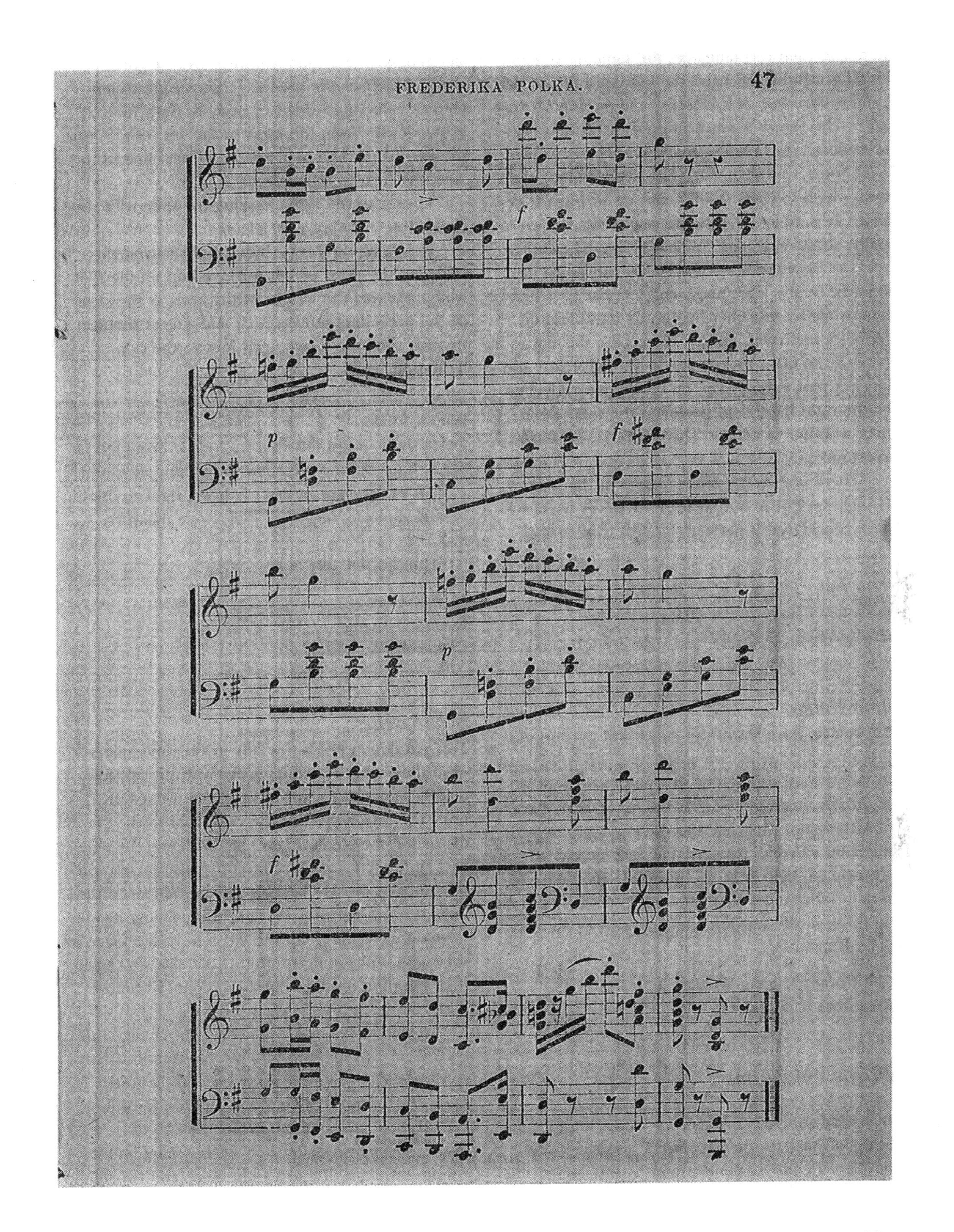
FREDERIKA POLKA.
47
f
p
f
p
f

step, and then recommences the same movement, holding with his left hand the left hand of the lady.

The Moulinet with following and turning his partner.—This figure is much more difficult than the preceding. The gentleman allows the lady to precede home, and then turns her while making the step, which the lady should execute with great celerity. It is, however, a figure impossible to describe sufficiently, and not suited for the saloons.

The Passe Double.—The gentleman holds his *danseuse* by the right hand, and lets her pass before him, while he takes her by the left hand and describes a half turn. Finally, to execute this figure in retiring, he takes his partner by the left hand and lets her pass behind him, he then again takes her by the right hand, and performs the same demi-turn with her as before. This figure is very easily executed.

There are several other figures in the true Hungarian Polka, but, as they are never used, we have considered it perfectly useless to describe them.

"The Polka Taught Without the Aid of a Master," in Godey's Magazine and Lady's Book *(Philadelphia, 1845), 223*

The Polka

Those who have learnt the dance will pardon our pointing out one or two vulgarisms which it is easy to fall into. A hopping or jumping movement is singularly ungraceful—so is the habit many have of kicking out their heels to the endangerment of the shins of other dancers. The feet should scarcely be lifted from the ground—the dancers sliding rather than hopping—and the steps should be taken in the smallest compass, and in the very neatest manner.

Ball-Room Dancing Without a Master *(New York, 1872), 20*

Polka Variations

GLIDE POLKA

Slide left foot to the side (2d). 1; draw right foot to left, and almost simultaneously slide left to the side (chasse), & 2; one measure. Draw right to left and slide left to the side, & 1; draw right to left (1st) transferring weight of body to right foot, 2; leap sidewise from the right to the left foot, 3; one measure. 1, & 2 to be made in a direct line to the side, the turn to be made on 1, 2, 3.

Repeat to the right, making the slide with the right foot.

In beginning a repetition of the movements, either to the right or left, make a hop on the foot which receives the weight of the body at the close of the preceding movements, and almost simultaneously slide the disengaged foot to the side (counting, & 1).

POLKA RUSSE

First Part:—Point left foot in 2nd, 1; bring left to 5th behind, 2; one measure. Polka, one measure, 1, 2, 3. Point right in 2nd, 1; bring right to 5th behind, 2; l one measure. Polka, one measure, 1, 2, 3.

Counterpart for lady.

M. B. Gilbert, Round Dancing *(Portland, Me, 1890), 66*

Schottische

The gentleman holds the lady in the same manner as in the Polka. He commences with the left foot, merely sliding it forward, (or side ways,) count one. Then he brings up the right foot to the place of the left foot (count two,) again sliding the left foot to the left, (count three,) then gently hop on the left foot (4). He repeats this movement to the right, beginning with the right foot, sliding it sideways right, bringing up the left foot to the place of the right, and sliding the right foot sideways again, then hopping on the same foot, count as before (4).

Immediately after, the movement changes into a series of double hops and double rotation. Thus, spring off left foot, (count 1) hop on the same foot, (2) turning half round; spring on right foot, (1) hop on right foot (2) turning half round—repeat the same with right foot, (2) turning half round—which will make eight beats and two whole

24
Herzblättchen.
Polka
(française)
Eduard Strauss, Op. 76.
Lento.
Tempo di Polka. (zum Concert etwas zurückgehalten.)
f
p
pp
poco ritard.
a tempo
p
pp
f
poco ritard.
1.
2.
p
mf
ff
1.
2.
rit.
a tempo
24106

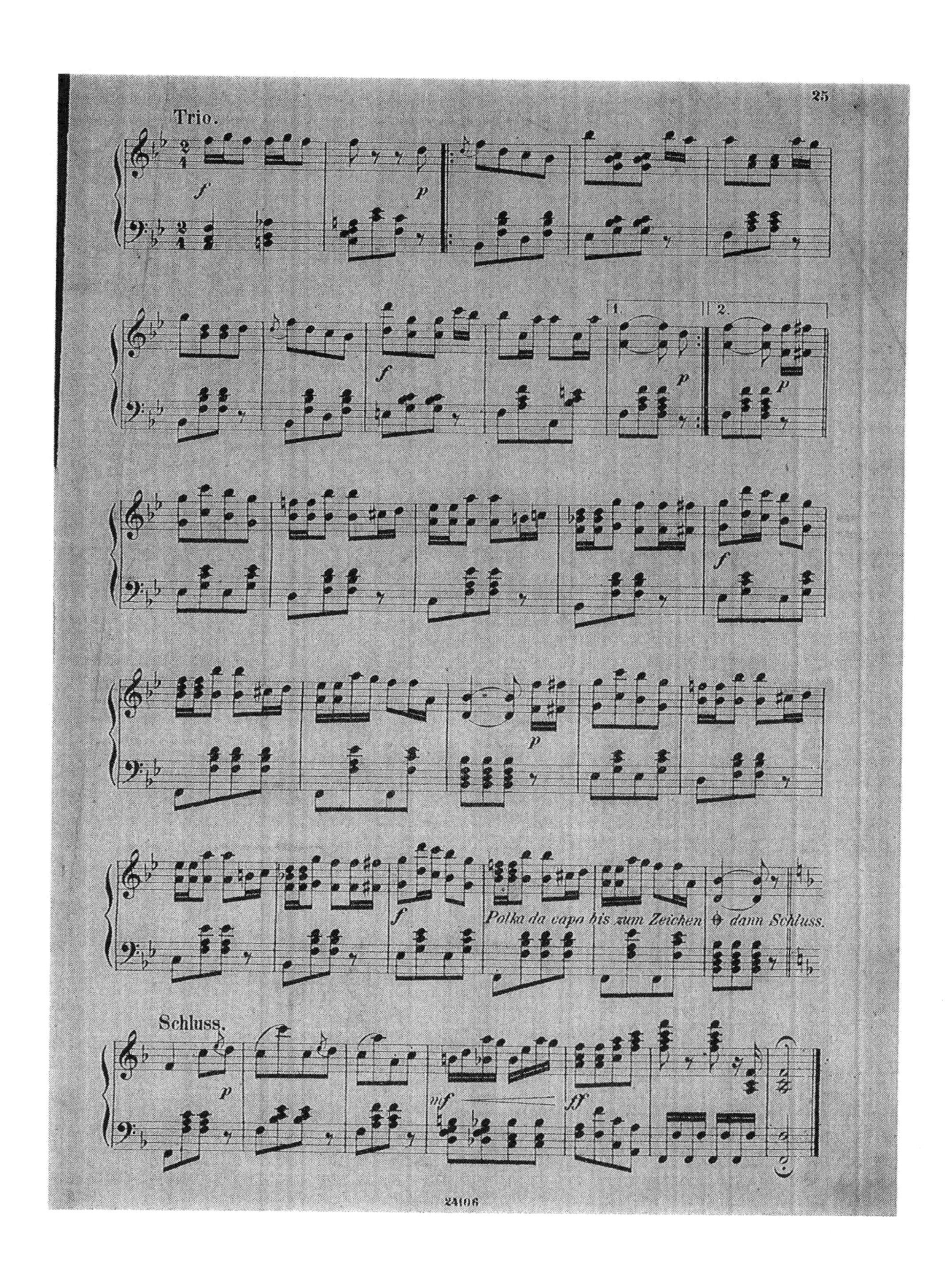
25
Trio.
Polka da capo bis zum Zeichen dann Schluss.
Schluss.
24106

turns. It is sometimes only done with one whole turn.

Then begin the balance again, (the first step) and circular step.

The lady's step is the counterpart of the gentleman's, she beginning with the right foot.

Charles Durang,
The Fashionable Dancer's Casket
(Philadelphia, 1856), 70–71

Galop

Music in 2/4 time—This is the easiest of all dances to learn, being, as the name implies, simply a gallop, though rapid in its movements.

It is said to have sprung from the Hungarians, and was introduced into France by Duchess of Berry during the carnival of 1829.

The Germans use it instead of the *chassez all* at the close of the quadrille, and bound off into the *gallop* with the greatest exuberance of spirit.

It can be made very pleasing and entertaining by the dancers, in couples, forming a column. The whole party then follows the leaders, or head couple, through a variety of serpentine courses, now winding themselves in circles, and anon unwinding to create new ones.

Edward Ferrero,
The Art of Dancing
(New York, 1859), 151

Part 3: Party Games: The German Cotillion ("The German")

Waltz Cotillon

Commence by six or eight couples waltzing round the room; a chair being placed in the centre, the first gentleman seats his partner in it, and presents each of the other gentlemen in succession; if the lady rejects, the gentleman discarded retires behind the chair, but with the favoured one she springs up, the tone and accent of the music being quickened, and off she waltzes with the chosen one; the other gentlemen resume their partners, and the circle is continued. All in turn go through the ceremony of presentation.

The Ball-Room Preceptor
(London, 1846), 72

Having described all the dances and waltzes that belong to the present fashion, it remains for me to speak of the cotillon, that, from the numerous elements of which it is composed, may be considered as the abstract of all the principal dances already detailed. The important place held by it in ballrooms is well known. We are all aware of the variety and animation it throws over the conclusion of balls, which can hardly be considered complete if they have not a cotillon for the epilogue, that always ends too soon to please the dancers.

To form a cotillon it is necessary to be seated

around the room in a semi-circle, or circle, according to the number of dancers, being careful to keep close to the walls, so as to leave in the middle of the room the greatest space possible.

The dancers are arranged in couples, the gentleman always having the lady on his right, and without leaving an interval between the seats.

The gentleman, who rises first to set, assumes the title of *conductor*; the place, which he occupies with his lady, represents what is called *the head of the cotillon*. . . .

The cotillon may consist of the waltze alone, the polka, or the mazurka. It often happens that the three are mingled, and that the dancers pass from one to the other for the sake of variety.

When the beginning is made with the waltze, the conducting couple set out first, and make the round of the room, followed by the others, who successively return to their places. The first couple rise again, and execute a figure according to their fancy, which the other couples must do one after the other to the extremity of the circle.

I do not hesitate to say that the fate of a cotillon is in a great measure in the hands of the conductor. Upon him more particularly depend the more or less animation and fire that prevail in the whole. It is he who gives the signal to the orchestra to begin, and warns the musicians when it is requisite to change the air in the cotillons blended with the waltze and polka. The orchestra should play on through the whole cotillon without ever stopping till it has been so ordered by the conductor.

Figures of the Cotillon

7. The Cushion—Le Coussin. (Waltze, polka, mazurka)

The first gentleman sets out, holding a cushion in his left hand. He makes the round of the room with his partner, and leaves the cushion to his partner, which she must present to several gentlemen, inviting them to kneel upon it. The lady should draw back quickly from the gentleman that she means to mock, and let it fall before the one that she intends to choose.

18. The Change of Ladies—Le Changement des Dames. (Waltze, polka, mazurka.)

Two couples set out with the waltze or promenade. After having made sundry circuits, they ought to approach each other, the gentlemen changing the ladies without losing the step or the time. After having danced with each other's lady, each takes back his own and regains his place.

23. The Ladies Mocked—Les Dames Trompees.

The first couple sets off. The gentleman takes his lady by the hand, promenades about the circle, and approaches several ladies pretending to invite them to waltz or dance. The moment the lady rises to accept his offer, he turns away quickly to address himself to another, on whom he plays off the same game, till he at last really makes a choice. The lady of the conductor dances or waltzes with the partner of the lady who has been elected.

47. The Fan—L'Eventail. (Waltze, polka.)
[See fig. 24]

Three chairs are placed in the middle of the room upon the same line. The two at the ends should be turned contrarywise to that in the centre, as in the figure of the *Glass of Champagne*. The first couple sets out in waltzing. The gentleman seats his lady upon the centre chair, and seeks two other gentlemen whom he places in the two other chairs. The lady offers her fan to one of the gentlemen at her side, and waltzes with the other. The gentleman with the fan must follow the waltzing couple, fanning them and hopping about the circle.

48. Blind-man's Bluff—La Colin Maillard. (Waltze, polka.)
[See fig.25]

Three chairs are placed on the same line in the middle of the room. The first couple sets off. The gentleman goes and takes another gentleman, whom he places in the centre chair, after having bound his eyes. The lady selects another gentleman, whom she leads on tiptoe to one of the chairs by the side of the Blind-Man, while she seats herself on the other. The first gentleman then invites the Blind-Man to choose the right or the left; if on the contrary he points to the gentleman, he

Figure 24

must waltze with him while the conductor waltzes with the lady.

Henri Cellarius,
The Drawing-Room Dances
(London, 1847), 81–83, 88–89, 92, 96–97, 109–10

The Figures of the Cotillon

The Sea During a Storm

Two rows of chairs are placed back to back, as in the game the name of which has been used to describe this figure. The first couple leads off. The gentleman conductor, if he has placed twelve chairs in the middle of the room, selects six ladies, including his own, and seats them on alternate chairs. He then selects six gentlemen, with whom he forms a chain, which he conducts. After having described a swift course in several parts of the room, and which he may prolong and vary as he thinks fit, he finishes by enveloping the rows of chairs on which are seated the ladies. When he takes a seat, every gentleman must instantly do the same, and dance with the lady on his right. In this figure there is a gentleman victim, who must return alone to his place.

Edward Ferrero,
The Art of Dancing
(New York, 1859), 165

In regard to favors, they should be suggestive and appropriate and placed where the leader may obtain them when necessary without delay or bustle.

Figure 25

Concerning this custom of "favoring," let there be the kindest feelings shown in the bestowal of favors. Do not present all your favors to the beautiful and good dancers, but glance around and "favor" those who seem to have been overlooked, and do not judge.

William B. DeGarmo,
The Dance of Society
(New York, 1875), 78

The "German" differs very little in its etiquette from that of the party. The leader of the dance is to be selected with discretion by the hostess, and the favors, which are always provided for the dancers, are chosen with individual and refined taste, always avoiding ostentatious display. The hostess is attentive to the ladies, observing if any timid or unattractive guest receives a noticeably small number of these trifles.

Generally the early part of the evening is spent with the waltz, and after supper the "German." Of course, nobody gives a "German" without being familiar with all the necessary and peculiar *etceteras*, which it is not in the province of etiquette to explain. The card of invitation is usually like that of a party, "The German" being engraved on the left-hand corner, with the hour when the dance is to commence. This mention of the time of opening this peculiar dance will be appreciated by all who are familiar with its requirements. If a *coterie* meets for practising the "German," it is customary for each lady member to invite all the members to her own house in turn, and as many other guests as is agreed upon by by-laws, from among her own particular friends.

Social Etiquette of New York
(New York, 1879), 89–90

The German, a dance known only to a favored few, is one of the most enjoyable of all dances. It is little danced, save in private coaches, and consists of a series of romps or games suitable for intimate friends and acquaintances.

In forming the "German" the dancers are seated round the room, each lady being placed at the right of her gentleman unless specially directed otherwise by the leader. If it be a private assemblage, the leader is appointed by the hostess. It is his duty to choose the various figures and lead them. In no other dance does the success so largely depend upon the perfect understanding, tact, judgment and good humor of a leader as does this, it being his especial privilege to select the divers figures and guide the musicians, it is necessary that he be of firm, even temper, good natured and above all patient. . . . It is well to begin with figures well known and moderate, and hold in reserve the more amusing until later in the evening when spirits flag, and the excitement and novelty begin to wear off; to provoke a climax, as if it were of gaiety and mirth, and thus render the final figure the most enjoyable of all and close with a feeling of kind regret that it should even end. For the complete success of the dance it is also necessary that the guests be as obedient to the leader as a soldier to his commander-in-chief. Nothing so thoroughly destroys the effect of the "German" as independence in the several dances, dancing after the signal has been given to be seated or out of turn when not properly up. If the leader should be inexperienced, shy or awkward, he is to be commiserated and every lady and gentleman should feel it his or her duty to aid him to the greatest possible extent by acquiescing in all his commands, however stupid or unadvisable and by never showing disapproval, by word or look, of the figures he has chosen however threadbare and monotonous they appear.

In regard to favors, they should be suggestive and appropriate and placed where the leader may obtain them when necessary without delay or bustle. Concerning this custom of "favoring," let there be the kindest feelings shown in the bestowal of favors. Do not present all your favors to the beauties and good dancers, but glance around and "favor" those who seem to have been overlooked, and do not judge that because all have partners and therefore all dance, your duty ends. Let no one be without a favor, this little bit of attention does more to establish joy and friendly feeling than all the elaborate and amusing figures of the most talented leader.

Nothing so disturbs and breaks up a *German* as where some couples, either from dislike to the figure or an inclination to be insubordinate and mischievous, branch off into something else or waltz with one another, when the rules of the game would dictate other partners. In such cases the leader must be firm and immovable and restore order to his ranks in a quiet but decisive manner.

5. The Rope

Three couples dance; the three gentlemen choose other ladies and the ladies other gentlemen. The ladies withdraw to one end of the room, while the gentlemen retire to the other. A rope is then stretched across and held by the leader and his partner over which every gentleman must leap in order to regain his partner. As the rope is managed so as to trip the gentleman as much as possible, great deal of amusement is afforded to the spectator.

56. Race

Whips and reins are the necessary properties for this figure. Each person is provided with whips and reins. Each couple dance. Partners are chosen and the ladies proceed to drive the gentlemen who race from one end of the room to the other, obedient to the whip and rein. All dance.

63. Hoop

Provide a number of light wooden hoops from thirteen to fifteen inches in diameter. Each lady is presented with a hoop which she gives to the partner she chooses. If the gentleman chosen desires to dance with her he slips the hoop over her head and on her shoulders. But should there be some other lady already on the floor with whom he prefers dancing, he so guides his partner as to be able to throw the hoop over her head, her partner endeavoring in the meanwhile to baffle the pursuer.

Samuel Baron,
Prof. Baron's Complete Instructor
(New York, ca. 1880), 16, 77, 79, 80, 87–88

Cotillion or German

This dance was introduced in New York about the year 1844. At that time the quadrille was the fashionable dance, but was known as the cotillion. To make a distinction between that and this dance, which was called the "German Cotillion," gradually the word cotillion was dropped, the dance becoming simply "The German."

Formerly it was customary for the music to play continuously throughout the whole duration of the cotillion. In later years, a desire, no doubt, to give rest to the ear for a short time, has established the custom of having the music cease at the end of each figure; that is to say, when a figure has completed its circle, and before the introduction of a second. This is no doubt, to many, a very acceptable change, as a short cessation of sound is a great relief at times, more especially when the same rhythm is maintained. Even the waltz becomes monotonous when too long continued, and so presses upon those hearing it as to become almost disagreeable. An occasional change of time has an excellent effect in promoting cheerfulness. This, however, rests with the conductor.

No. 163. The Mirror

A lady is seated, provided with a hand-mirror; the conductor presents successively a number of gentlemen, each one in turn looking over the lady's shoulder from behind, so that she may see the face reflected in the mirror, in rejecting the gentlemen she rubs the surface of the mirror; the rejected gentlemen place themselves one behind the other at the back of the lady's chair; when the lady makes a choice she rises, and places the mirror upon the chair; the rejected gentlemen then search for partners. Sometimes the gentlemen stand in front of the lady, and sometimes a gentleman takes the chair and the ladies perform the figure.

No. 192. L'Adresse

A lady presents to five or six ladies rosettes of different colors; a gentleman places an equal number of dolls in a line, not too close together, at the other end of the room; a ball is given to a gentleman, who rolls it the length of the room and, if he succeeds in knocking one of the dolls down, he dances with the lady having the rosette of the same color as the doll. Upon ceasing to dance, the lady presents her rosette to another lady.

Allen Dodworth,
Dancing and Its Relations to . . . Social Life
(New York, 1885), [145], 153–54, 232–33, 242

It Is Not the Correct Thing—For a gentleman who is not an expert dancer, or who is not thoroughly acquainted with the figures of the german, to undertake to lead the cotillion.

For people to dance in the german when it is not their turn, particularly where the leader requests that this shall not be done.

It Is the Correct Thing—For a good waltzer to dance the german, even if he do not know its figures. In this case he should sit near the foot, and watch carefully the evolutions of those who precede him.

For a hostess to provide favors and bouquets for the german.

Florence Marion Hall,
The Correct Thing in Good Society
(Boston, ca. 1888), 119–20

Notes

Preface

1 Thomas Wilson, *An Analysis of Country Dancing* (London: W. Calvert, 1808), xiv–xv.

2 Arthur M. Schlesinger, *Learning How to Behave. A Historical Study of American Etiquette Books* (New York: MacMillan Co., 1946), ix.

Introduction

Upward Mobility

1 Southern plantation society made a conscious effort to emulate European aristocracy, so the rise of its society and class system was quite different from that of the North.

2 Mrs. John Sherwood, *Manners and Social Usages* (New York: Harper & Bros., 1884), [3].

3 Oscar Handlin, *America—A History* (New York: Holt, Rinehart and Winston, 1968), 103.

4 In fact, Andrew Jackson won the popular vote in the election of 1824. However, none of the four candidates—Jackson, John Quincy Adams, William Harris Crawford, or Henry Clay—received a majority of the electoral votes; therefore the House of Representatives chose the winner. When Henry Clay's supporters gave their votes to Adams, the result was 13 votes for Adams, 7 for Jackson, and 4 for Crawford.

5 Schlesinger, *Learning How to Behave,* 17.

6 *The Laws of Etiquette. By A Gentleman* (Philadelphia: Carey, Lea, and Blanchard, 1836), 9.

7 Mrs. John Sherwood, *Manners and Social Usages,* 177.

8 Ibid., 182. These comments demonstrate the shifting attitude toward the display of one's wealth through luxurious furnishings during the last thirty-five years of the century. In a sharp contrast to the splendor of Mrs. Sherwood's description, *The Habits of Good Society,* published twenty-four years earlier, denounced the use of gold dinner plates as vulgar.

9 Arthur Meier Schlesinger, *Political and Social History of the United States, 1829–1925* (New York: The MacMillan Company, 1927), 2:130.

10 Fon W. Boardman, Jr., noted, in *America and the Gilded Age: 1876–1900* (New York: Henry Z. Walck, 1972), that between 1860 and 1900 the farm population of the U.S.A. increased by 50 percent but the urban population increased by 400 percent!

11 "Owners of the United States," *The Forum* 8 (November 1889): 269.

Sex Roles in Society

12 Madame Zuingle, *Petits Secrets* (Edinburgh: Andrew Murray, 1848), 7.

13 Ann Douglas, *The Feminization of American Culture* (New York: Alfred A. Knopf, 1977), 50–51.

14 Gerda Lerner, "The Lady and the Mill Girl: Changes in the Status of Women in the Age of Jackson," *Midcontinent American Studies Journal* 10, no. 1 (Spring 1969): 5.

15 Nancy S. Cott, *The Root of Bitterness* (Boston: Northeastern University Press, 1986), 18–19.

16 As American industrialization expanded, poor women took the spinning and weaving they had previously done at home to the factories and mill towns. A shortage of factory labor created opportunities for these women to earn comparatively high wages as well as maintain respectability. The quest for self-help was important for the workers of these industrial centers, and in 1843 *The Ladies' Vase* (p. 201) was published in Lowell, Massachusetts, for its mill girls.

17 The "Lady" author in this case was Eliza Ware Farrar.

18 Mrs. Manners, *At Home and Abroad* (New York: Evans and Brittan, 1853), 128.

19 [Eliza Ware Farrar], *The Young Lady's Friend. By a Lady* (Boston: American Stationers' Company, 1836).

20 *The Young Man's Own Book* (Philadelphia: Key & Biddle, 1832), 177, 180–81.

21 *The American Code of Manners* (New York: W. R. Andrews, 1880), 10.

22 Women whose families had the means to educate them were, in fact, highly cultured and knowledgeable in the humanities and fine arts. For example, the abilities of women as musicians and composers is illuminated extremely well by Judith Tick in *American Women Composers before 1870* (Ann Arbor, Mich.: UMI Research Press, 1982).

23 I. J. Benjamin II, *Drei Jahre in Amerika 1859–1862. 1 Theil* (Hanover: Selbstverlag des Verfassers, 1862), and quoted in Oscar Handlin, *This Was America* (Cambridge, Mass.: Harvard University Press, 1949), 274.

24 Giovanni Grassi, *Notizie varie sullo stato presente della Repubblica degli Stati Uniti dell'America* (Milan: Giovanni Silvestri, 1819), quoted in Handlin, *This Was America,* 143.

25 Isidore Löwenstern, *Les États-Unis et la Havane: Souvenirs d'un Voyage* (Paris: Arthur Bertrand, 1842), and quoted in Handlin, 181.

26 Harriet Martineau, *Society in America* (London: Saunders and Otley, 1837), 2:249.

27 *American Code of Manners,* 11–12.

28 Josiah Holbrook, *American Lyceum* (Boston: Perkins & Marvin, 1829), [3].

29 Ibid., 4.

30 J. C. Furnas, *The Americans, A Social History of the United States, 1587–1914* (New York: G. P. Putnam's Sons, 1969), 561.

31 John Robert Godley, *Letters from America* (London: John Murray, 1844), 48–49.

32 *The Young Lady's Book,* ed. Abel Bowen, American ed. (Boston: A. Bowen and Carter & Mendee, 1830), 391.

33 *The Young Lady's Friend,* 317–18.

34 Two of the few occasions upon which women were admitted to the Philadelphia Club during the nineteenth century were for balls in 1851 and 1869.

35 Madame Lola Montez, *The Arts of Beauty* (New York: Dick & Fitzgerald, ca. 1858), 116.

36 [Abby Buchanan Longstreet], *Social Etiquette of New York* (New York: D. Appleton & Co., 1879), 123.

37 Carlo Gardini, *Gli Stati Uniti: Ricordi con 76 Illustrazionie Carte,* 2d ed. (Bologna: Nicola Zanichelli, 1891), and quoted in Handlin, 347.

38 *The Hand-Book of Etiquette* (London: Cassell, Petter, and Galpin, 1860), 42.

39 *Mixing in Society* (London and New York: George Routledge & Sons, 1860), 166.

40 Florence Howe Hall, *Social Customs* (Boston: Estes and Laureat, 1881), 140.

41 Ingersoll Lockwood, *The P.G., or, Perfect Gentleman* (New York: G. W. Dillingham, 1887), 33.

Book Publishers, Manuals and Their Audience

42 Grassi, *Notizie varie,* and quoted in Handlin, 145.
43 Gerard R. Wolfe, *The House of Appleton* (Metuchen, N.J., and London: The Scarecrow Press, 1981), 67.
44 Sherwood, *Manners and Social Usages,* [3].
45 Patrick Williams, *The American Public Library and the Problem of Purpose* (New York, Westport, Connecticut, and London: Greenwood Press, n.d.), 7–8.
46 Saltator, *A Treatise on Dancing* (Boston: The Commercial Gazette, 1802), 11, 18, 26.
47 Also leaving nothing to chance in its explanations, *The Illustrated Manners Book* of 1855 offered an apology for being blunt: "We must run the risk of executing a feeling of disgust in some readers, that we may give to others the instructions they need" (24).
48 Charles Durang, *The Dancer's Own Book and Ball-Room Companion* (Philadelphia, Baltimore, et al.: Fisher & Brother, 1855), 179.
49 Many dance manuals included glossaries of French dance terminology, and in 1833 E. Woodward Masters took the concept one step further by supplying phonetic pronunciation aids. Thus, the word *alignment* was followed by "alleenmang" and *Cotillon* by "Koteeyong."
50 Allen Dodworth, *Dancing and Its Relations to Education and Social Life* (New York: Harper and Brothers, 1885), 13.
51 *The American Catalogue. Subject Entries of Books in Print and for Sale Including Reprints and Importations July 1, 1876,* comp. Lynds E. Jones (New York: Peter Smith, 1941).
52 *American Code,* i.
53 *Good Manners* (New York: The Butterick Publishing Co., 1888), i.
54 [Abby Longstreet], *Social Etiquette of New York,* [7].
55 *Dick's Quadrille Call-Book* (New York: Dick & Fitzgerald, 1878), [9].
56 *The Ball-Room Instructor* (New York: Huestis & Croft, 1841), [15].
57 *The Ball-Room Bijou and Art of Dancing* (New York and Philadelphia: Turner & Fisher, 1848), title page.
58 George E. Wilson, *Wilson's Ball-Room Guide and Call Book, or, Dancing Self Taught* (New York: Excelsior Publishing House, 1884), 11–12.
59 *Cartier and Baron's Practical Illustrated Waltz Instructor* (New York: Clinton T. DeWitt, 1879), [3].
60 William B. DeGarmo, *The Prompter,* 4th ed. (New York: Wm. A Pond & Co., 1868), [1].
61 Grassi, *Notizie varie,* quoted in Handlin, 143.
62 Mrs. Hale, *Manners; or Happy Homes and Good Society All the Year Round* (Boston: Lee, 1867), 177.
63 Eliza Leslie, *The Behavior Book* (Philadelphia: Willis P. Hazard, 1853), 312–13.
64 *Social Etiquette and Home Culture* (New York: Harper & Brothers, 1881), 7.
65 *The Mirror of the Graces; or, The English Lady's Costume. By a Lady of Distinction* (New York: C. Wiley, 1813), 182. *Social Etiquette and Home Culture,* 7.
66 Mrs. Hale, *Manners,* 181.
67 *Social Etiquette and Home Culture,* 7.
68 Mrs. Hale, 181.
69 *Social Etiquette and Home Culture,* 6.
70 *True Politeness. A Hand-Book of Etiquette for Ladies. By an American Lady* (New York: Manhattan Publishing Co., 184–), 43.
71 Thomas Wilson, *A Companion to the Ball Room* (London: Button, Whittaker, & Co., 1816), xx.
72 *Elements and Principles of the Art of Dancing . . . By V.G.* (Philadelphia: J. F. Hurtel, 1817), 74–75.
73 E. Woodward Masters, *The Standard Dance Album* (Boston: By the Author, 1883) 37.
74 *The Ball-Room Guide, A Handy Manual* (New York and London: Frederick Warne & Co., 186–), 19.
75 For example, Stephen Foster, *The Social Orchestra for Flute or Violin* (New York: Firth and Pond, 1854).
76 G. W. E. Friederick, arr., *The Orchestra Journal* (New York: Firth and Pond, 1856). This is an example of a collection aimed at larger, mixed ensembles.

Group Dances

THE ENGLISH COUNTRY DANCE

77 John Playford, *The English Dancing Master* (London: Thomas Harper, 1651).

78 Leslie, *The Behaviour Book,* 321.

79 After the first quarter of the nineteenth century, English country dances were never very popular in the context of urban settings because of their informal structure. However, rural areas were dependent on the dance manuals that booksellers sent from the urban publishing centers. Feeling the dances in these manuals did not reflect the desires of their rural community, the village of Belfast, Maine, published its own manual in 1866. Entitled *The Ball-Room Manual of Contra Dances and Social Cotillons, with Remarks on Quadrilles and Spanish Dance,* the preface stated: "The dancing public have been supplied with 'Ball Room Instructors,' and 'Guides,' embracing the figures of 'Quadrilles,' 'Polkas,' 'Cotillons,' &c., &c., with 'hints' on 'dress' and 'address,' but containing very few, of the good old contra dances of our ancestors, as enjoyed by them in their hours of relaxation and amusement" [iii].

80 Saltator, *Treatise on Dancing,* 85.

81 *The Mirror of the Graces,* 168.

82 Barclay Dun, *A Translation of 9 of the Most Fashionable Quadrilles* (Edinburgh: William Wilson & Company, 1818), v.

83 Francis Peacock, *Sketches Relative to the History and Theory, But More Especially to the Practice of Dancing* (Aberdeen: J. Chalmers & Co., 1805), 92.

COTILLION AND QUADRILLE

84 Giovanni-Andrea Gallini, *Critical Observations* (London: For the Author, 1770?).

85 Saltator, *Treatise on Dancing,* 79. The ten cotillion changes are provided by Saltator on page 141 and cotillion figures are given both by Saltator and E. H. Conway on page 143.

86 *A Selection of Favorite Quadrilles* (London: C. Wheatstone, 181–), 1.

87 Thomas Wilson, *The Quadrille and Cotillion Panorama* (London: R. & E. Williamson, ca. 1818), 1.

88 Mrs. Trollope, *Domestic Manners of the Americans* (New York: Reprinted for the Booksellers, 1832), 130.

89 *The Ball-Room Preceptor and Polka Guide,* 6th ed. (London: David Bogue, 1846), 13.

90 Gourdoux-Daux, *Principles et Notions Elementaires sur L'Art de la Danse Pour la Ville* (Parish, Chez l'auteur, 1804).

91 Gourdoux-Daux, *De L'Art de la Danse* (Paris: Chez l'auteur, 1823), and *Recueil d'un Genre Nouveau de Contredanses et Walses* (Paris, Chez l'auteur, 1819).

92 Edward Ferrero, *The Art of Dancing* (New York: The Author, 1859), 121.

93 Mrs. Trollope, *Domestic Manners,* 130.

94 C. H. Cleveland, Jr., *Dancing at Home and Abroad* (Boston: Oliver Ditson & Co., 1878), 29.

THE COTILLION, GERMAN COTILLION, OR THE GERMAN

95 Henri Cellarius, *The Drawing-Room Dances* (London: E. Churton, 1847), 83.

96 *Prof. Baron's Complete Instructor in all the Society Dances* (New York: J. Young, ca. 1880), 79.

97 William B. DeGarmo, *The Dance of Society* (New York: William A. Pond & Co., 1875), 78.

98 William E. Greene, *The Terpsichorean Monitor* (Providence, R.I.: E. A. Johnson & Co., 1889), 14.

99 Cleveland, *Dancing at Home and Abroad,* 85.

100 Ibid., 90.

101 [Florence Hall], *The Correct Thing in Good Society* (Boston: Estes and Lauriat, ca. 1888), 144.

102 Ibid., 120.

103 DeGarmo, *The Dance of Society,* 78.

104 [Abby Buchanan Longstreet], *Social Etiquette of New York,* 90.

105 Mrs. John Sherwood, *Manners and Social Usages,* 193, 198.

106 Cleveland, 35.

107 *Manners and Tone of Good Society,* 3d ed.

(London: Frederick Warne and Co., ca. 1879), 122.

108 *True Politeness. A Hand-Book of Etiquette for Ladies,* 38.

THE WALTZ

109 Dauternaux, *Recueil d'Airs de Contre-Danses* (Paris, 1778). The ca. 1810 *Waltz Cotillion,* page 181, is an example of the waltz used within a group dance.

110 *The Mirror of the Graces,* 177.

111 Donald Walker, *Exercises for Ladies* (London: Thomas Hurst, 1836), 149.

112 Dio Lewis, *Our Girls* (New York, 1871), and quoted in Thomas Woody, *A History of Women's Education in the U.S. in Two Volumes* (New York & Lancaster, Pa.: The Science Press, 1929), 2:102–3.

113 Donald Walker, *Exercises for Ladies,* 149.

114 Mme. Celnart, *The Gentleman and Lady's Book of Politeness,* 2d American ed. (Boston: Allen and Ticknor and Carter, Hendee, & Co., 1833).

115 *The Illustrated Manners Book* (New York: Leland Clay & Co., 1855), 397–98.

116 Ibid., 398.

117 Cellarius, *The Drawing-Room Dances,* 26.

118 Ibid., 34.

119 *The Ball-Room Guide* (London: Frederick Warne, 1868), 63.

120 Edward Scott, *The Art of Waltzing and Guide to the Ball-Room* (London: Ward & Downey, 1885), 25.

121 Allen Dodworth, *Dancing and Its Relations to Education and Social Life,* 47.

122 *The Ball-Room Guide and Call Book* (New York: G. Blackie & Co., 1860), 58.

123 Ibid., p. 59.

124 Dodworth, 73.

125 Ibid., 62.

Fashion

126 Abby Buchanan Longstreet, *Manners, Good and Bad* (New York: Frederick A. Stokes Company, 1890), 53.

127 Mrs. Hale, *Manners,* 241.

128 John Young, *Our Deportment or the Manners, Conduct and Dress of the Most Refined Society* (Detroit, St. Louis, et al.: F. B. Dickerson & Co., 1879), 325–40.

129 Carlo Gardini, *Gli Stati Uniti: Ricordi con 76 Illustrazionie Carte,* quoted by Handlin, *America—A History,* 374.

130 *The Mirror of the Graces,* 181.

131 Isidore Löwenstern, *Les Etats-Unis et la Havane: Souvenirs d'un Voyage,* quoted in Handlin, 183.

132 Ibid.

133 [Farrar], *The Young Lady's Friend,* 199.

134 *The Art of Good Behaviour* (New York: C. P. Huestis, ca. 1845), 16.

135 John Robert Godley, *Letters from America,* 44.

136 Vanda Foster, *A Visual History of Costume* (London: B. T. Bulsford, 1984), 13.

137 Geoffrey Squire, *Dress and Society* (New York: Viking Press, 1974), 159.

138 Carol McD. Wallace, Don McDonagh, et al., *Dance: A Very Social History* (New York: Rizzoli, 1986), 89.

139 Mrs. Hale, *Manners,* 241.

140 Professor Bland, *Etiquette of the Ballroom* (London: Milner & Co., 1870), 10.

141 *Offenbach's Dancing Without a Master* (New York: Hurst & Co., 1876), 20.

142 Cleveland, *Dancing at Home and Abroad,* 30, 35.

143 *Manners and Tone of Good Society,* 125.

144 John Young, *Our Deportment,* 348–49.

145 Ole Munch Roeder, *America in the Forties from the letters of Ole Munch Roeder.* Translated and edited by C. J. Malmir (Minneapolis: University of Minnesota Press, 1929), quoted in Handlin, *This was America,* 205.

146 Edward Ferrero, *The Art of Dancing,* 92.

147 *Mixing in Society,* 126.

148 *The Ball-Room Guide, A Handy Manual,* 25.

149 Abba Louisa Woolson, *Dress-Reform* (Boston: Roberts Bros., 1874), 149–51.

150 *True Politeness* (New York: Leavitt and Allen, 1848), 15.

151 [Oliver Bell Bunce], *Don't: A Manual of Mistakes & Improprieties* (New York: D. Appleton, 1883), 16.

152 Abby Buchanan Longstreet, *Manners, Good and Bad,* 53.

153 T. Wilson, *An Analysis of Country Dancing* (London: W. Calvert, 1808), 16.
154 T. Wilson, *A Companion to the Ballroom,* 220.
155 *The Art of Good Behaviour,* 14.
156 Mme. Celnart, *The Gentleman and Lady's Book of Politeness,* 183.
157 *The Ball-Room Instructor,* 40.
158 *The Art of Good Behaviour,* 15.
159 Ibid., 14.
160 G. M. S. Chivers, *A Pocket Companion to French and English Dancing,* 2d ed. (London: T. Denham, 1821?), 37.
161 Wilson, *An Analysis of Country Dancing,* 135.
162 *The Art of Good Behaviour,* 15.
163 Cecil B. Hartley, *The Gentlemen's Book of Etiquette* (Boston: G. W. Cottrell, Publisher, ca. 1860), 16.
164 Ibid., 60.
165 Longstreet, *Manners, Good and Bad,* 53.
166 Hudson K. Lyverthey, *Our Etiquette and Social Observances* (Grand Rapids, Mich.: Chubb & Reynders, 1881), 63.
167 Daniel R. Shafer, *Secrets of Life Unveiled; or Book of Fate* (St. Louis, et al.: Shafer & Co., 1877), 233. Glove flirtations, as well as handkerchief, fan, and parasol flirtations, are quoted in their entirety on pages 103–5.

Select Bibliography

American Bibliography. A Preliminary Checklist for 1801–1819. 22 vols. Compiled by Ralph R. Shaw and Richard M. Shoemacker. New York: The Scarecrow Press, 1958–65.

The American Catalogue. Under the Direction of F. Leypoldt. Books in Print and for Sale July 1, 1876. Lynds E. Jones, comp. New York: Peter Smith, 1941.

The American Catalogue. Founded by F. Leypoldt, 1876–1884. Books Recorded (Including Reprints and Importations) July 1, 1876–June 30, 1884. Compiled under the editorial direction of R. R. Bowker. New York: Peter Smith, 1941.

The American Catalogue. Founded by F. Leypoldt, 1890–1895. Books Recorded (Including Reprints and Importations) July 1, 1890–June 30, 1895. Compiled under the editorial direction of R. R. Bowker. New York: Peter Smith, 1941.

The American Catalogue of Books (originals and reprints,) Published In the United States from Jan., 1861, to Jan., 1866, with Date of Publication, Size, Price and Publisher's Name. Compiled and arranged by James Kelly. New York: Peter Smith, 1838.

The American Catalogue of Books Recorded July 1, 1884 to June 30, 1890. Compiled under the editorial direction of R. R. Bowker. New York: Peter Smith, 1941.

The American Code of Manners. New York: W. R. Andrews, 1880.

Aresty, Esther B. *The Best Behavior.* New York: Simon & Schuster, 1970.

The Art of Good Behaviour. New York: C. P. Huestis, ca. 1845.

Arthur and Elizabeth Schlesinger Library on the History of Women in America. The Manuscript Inventories and the Catalogues of Manuscripts, Books and Pictures. 3 vols. Boston: G. K. Hall, 1973.

The Ball-Room Guide, A Handy Manual for all Classes of Society. New York and London: Frederick Warne & Co., 186–.

The Ball-Room Guide and Call Book. New York: G. Blackie & Co., 1860.

The Ball-Room Instructor; Containing a Complete Description of Cotillons and Other Popular Dances. New York: Huestis & Croft, 1841.

The Ball-Room Manual of Contra Dances and Social Cotillons, with Remarks on Quadrilles and Spanish Dance. Belfast, Maine, 1866.

The Ball-Room Preceptor and Polka Guide. 6th ed. London: David Bogue, 1846.

Beard, Charles, and Mary Beard. *Rise of American Civilization.* New York: The MacMillan Co., 1956.

Biblioteca Americana. Catalogue of American Publications, Including Reprints and Original works, from 1820 to 1852, Inclusive. Compiled and arranged by O. A. Roorbach. New York: Peter Smith, 1939.

Supplement to the Biblioteca Americana, A Catalogue of American Publications (Reprints and Original Works). Compiled and arranged by O. A. Roorbach. New York: Peter Smith, 1939.

Bland, Professor. *Etiquette of the Ballroom.* London: Milner & Co., 1870.

Boardman, Fon. W., Jr. *America and the Guilded Age: 1876–1900.* New York: Henry Z. Walck, 1972.

Bobbitt, Mary Reed, comp. *A Bibliography of Etiquette Books Published in America before 1900.* New York: The New York Public Library, 1947.

Bowen, Abel, ed. *The Young Lady's Book.* Boston: A. Bowen and Carter & Mendee, 1830.

Brooke, Iris. *Footwear, A Short History of European and American Shoes.* New York: Theatre Arts Books, 1971.

Buck, Anne. *Victorian Costume and Costume Accessories.* New York: Thomas Nelson & Sons, 1961.

Bunce, Oliver Bell. *Don't: A Manual of Mistakes & Improprieties.* New York: D. Appleton, 1883.

Bussy, R. Kenneth. *Two Hundred Years of Publishing.* Philadelphia: Lea & Febiger, 1985.

Carson, Gerald. *The Polite Americans—A Wide-Angle View of Our More or Less Good Manners Over 300 Years.* New York: William Morrow & Co., 1966.

Cartier and Baron's Practical Illustrated Waltz Instructor. New York: Clinton T. DeWitt, 1879.

Cellarius, Henri. *The Drawing-Room Dances.* London: E. Churton, 1847.

Celnart, Mme. *The Gentleman and Lady's Book of Politeness.* 2d American ed. Boston: Allen and Ticknor and Carter, Hendee, & Co., 1833.

A Checklist of American Imprints for 1820–1839. Compiled by Richard H. Shoemaker et al. Metuchen, N.J.: The Scarecrow Press, 1966–88.

Chivers, G. M. S. 2d ed. *A Pocket Companion to French and English Dancing.* London: T. Denham, 1821(?).

Cleveland, C. H., Jr. *Dancing at Home and Abroad.* Boston: Oliver Ditson & Co., 1878.

Cott, Nancy S. *The Root of Bitterness.* Boston: Northeastern University Press, 1986.

Cunnington, C. Willett. *English Women's Clothing in the Nineteenth Century.* New York: Thomas Yoseloft, 1958.

Dauternaux. *Recueil d'Airs de Contre-Danses.* Paris: 1778.

DeGarmo, William B. *The Dance of Society.* New York: William A. Pond & Co., 1875.

———. *The Prompter.* 4th ed. New York: Wm. A. Pond & Co., 1868.

Dick's Quadrille Call-Book. Boston: Dick & Fitzgerald, 1878.

Dictionary Catalogue of the Research Libraries. A Cumulative List of Authors, Titles, and Subjects Representing Materials Added to the Collections Beginning January 1, 1972, Issued January, 1980. New York: The New York Public Library, Astor, Lenox and Tilden Foundations, 1979.

Dictionary Catalogue of the Research Libraries of the New York Public Library, 1911–1971. New York: The New York Public Library, Astor, Lenox and Tilden Foundations, 1979.

Dodworth, Allen. *Dancing and Its Relations to Education and Social Life.* New York: Harper and Brothers, 1885.

Douglas, Ann. *The Feminization of American Culture.* New York: Alfred A. Knopf, 1977.

Dun, Barclay. *A Translation of 9 of the Most Fashionable Quadrilles.* Edinburgh: William Wilson & Company, 1818.

Durang, Charles. *The Ball-Room Bijou and Art of Dancing.* New York and Philadelphia: Turner & Fisher, 1848.

———. *The Dancer's Own Book and Ball-Room Companion.* Philadelphia, Baltimore, et al.: Fisher & Brother, 1855.

Elements and Principles of the Art of Dancing . . . By V.G. Philadelphia: J. F. Hurtel, 1817.

[Farrar, Eliza Ware]. *The Young Lady's Friend. By a Lady.* Boston: American Stationers' Company, 1837.

Feather, John. *A History of British Publishing.* London, New York, and Sydney: Crom Helm, 1988.

Ferrero, Edward. *The Art of Dancing, Historically Illustrated.* New York: The Author, 1859.

Foster, Stephen. *The Social Orchestra for Flute or Violin.* New York: Firth and Pond, 1854.

Foster, Vanda. *A Visual History of Costume.* London: B. T. Bulsford, 1984.

Friederick, G. W. E., arr. *The Orchestra Journal.* New York: Firth and Pond, 1856.

Furnas, J. C. *The Americans: A Social History of the United States, 1587–1914.* New York: G. P. Putnam's Sons, 1979.

Godley, John Robert. *Letters from America*. London: John Murray, 1844.

Good Manners. New York: The Butterick Publishing Co., 1888.

Gourdoux-Daux. *De L'Art de la Danse*. Paris: Chez l'auteur, 1823.

———. *Principles et Notions Élémentaires sur L'Arte de la Danse Pour La Ville*. Paris: Chez l'auteur 1804.

———. *Recueil d'un Genre Nouveau de Contre-danses et Walses*. Paris: Chez l'auteur 1819.

Greene, William E. *The Terpsichorean Monitor*. Providence, R.I.: E. A. Johnson & Co., 1889.

Hale, Mrs. *Manners; or Happy Homes and Good Society all the Year Round*. Boston: Lee, 1867.

Hall, Florence Howe. *The Correct Thing in Good Society*. Boston: Estes and Lauriat, ca. 1888.

———. *Social Customs*. Boston: Estes and Lauriat, 1887.

Hand-Book of Etiquette. London: Cassell, Petter, and Galpin, 1860.

Handlin, Oscar. *America—A History*. New York: Holt, Rinehart and Winston, 1968.

———. *This was America; true accounts of people and places, manners and customs, as recorded by European travelers to the western shores in the eighteenth, nineteenth and twentieth centuries*. Cambridge: Harvard University Press, 1949.

Hartley, Cecil B. *The Gentlemen's Book of Etiquette*. Boston: G. W. Cottrell, Publisher, ca. 1860.

Hill, Thos. E. *Hills' Manual of Social & Business Forms: Guide to Correct Writing*. Chicago: Moses Warner & Co., 1877.

Holbrook, Josiah. *American Lyceum*. Boston: Perkins & Marvin, 1829.

Humphreys, Nancy K. *American Women's Magazines, An Annotated Historical Guide*. New York and London: Garland Publishing, 1989.

The Illustrated Manners Book. New York: Leland Clay & Co., 1855.

Jones, Michael Wynn. *The World 100 Years Ago*. London: Macmillan London Limited, 1976.

King, Cornelia S., comp. *American Education 1622–1860*. New York and London: Garland Publishing, 1984.

Laver, James. *The Age of Illusion, Manners and Morals, 1750–1848*. New York: David McKay Co., 1972.

The Laws of Etiquette. By A Gentleman. Philadelphia: Carey, Lea, and Blanchard, 1836.

Lehmann-Haupt, Hellmut. In collaboration with Laurence C. Worth and Rollo G. Silver. *The Book in America, A History of Making and Selling of Books in the United States*. New York: R. R. Bowker Co., 1952.

Lerner, Gerda. "The Lady and the Mill Girl: Changes in the Status of Women in the Age of Jackson." *Midcontinent American Studies Journal* 10, no. 1 (Spring 1969).

Leslie, Eliza. *The Behaviour Book*. Philadelphia: Willis P. Hazard, 1853.

Lockwood, Ingersoll. *The P.G., or, Perfect Gentleman*. New York: G. W. Dillingham, 1887.

Longstreet, Abby Buchanan. *Manners, Good and Bad*. New York: Frederick A. Stokes Company, 1890.

[Longstreet, Abby Buchanan]. *Social Etiquette of New York*. New York: D. Appleton & Co., 1879.

Lyverthey, Hudson K. *Our Etiquette and Social Observances*. Grand Rapids, Mich.: Chubb & Reynders, 1881.

McClellan, Elizabeth. *Historic Dress In America*. Rev. ed. New York and London: Benjamin Blom, 1969.

Manners, Mrs. *At Home and Abroad; or, How to Behave*. New York: Evans and Brittan, 1853.

Manners and Tone of Good Society. 3d ed. London: Frederick Warne and Co., ca. 1879.

Martineau, Harriet. *Society in America*. London: Saunders and Otley, 1847.

Masters, E. Woodward. *The Standard Dance Album*. Boston: By the Author, 1883.

The Mirror of the Graces; or, The English Lady's Costume. By a Lady of Distinction. New York: C. Wiley, 1810.

Mixing in Society. London and New York: George Routledge & Sons, 1860.

Montez, Madame Lola. *The Arts of Beauty*. New York: Dick & Fitzgerald, ca. 1858.

The National Union Catalogue, Pre-1956 Imprints. London: Mansell, 1968.

Nineteenth Century Short Title Catalogue. Series I Phase I, 1801–1815. Extracted from the Catalogues of the Bodleian Library, the British Library, the Library of Trinity College, Dublin, the National Library of Scotland, and the University Libraries of Cambridge and

Newcastle. 6 vols. Newcastle-upon-Tyne: Avero Publications, 1984–1986.

Offenbach's Dancing Without a Master. New York: Hurst & Co., 1876.

Peacock, Francis. *Sketches Relative to the History and Theory, But More Especially to the Practice of Dancing.* Aberdeen: J. Chalmers & Co., 1805.

Peddie, R. A. *Subject Index of Books Published Before 1880, A–Z.* London: Grafton & Co., 1933.

———. *Subject Index of Books Published up to and Including 1880.* 3d ser., A–Z. London: Grafton & Co., 1939.

Playford, John. *The English Dancing Master.* London: Thomas Harper, 1651.

Prof. Baron's Complete Instructor in all the Society Dances. New York: J. Young, ca. 1880.

Risenberg, Carroll Smith. "Beauty, the Beast and the Militant Woman: A Case Study in Sex Roles and Social Stress in Jacksonian America." *American Quarterly* 23, no. 4 (1971).

Saltator. *A Treatise on Dancing.* Boston: The Commercial Gazette, 1802.

Schlesinger, Arthur M. *Learning How to Behave, A Historical Study of American Etiquette Books.* New York: MacMillan Co., 1946.

———. *Political and Social History of the United States, 1829–1925.* vol. 2. New York: The MacMillan Co., 1927.

Scott, Edward. *The Art of Waltzing and Guide to the Ball-Room.* London: Ward & Downey, 1885.

A Selection of Favorite Quadrilles. London: C. Wheatstone, 181–.

Shafer, Daniel R. *Secrets of Life Unveiled; or Book of Fate.* St. Louis et al.: Shafer & Co., 1877.

Sherwood, Mrs. John. *Manners and Social Usages.* New York: Harper & Bros., 1884.

Social Etiquette and Home Culture. New York: Harper & Brothers, 1881.

Squire, Geoffrey. *Dress and Society.* New York: Viking Press, 1974.

Stern, Madeleine B. *Books and Book People in 19th-century America.* New York and London: R. R. Bowker Company, 1978.

———, ed. *Publishers for Mass Entertainment in Nineteenth-Century America.* Boston: G. K. Hall & Co., 1980.

Tebbel, John. *Between Covers. The Rise and Transformation of Book Publishing in America.* New York and Oxford: Oxford University Press, 1987.

Thompson, Eleanor Wolf. *Education for Ladies, 1830–1860.* New York: King's Crown Press, 1947.

Thornwell, Emily. *The Lady's Guide to Perfect Gentility, In Manners, Dress, and Conversation, In the Family, In Company at the Piano Forte, the Table, In the Street, and in Gentlemen's Society.* New York: Derby & Jackson, 1856.

Tick, Judith. *American Women Composers before 1870.* Ann Arbor, Mich.: UMI Research Press, 1982.

Trollope, Mrs. *Domestic Manners of the Americans.* New York: Reprinted for the Booksellers, 1832.

True Politeness. New York: Leavitt and Allen, 1847.

True Politeness. A Hand-Book of Etiquette for Ladies. By an American Lady. New York: Manhattan Publishing Col., 184–.

Walker, Donald. *Exercises for Ladies.* London: Thomas Hurst, 1836.

Wallace, Carol McD., Don McDonagh, et al. *Dance: A Very Social History.* New York: Rizzoli, 1986.

Wecter, Dixon. *The Saga of American Society, A Record of Social Aspiration.* New York: Charles Scribner's Sons, 1937.

Wiegant, Wayne A. *The Politics of an Emerging Profession: The American Library Association.* New York, Westport, Conn., and London: Greenwood Press, 1986.

Wildeblood, Joan, and Peter Brimson. *The Polite World. A Guide to English Manners and Deportment from the Thirteenth to the Nineteenth Century.* London: Oxford University Press, 1965.

Williams, Patrick. *The American Publick Library and the Problem of Purpose.* New York and Westport, Conn., and London: Greenwood Press, n.d.

Wilson, George E. *Wilson's Ball-Room Guide and Call Book, or Dancing Self Taught.* New York: Excelsior Publishing House, 1884.

Wilson, T. *An Analysis of Country Dancing.* London: W. Calvert, 1808.

———. *A Companion to the Ballroom.* London: Button, Whittaker, & Co., 1816.

———. *The Quadrille and Cotillion Panorama.* London: R. & E. Williamson, ca. 1818.

Wolfe, Gerard R. *The House of Appleton: The History of a Publishing House and its Relationship to the Cultural, Social, and Political Events that Helped Shape the Destiny of New York City.* Metuchen, N.J., and London: The Scarecrow Press, 1981.

Woody, Thomas. *A History of Women's Education in the U.S.* 2 vols. New York and Lancaster, Pa.: The Science Press, 1929.

Woolson, Abba Louisa. *Dress-Reform; A Series of Lectures Delivered in Boston, on Dress as it Affects the Health of Women.* Boston: Roberts Bros., 1874.

Young, John. *Our Deportment of the Manners, Conduct and Dress of the Most Refined Society.* Detroit, St. Louis, et al.: F. B. Dickerson & Co., 1879.

The Young Man's Own Book. Philadelphia: Key & Biddle, 1832.

Zuingle, Madame. *Petits Secrets.* Edinburgh: Andrew Murray, 1848.

Annotated Bibliography

Etiquette Manuals

The School of Good Manners. Composed for the Help of Parents in Teaching Their Children How to Carry It In Their Places During Their Minority. [New London, Conn.]: n.p., 1801.

In 1595 William Fiston translated into English a 1564 French treatise entitled *L'A, B, C, ou Instruction pour les petis Enfans.* The first surviving edition of this manual was published in London in 1609 under the title, *The School of Good Manners: or, a new School of Virtue.* It seems probable that Fiston also added to this work materials from Francis Seager's 1557 *The School of Vertue, and Book of Good Nourture for Chyldren and Youth.* In 1685 Fiston's work was republished as *The School of Good Manners. By the author of English Exercises.*

Addressed to children, the manual's first American edition appeared in 1715 under the title, *The School of Good Manners. Containing Children's Behaviour at the Meeting House, at Home, at the Table, in Company, in Discourse, at School, Abroad: with an Admonition to Children . . . Some Prayers for Children; with Graces before and after Meat.* The fifth American edition of 1754 states that the work was "compiled (chiefly) by Mr. Eleazar Moody, late a famous School-Master in Boston." By the late eighteenth century the "Preceptor of the Ladies' Academy in New London" was taking credit for the manual and more text changes were made. During the 131 years of its American printing history (thirty-four editions between 1715 and 1846, nearly half published in the nineteenth century), the manual continually went through extensive editing, reflecting subtle changes in etiquette and terminology. For example, by 1827 the word *bow* was replaced by the word *courtsey*, and requests to spit in a corner were replaced by the admonition to spit, instead, in the fireplace.

The Mirror of the Graces; or, The English Lady's Costume. By a Lady of Distinction. New York: C. Wiley, printer, 1813.

Originally published in London in 1810 and reprinted in 1811, *The Mirror of the Graces* was published three times in the United States (1813, 1815, and 1831). The manual also appeared in Scottish editions in 1830 and 1840. Many sections of this manual appear later in *Etiquette for Ladies* (Philadelphia, 1838).

Important Trifles: Chiefly Appropriate to Females on their Entrance into Society. By Emma Parker. London: T. Egerton, 1817.

This thirty-chapter manual covers such topics as "The Influence of Dress and Manners," "Heartless Mirth," "The Ball," "Seasonable Words," and "Rage—with an Anecdote."

The American Chesterfield, or Way to Wealth, Honour and Distinction: Being Selections from the Letters of Lord Chesterfield to his Son; and Extracts from Other Eminent Authors, on the Subject of Politeness. With Alternations and Additions, Suited to the Youth of the United States. By a Member of the Philadelphia Bar. Philadelphia: John Grigg, 1827.

Probably the most important behavior manual published in England during the eighteenth century, Lord Chesterfield's *Letters* first appeared in 1744 under the title *Letters written by the right honourable Philip Dormer Stanhope, Earl of Chesterfield, to his son, Philip Stanhope, Esq., late envoy extraordinary to the Court of Dresden. Published by Mrs. Eugenia Stanhope from the originals in her possession.* Between 1774 and 1803 the volume was published in twelve editions and formed the basis for virtually all early nineteenth-century writings on etiquette. Chesterfield's work saw thirty-one printings, including six new editions in early nineteenth-century America. With each new edition unknown editors altered the original text until the volume was once again offered to the American public in 1827 as *The American Chesterfield.* Versions of *The American Chesterfield* were published fifteen times through the 1870s, and *The American Catalogue* listed six different editions available in 1876, ranging in price from seventy-five cents to ten dollars.

Chapters in *The American Chesterfield* include "Vanity," "Lying," "Genteel Carriage," "Knowledge of the World," "Dignity of Manners," "Sundry Little Accomplishments," "Pedantry," and "A Chapter Addressed to Americans." This last chapter exposes many of the violations frequently decried by European visitors: the chewing of tobacco, "reaching across a table, or across three or four persons setting next to him who wishes for some particular dish" (203), and "the ungentlemanly and abominable habit of spitting" (202). The last quarter of the manual is devoted to three essays: "Dr. Watts' Advice to a Young Man on His Entrance to the World;" "Ten Precepts, Given by William Lord Burghley . . . to his Son Robert Cecil . . . ;" and *The Honours of the Table, or rules for behaviour during meals; with the Whole Art of Carving, Illustrated with a variety of Cuts.* This last essay was a separate publication issued by John Grigg and inserted into this edition.

The Young Lady's Book, a Manual of Elegant Recreations, Exercises, and a Manual of Elegant Recreations, Exercises, and Pursuits. Edited by Abel Bowen. American Edition. Boston: A. Bowen and Carter & Mendee, and Philadelphia: Carey & Lea, 1830.

This manual was based on an English manual titled *The Young Lady's Book; a Manual of Elegant Recreations, Exercises, and Pursuits,* published in 1829 and 1832. The American version went through five editions, the last published in 1837.

The Gentleman and Lady's Book of Politeness and Propriety of Deportment, Dedicated to the Youth of Both Sexes. Translated from the Sixth Paris Edition, Enlarged and Improved. By Mme. Celnart. 2d American ed. Boston: Allen and Ticknor and Carter, Hendee & Co., 1833.

Elisabeth Félice Bayle-Mouillard's (1796–1865) popular manual was first published in the United States in 1833. By 1872 it had gone through thirteen editions and was still available in 1876 for seventy-five cents. Many of her works were translated from French into English and German. Bayle-Mouillard's second book to be translated into English was entitled *Perfumery; its Manufacture and Use* (French ed. 1845, English eds. in 1847 and 1853). The preface to *The Gentleman and Lady's Book* comments that some "rules [were] founded on customs and usages peculiar to France and other countries. . . . In our liberal and tolerant country, these peculiarities will give offence to none; while to many their novelty, at least, will be interesting." Sections of *The Gentleman and Lady's Book* appear later in Emily Thornwell's 1856 *Lady's Guide* and *Howe's Complete Ball-Room Handbook* of 1858.

The Laws of Etiquette: Or, Short Rules and Reflections for Conduct in Society. By A Gentleman. Philadelphia: Carey, Lea, and Blanchard, 1836.

The Laws of Etiquette, available for fifty cents in 1836, was reissued in 1838. In 1839 the manual was published under the title *Canons for Good Breeding,* and during the 1840s it was expanded and printed under yet another name, *Etiquette for Gentlemen.* The straightforward chapter titles in this manual include: "Good Breeding," "Dress," "Visits," "Dinner," "Balls," "Funerals," "Servants" ("a necessary evil," 119), and "Fashion" ("A man of fashion must never allow himself to be pleased," 129). *The Laws of Etiquette* contains some paraphrasing of text from Mme. Celnart's *The Gentleman and Lady's Book* (1833).

The Young Lady's Friend. By a Lady [Eliza Ware Farrar]. Boston: American Stationers' Company, 1836.

This 432–page, twenty-chapter manual addresses numerous topics thought to be of importance in the education of a well-rounded young lady. A chapter entitled "Domestic Economy" includes discussions on "Woman's Peculiar Calling," "Pouring out Tea and Coffee," "Expense," and "Uncertainty of Riches." Other chapters include "Means of Preserving Health," "Nursing the Sick," and "Behavior to Gentlemen," which offered comments on "A Good Listener," "Perpetual Smiles," "Offers and Refusals," and "Religion: the only Cure for a Wounded Heart." Eliza Ware Farrar's popular manual was reprinted in 1837, 1838, 1841,1843, 1860, and 1870. In 1873 it appeared again, revised by an unknown author. Mrs. Clara Bloomfield-Moore reissued the manual in 1880 under the pseudonym of Harriet O. Ward.

Ladies' Vase; or Polite Manual for Young Ladies; Original and Selected. By an American Lady. Lowell, Mass.: N. L. Dayton, 1843.

In 1820 the town of Lowell, Massachusetts, had a population of only 250; ten years later it was over 15,000. Lowell's strategic location on the Merrimac River made it possible for the sleepy hamlet to become a thriving milltown. Young women from all over the East Coast came to work and, although hours were long, pay was relatively high. The "overseers" of the mills provided churches and libraries and encouraged their workers to continue their quest for self-improvement.

Etiquette for Gentlemen, or, Short Rules and Reflections for Conduct in Society. By A Gentleman. Philadelphia: Lindsay and Blakiston, 1844.

Sold as part of Lindsay and Blakiston's "Chesterfieldian Library," *Etiquette for Gentlemen* was reprinted in 1845, 1846, 1847, and 1849. It was still offered for sale by two different publishers in 1876. Scribner's sold the manual for twenty-five cents and Routledge offered it for a slightly better price, twenty cents. (At its 1844 publication date, *Etiquette for Gentlemen* was sold for fifty cents.) This manual was a revised and expanded edition of *The Canons of Good Breeding* (1839), which was revised again in 1841 and published as *The Laws of Etiquette.* In a section regarding "Americanisms," *Etiquette for Gentlemen* complains that the language of Americans is "too studied, too elevated, too bookish, not natural and plain enough" (197). In addition, the author warns against the use of incorrect words such as speaking of a "cotillion" instead of "quadrille" (199).

Etiquette, or, A Guide to the Usages of Society; with a Glance at Bad Habits. Adapted to American Society. Boston: William D. Ticknor, Co., 1844.

Originally published in London ca. 1834 as *Hints on Etiquette and the Usages of Society,* by Charles William Day, the manual's second edition appeared in 1836, 19th edition in 1839, and 26th edition in 1849. In 1843 the manual was published in Philadelphia under the title *Etiquette; or, A Guide to the Usages of Society.* It was also published in New York as part of the "Brother Jonathan Monthly Library" (Wilson & Co.) in 1843 under the title *Etiquette; or, A Guide to the Usages of Society, with a Glance at Bad Habits. By Count Alfred D'Orsay.* This version was reprinted in 1845, 1846, and 1848. The manual can also be found under the title of *American Ladies' and Gentlemen's Manual of Elegance,* published in 1849 and reprinted in 1850, 1852, 1853, 1854, 1856, and 1859. Under the section entitled *Dinners,* Day made reference to the "filthy custom of gargling" water from finger glasses. This was an example of the difference between customs, as Day was referring to a French practice dating from medieval times of rinsing the mouth at the table. Text from this treatise was frequently quoted in etiquette and dance manuals published throughout the century.

The Ladies' Science of Etiquette by an English Lady of Rank. To Which is Added, the Ladies' Hand-Book of the Toilet; a Manual of Elegance and Fashion. By E. C. de Calabrella, "baroness." New York: Wilson, 1844.

Baroness E. C. de Calabrella also edited *Evenings at Haddan Hall; a Series of Romantic Tales of the Olden Time.* This popular volume was published in 1850, and its last printing was in 1893. *The Ladies' Science of Etiquette* was last reissued in 1853 but was still available in 1876 for twenty-five cents. The sections on dance were taken from *Gentleman and Lady's Book,* 1833. Emily Thornwell used *The Ladies' Science* as a reference for her *Lady's Guide to Perfect Gentility,* published in 1856.

The Art of Good Behaviour; and Letter Writer, on Love, Courtship, and Marriage: A Complete Guide for Ladies and Gentlemen, Particularly Those Who Have Not Enjoyed the Advantages of Fashionable Life: Containing Directions for Giving and Attending Parties, Balls, Weddings, Dinners &c., Including the Necessary Preparations and Arrangements for the Marriage Ceremony. New York: C. F. Huestis, ca. 1845.

This nineteen-chapter manual was aimed at both ladies and gentlemen and contains a separate chapter called "Parties and Balls." In "A Chapter of Vulgarities; or, things to be Avoided," the author offers the following unsavory profile of a vulgar man: "When talking to you he picks his nose with his fingers, scratches his head, belches in our face, or hawks up his saliva. He blows his nose with his fingers and wipes them upon his clothes" (57). *The Art of Good Behaviour* was reprinted in 1848 and 1850 and was still available in 1876 for ten cents, making it the least expensive etiquette manual listed in *The American Catalogue.* C. F. Huestis took much of this manual from Mme. Celnart's *The Gentleman and Lady's Book* (1833).

Morals of Manners; or, Hints For Our Young People. By Miss Sedgwick. New York: Wiley & Putnam, 1846.

Catherine Maria Sedgwick (1789–1867) published her first novel, *A New England Tale,* in 1822. Like authoress Lydia Child, Sedgwick's social concerns were well known: prison reform, religion, the poor, duelling, antislavery and secession. She wrote novels and published short stories which appeared in over twenty-five periodicals, including *Lady Godey's, Harper's New Monthly Magazine, The New Yorker, Atlantic Souvenir,* and *The Boston Pearl and Literary Gazette. Morals of Manners* was reissued in 1847 and 1854. In 1864 the manual was newly revised, and it was last published in 1873.

True Politeness. A Hand-Book of Etiquette for Ladies. By An American Lady. New York: Manhattan Publishing Co., 184–.

A companion to the 1847 *True Politeness, a Hand-Book of Etiquette for Gentlemen,* this ladies' version was based on the 1840 London edition of *True Politeness; or, Etiquette for Everybody. Part II. Ladies.* An extremely popular manual, the American version was reprinted yearly from 1847 to 1854.

True Politeness, a Hand-Book of Etiquette for Gentlemen. By an American Gentleman. New York: Leavitt and Allen, 1847.

True Politeness was based on the 1840 London edition of *True Politeness; or, Etiquette.* This American version was very popular and was reprinted yearly from 1847 to 1853. This manual, which reduced the rules of etiquette to numbered sections of one or two sentences, was available for twenty-five cents.

Woman in her Various Relations: containing Practical Rules for American Females, the best method for dinners and social parties—a chapter for Young Ladies, Mothers, and Invalids—Hints on the body, mind and character—with a Glance at Woman's Rights and Wrongs, Professions, Costume, etc. etc. By Mrs. L. G. Abel. New York: W. Holdredge, 1851.

Much in this manual was taken from Eliza Ware Farrar's 1838 edition of *The Young Lady's Friend. Woman in her Various Relations* was reissued in 1855 and sold for seventy-five cents.

At Home and Abroad; or, How to Behave. By Mrs. Manners. New York: Evans and Brittan, 1853.

Writing under the pseudonym of "Mrs. Manners," Cornelia Bradley Richards (1822–92) also authored *Segemoor: or, Home Lessons* (1857) and *Aspiration: An Autobiography of Girlhood* (1855). Mrs. Manners' thirty-two-chapter book has "for its sole aim, the benefit of the young." In the introduction she covers topics such as "Why We Should Learn to Behave," "Behaviour at the Table," "The Careless Guest," and "Personal Habits." A chapter entitled "A Night in a Sea Steamer" relates the perils of one of the most popular modes of travel: "When night came on, and the sea-sickness only grew more unbearable, the confusion became greater, and the scene was sometimes ludicrous and sometimes shocking. One lady lost her false hair, [and] with her side-combs, went rolling on the cabin floor . . . " (102–3). *At Home and Abroad*, available for fifty cents, was reprinted in 1854 and 1855.

The Behaviour Book: A Manual for Ladies. By Miss Leslie. 3d ed. Philadelphia: Willis P. Hazard, 1853.

Eliza Leslie (1787–1858) frequently wrote for *Godey's Magazine*, and her first popular book, consisting of recipes she had learned at Mrs. Goodfellow's Philadelphia cooking school, was published in 1828. The author of numerous other cookbooks, Eliza Leslie also wrote *Directions for Cookery in its Various Branches*. Published in 1840, this cookbook was in its 60th edition by 1870. Additional home-centered manuals included *The Housebook, or, A Manual of Domestic Economy* (1840, 1844), and she was the editor of *Miss Leslie's Magazine: Home Book of Fashions, Literature and Domestic Ecomony* (1843). *The Behaviour Book* was published again in 1854, 1855, and 1857. In 1859 the manual appeared as *Miss Leslie's Behaviour Book,* and in 1864 as *The Ladies' Guide to True Politeness and Perfect Manners; or, Miss Leslie's Behaviour Book.*

The Illustrated Manners Book, A Manual of Good Behaviour and Polite Accomplishments. New York: Leland Clay & Co., 1855.

The Illustrated Manners Book contains a chapter entitled "Gymnastics and Dancing," which provides a long discussion of the social dances popular during the 1850s. This manual was reissued in 1865 by Robert De Valcourt, and in 1866 the book appeared under a new title, *The Illustrated Book of Manners: A Manual of Good Behaviour and Polite Accomplishments.*

Hand-Books for Home Improvement, Comprising How To Write. How To Talk. How to Behave. How To Do Business. Complete in One Volume. New York: Fowler and Wells, ca. 1856.

The behavior section of this volume was also published under the title *How to Behave, A Pocket Manual of Republician Etiquette and Guide to Correct Personal Habits*, which appeared in 1856, 1857, and 1872. Much of the text in this manual is taken from Mrs. Manners's *At Home and Abroad* (1853). The unknown compiler of this volume devotes a chapter to "Maxims from Chesterfield," demonstrating the continuing influence of Lord Chesterfield's eighteenth-century work.

The Lady's Guide to Perfect Gentility, In Manners, Dress, and Conversation, In the Family, In Company at the Piano Forte, the Table, in the Street, and in Gentlemen's Society. By Emily Thornwell. New York: Derby & Jackson, 1856.

Emily Thornwell was the editor of several poetry and prose anthologies, including *The Rainbow Around the Tomb; or, Rays of Hope for those who Mourn* (1857). The seven chapters of *The Lady's Guide to Perfect Gentility* cover a wide range of topics from "Agreeableness and Beauty of Person" to "The Art of Conversing with Fluency and Propriety." Dress, refinement of manners, needlework, and dressmaking are also discussed. *The Lady's Guide* was reissued ten times between 1857 and 1890. Thornwell took text from *The Gentleman and Lady's Book* of 1833 and E. C. de Calabrella's *The Ladies' Science of Etiquette*, 1844. Entire sections of Thornwell's manual were inserted into *Martine's Hand-Book of Etiquette, and Guide to True Politeness*, ca. 1866.

The American Gentleman's Guide to Politeness and Fashion; or, Familiar Letters to His Nephews, Containing Rules of Etiquette, Directions for the Formation of Character, etc., etc., illustrated by Sketches Drawn from Life, of the Men and Manners of Our Times. By Henry Lunettes. New York: Derby & Jackson and Cincinnati: H. W. Derby & Co., 1857.

Written by Margaret Cockburn Conkling (1814–90), this manual is one of the few nineteenth-century etiquette guides authored by a woman using a male pseudonym. Conkling also wrote *Memoirs of the Mother and Wife of Washington* (1850) and a play, *The Widower's Stratagem* (1860). *The American Gentleman's Guide* was reprinted in 1858, 1860, 1863, 1866, 1868, and 1876, when it was offered for a dollar fifty.

The Habits of Good Society: A Handbook for Ladies and Gentlemen. (From the last London Edition). New York: Rudd & Carleton, 1860.

Based on an 1859 English manual of the same name, this Americanized version was popular enough to be reprinted an astounding seventeen times between 1860 and 1890. In 1879 the manual appeared for one printing under the title *The Ladies' and Gentlemen's Etiquette Book of the Best Society,* and again in 1882 as *Sensible Etiquette and Good Manners of the Best Society*. One of the best manuals for comments on dance and balls, more than 10 percent of the 430 pages of *The Habits of Good Society* focuses on these topics.

The Hand-Book of Etiquette: Being a Complete Guide to the Usages of Polite Society. London: Cassell, Petter, and Galpin, 1860.

*Mixing in Society. A Complete Manual of Manners, by the Right Hon. Countess of **.* London and New York: George Routledge & Sons, 1860.

Mixing in Society opens with a discussion on good manners, their rise, progress and social importance. The book's fifteen chapters, addressed to both ladies and gentlemen, include "The Arrangement of a Lady's House and the Management of Servants," "The Lady's Toilet," "The Gentleman's Toilet," "Riding and Driving—The Promenade," "The Ball," and "Engagement and Marriage." The manual concludes with nine appendices that display an eclectic array of subjects: "The Rules of Presentation at Court, Foreign Courts, Papal Court," "Formal Mode of Address," "One Hundred Selected Toasts," "Language of Flowers," and "Hints on Carving." *Mixing in Society* was reprinted in 1869, 1870, 1874, and 1879.

The Perfect Gentleman; or Etiquette and Eloquence. By a Gentleman. New York: Dick & Fitzgerald, Publishers, 1860.

This manual was reissued in 1862 and 1864. Much of the text in *The Perfect Gentleman* is paraphrased from Charles William Day's *Hints on Etiquette and the Usages of Society* (ca. 1834).

The Gentlemen's Book of Etiquette, and Manual of Politeness; Being a Complete Guide for A Gentleman's Conduct in All His Relations Towards Society. From the Best French, English and American Authors. By Cecil B. Hartley. Boston: G. W. Cottrell, Publisher, ca. 1860.

Cecil B. Hartley, biographer of Daniel Boone, General Henry Lee, and Empress Josephine, wrote on diverse subjects ranging from etiquette to books on hunting in the West. *The Gentlemen's Book* was reissued in 1873, 1874, 1875, and 1876.

Manners; or Happy Homes and Good Society All the Year Round. By Mrs. Hale. Boston: Lee, 1867. Reprinted in 1868, 1874, and 1889.

The Young Lady at Home and in Society. By Mrs. L. C. Tuthill. New York: Allen Bros., 1869.

Louisa Caroline (Huggins) Tuthill (1798–1879) was a well-known author. Her children's books included *The Boarding-School Girl* (1848) and *Edith, the Backwoods Girl; A Story for Girls* (1859). She also wrote *The Belle, the Blue and the Bigot; or Three Fields for Women's Influence* (1844) and *History of Architecture* (1848). Under the category of self-help and etiquette she authored *I Will be a Gentleman: a Book for Boys* (1844), *I Will be a Lady: a Book for Girls* (1844), *The Nursery Book: for Young Mothers* (1849), and *The Young Lady's Home* (1839). *I Will be a Gentleman* reached a 37th edition in 1868, and *I Will be a Lady* saw a 30th edition in 1863 and continued to be published until 1876.

The Young Lady at Home and in Society covered, in thirty-two chapters, those aspects Mrs. Tuthill considered important to the training and character formation of a young lady. Included are chapters titled "Leaving School," "Physical Education," "Dress"; five chapters on "Christian Duty," "English Literature," "History"; and "The Economy of Home." Concerning languages, Mrs. Tuthill recommended that young ladies have a "good knowledge" of Latin. She also states that French is "indispensible . . . Italian is easily acquired after the French. . . . The Spanish can be added with so little trouble, after French and Italian, that it should not be neglected . . . " (70–71).

The Bazar Book of Decorum. New York: Harper & Brothers, 1870.

Published almost yearly until 1878, this one-dollar manual, written by Robert Tomes (1817–82), was still being offered to the public in 1884. Several of the sections were originally published in "Harper's Bazar," and a portion appeared in *How to Behave: a Pocket Manual of Republican Etiquette.* Much of the text in this manual was based on the nineteenth-century editions of Lord Chesterfield's *Letters.* Tomes also wrote *Battles of America by Sea and Land,* first published in 1861.

Sensible Etiquette of the Best Society, Customs, Manners, Morals, and Home Culture. Compiled from the Best Authorities by Mrs. H. O. Ward. 16th rev. ed. Philadelphia: Porter & Coates, 1878.

Mrs. Clara Sophia Bloomfield-Moore (1824–99), the compiler of this volume, also wrote under the pseudonym of Mrs. Clara Moreton. On the subject of etiquette she also authored *Social Ethics and Society Duties* (1892) and wrote an introduction for a reprint of Eliza Farrar's *The Young Lady's Friend* (1880). Other titles included: *First Requisites in Physician and Nurse for the Cure of Insanity* (1881, 1883); *Nancy Lee Songster; Containing a Complete . . . Collection of the Latest and Best Serio-Comic and Sentimental Songs of the Day* (1879); and a novel, *On Dangerous Ground; or, Agatha's Friendship. A Romance of American Society* (1876).

Numbering 567 pages, *Sensible Etiquette* is one of the longest of the self-help manuals. Each of its twenty-seven chapters contains a number of subtopics, for example, chapter 10, "Home Education—Company Manners—Genealogy—Requisites for Success—The Test of Nobleness—Societies Pin-Pricks—Noble and Ignoble Patience—True Education—Life's Shipwrecks." *Sensible Etiquette* was one of the most popular etiquette books of its time and went through twenty editions in 1878. It was republished in 1892.

Manners and Tone of Good Society or Solecisms to be Avoided. 3d ed. By a Member of the Aristocracy. London: Frederick Warne and Co., ca. 1879.

This manual was offered at the price of a dollar in the United States by Scribner in 1880. Subsequent London editions were published in 1880, 1881, 1910, and 192–. The unknown author also wrote *Management of Servants: a Practical Guide to the Routine of Domestic Service,* published in the late 1880s.

Our Deportment or the Manners, Conduct and Dress of the Most Refined Society; including Forms for Letters, Invitations, Etc., Etc. Also, Valuable Suggestions on Home Culture and Training. By John H. Young. Detroit, St. Louis, Cincinnati, Chicago: F. B. Dickerson & Co., 1879.

John H. Young's thirty-six chapters cover a variety of subjects, including manners, visiting etiquette, etiquette of cards, table etiquette, wedding etiquette, woman's higher education, etiquette at Washington, dress, language of flowers, and significance of precious stones. *Our Deportment* was reprinted in 1880, revised in 1881, and published yearly from 1882 to 1885.

Social Etiquette of New York. [Abby Buchanan Longstreet]. New York: D. Appleton & Company, 1879.

Abby Buchanan Longstreet wrote numerous etiquette and home manuals, including *Cards, their Significance* (1889), *Dinners, Ceremonious and Unceremonious* (1889, 1890 1891, 1899), *Hospitality in Town and Country* (1892), *Weddings* (1891), *Health; How to be Well and Live Long* (1896), and *Manners, Good and Bad* (1890). *Social Etiquette of New York,* available for one dollar, was reprinted yearly until 1885; thereafter it was published in 1887, 1892, and 1897.

The American Code of Manners: A Study of the Usages, Laws and Observances which Govern Intercourse in the Best Social Circles, and of the Principles which Underlie Them. Reprinted from "Andrews' American Queen." New York: W. R. Andrews, 1880.

"Andrews' American Queen" was published every Saturday and contained reports on society balls, receptions, banquets, and weddings.

Our Etiquette and Social Observances. For Ladies and Gentlemen. By Hudson K. Lyverthey [George Lamont Chubb]. Grand Rapids, Mich.: Chubb & Reynders, 1881.

Franklin Square Library, "Social Etiquette and Home Culture. The Glass of Fashion: A Universal

Hand-Book of Social Etiquette and Home Culture for Ladies and Gentlemen. With Copious and Practical Hints upon the Manners and Ceremonies of Every Relation in Life, at Home, in Society, and at Court. Interspersed with Numerous Anecdotes." No. 164 (March 4). By the Lounger in Society. New York: Harper & Brothers, 1881.

Originally published in 1878, this paperback was Harper & Brothers' entry into the realm of reprinting cheap paper editions. This edition of the *Franklin Square Library* was available for only twenty cents.

Social Customs. By Florence Howe Hall. Boston: n.p. [1881].

Daughter of Julia Ward Howe, Florence Howe Hall (1845–1922) was a novelist, writer of children's stories, and editor of Julia Ward Howe's speeches and essays. She also wrote several etiquette and self-help books, including *The Correct Thing in Society* (1887), *Social Usages at Washington* (1906), *Good Form for all Occasions* (1914), *A-B-C of Correct Speech* (1916), and *Manners for Boys and Girls* (1913). A portion of *Social Customs* appears in Butterick's *Good Manners*, published in 1888. *Social Customs* was reprinted in 1887, 1897, and 1911.

Don't: A Manual of Mistakes & Improprieties More or Less Prevalent in Conduct & Speech. By Censor. New York: D. Appleton, 1883.

The first word of every paragraph in this 72–page, ten-chapter book begins with the word, "Don't." Other editions of *Don't,* offered at thirty cents, appeared in 1885, 1886, and 1888. The author, Oliver Bell Bunce (1828–90), was a writer of fiction, historical novels, essays, and a discourse on Booth's Theatre entitled *Behind the Scenes: Booth's Theatre* (1872). Under the pseudonym of "Censor," Bunce's second *Don't* manual was entitled *Don't: or Directions for Avoiding Improprieties in Conduct and Common Errors of Speech* (1886) and was reprinted numerous times through 1921.

Manners and Social Usages. By Mrs. John Sherwood. New York: Harper & Bros. 1884.

Mary Elizabeth Wilson Sherwood (1830–1903) wrote two additional etiquette manuals, *The Art of Entertaining* (1892, 1893, 1894) and *Etiquette, the American Code of Manners* (1884). She was also the author of *Amenities of Home* (1881, 1882, 1884) and *Home Amusements* (1881, 1884), as well as numerous novels including *Henrietta's Heroism by M.E.W.S. and other Stories* (1881) and *History of Henry Milner, a little Boy who was not Brought up according to the Fashions of this World* (1858). Mrs. Sherwood was the first woman to be awarded the insignia of Officier d'Académie de France.

Mrs. Sherwood's massive, 59–chapter manual contains two chapters devoted to dancing and balls. It also discusses "Laying the Dinner Table," "Napkins and Tableclothes," "How to Treat a Guest," and "How to Treat English People." Revised in 1887, *Manners and Social Usages* was published seven more times, in 1888, 1894, 1897, 1902, 1903, 1907, and 1918.

The P.G., or, Perfect Gentleman. By Ingersoll Lockwood. New York: G. W. Dillingham, and London: S. Low, Son & Co., 1887.

Ingersoll Lockwood (1841–1918), playwright and novelist, also translated a number of works from French into English, including *Letters on Wine* (1865). His colorful titles included the children's novel *Wonder Deeds and Doings of Little Grant Boab and his Talking Raven Tabb* (1891) and *1000 Legal Don'ts; or The Lawyer's Occupation Gone; a Legal Remembrancer, Instructor and Advisor for Those who Have no Time to Read Big Books* (1887, 1889).

The Correct Thing in Good Society, by the Author of "Social Customs." [Florence Marion Hall]. Boston: Estes and Lauriat, ca. 1888.

"Good Form" In England. By an American Resident in the United Kingdom. [L. J. Ransone]. New York: D. Appleton and Company, 1888.

Social Mirror; a Complete Treatise on the Laws, Rules and Usages that Govern Our Most Refined Homes and Social Circles. Introduced by Rose E. Cleveland. St. Louis, Mo.: L. W. Dickerson, 1888.

Rose E. Cleveland's (1846–1918) popular anthology, *George Eliot's Poetry, and Other Studies,* saw twelve editions in 1885. *Social Mirror* was republished in 1881 under the new title, *Our Society, A Complete Treatise of the Usages that Govern the Most*

Refined Homes and Social Circles. The manual was concerned with the etiquette of introductions, conduct in the street, and at soirees, matinees, and musicals, and manners while traveling. Also included was a chapter entitled *Keep Your Daughters Near You.*

Every-Day Etiquette, a Manual of Good Manners. By Louise Fiske Bryson. New York: W. D. Kerr, 1890.

According to Louise Fiske Bryson, the information in this manual was "gathered from many sources." She itemized twenty-five manuals, including *Social Etiquette of New York, Don't, The Correct Thing,* and *Good Behaviour,* as some of the sources. The manual was republished in 1899.

Manners, Good and Bad, at Home and in Society with Remarks upon the Values of Tact, Courtesy, and Conventionality. By Abby B. Longstreet. New York: Frederick A. Stokes Company, 1890.

Dance Manuals

A Treatise on Dancing; and on Various Other Matters, which are connected with that accomplishment; to make youth well received, and regulate their behavior in company. Together with a full description of dancing in General—lessons, steps, figures, &c. By Saltator [pseud.] Boston: The Commercial Gazette, 1802.

Continuing to reflect eighteenth-century attitudes, nearly half of Saltator's manual includes chapters such as "Observations on the Employment of Time," "Choice of Companions," "Observations on Conversation," "View of the Passions," and "Observations on Dancing" (where Saltator borrows liberally from eighteenth-century dance writers Giovanni-Andrea Gallini and Jean-Georges Noverre). An important aspect of this treatise is the description of twenty steps appropriate for either English country dances or cotillions. Bows, curtseys, positions of the feet, and a description of several English country dances are also included. A second edition was published in 1807.

Sketches Relative to the History and Theory, But More Especially to the Practice of Dancing; as a Necessary Accomplishment to the Youth of Both Sexes; Together with Remarks on the Defects and Bad Habits they are Liable to in Early Life; and the Best Means of Correcting or Preventing Them. Intended as Hints to the Young Teachers of the Art of Dancing. By Francis Peacock. Aberdeen: J. Chalmers & Co., 1805.

Francis Peacock (1723–1807) was also the compiler of *Fifty Favorite Scotch Airs for a Violin, German-Flute and Violoncello with a Thorough Bass of the Harpsichord,* 1762.

The most popular *danse à deux* of the eighteenth century, the minuet changed dramatically during the last decades of the century. By the early nineteenth century, it was rarely seen in the ballroom except as a specialty dance choreographed by a dancing master. Francis Peacock's remarks on the declining popularity of the minuet are especially interesting, as the time-span of his life would indicate that he witnessed changes not only in the early-nineteenth-century but in the eighteenth-century minuet as well. The majority of his manual is devoted to the description and performance of steps appropriate for the Scotch reel. The reel was a popular group dance in late-eighteenth-century ballrooms, most commonly performed by three or six dancers and with a variety of special steps. The universal figure of the reel was an interweaving pattern called the "hey."

An Analysis of Country Dancing: Wherein are Displayed all the Figures Ever Used in Country Dances, In a Way so Easy & Familiar that Persons of the Meanest Capacity May in a Short Time Acquire (Without the Aid of a Master) a Complete Knowledge of that Rational & Polite Amusement. To which are Added, Instructions for Dancing some Entire new Reels: Together with the Rules, Regulations, and Complete Etiquette of the Ball Room. By T. Wilson. London: W. Calvert, 1808.

Thomas Wilson, dancing master from the King's Theatre in London, wrote a number of dance manuals that were available through the 1850s. Wilson was the author of at least fifteen dance texts, which included *The Complete System of English Country Dancing* (1815), *Quadrille Fan* (ca. 1820), *Treasures of Terpsichore* (1809), and *The Art of Dancing* (1824). He is represented in this collection by four additional dance treatises: *A Description of the Correct Method of Waltzing, The Quadrille and Cotillion Panorama, A Companion to the Ball Room,* and *Analysis of the London Ball-Room.* He was also the author of a poem, *The Danciad* (1824), and a play entitled *Plot Against Plot* (1821). For the second edition of *An Analysis of Country Dancing* published in 1811, the title was altered to *An Analysis of Country Dancing, wherein all the Figures in that Polite Amusement are Rendered Familiar by Engraved Lines.* The manual was also published a third time in 1822.

A Treatise on the Theory and Practice of Dancing, with an appropriate Poem, in Two Cantos, and Plates Illustrative of the Art. By James P. Cassidy. Dublin: William Folds, 1810.

Cassidy's treatise is divided into two "books." The first book of six chapters covers such topics as "On the Necessity of Exercise," "Effects of Music on Animate and Inanimate Bodies," and "Universality of Dancing among Ancient and Modern Nations." Book 2 discusses, in nine chapters, "Steps," "Positions and Attitudes," "On the Deportment of the Body," "Reflections on the Minuet, Reel and Country Dance," and "On Graceful Movements in Bowing, Courtesying and Addressing."

A Selection of Favorite Quadrilles or Fashionable French Dances, with Preliminary Remarks & Figures the Same as performed by Paines Band at Almack's, Argyle Rooms and at the Nobilities Balls, arranged for the Piano Forte or Flute. Vol I. London: C. Wheatstone, 181–.

A Selection of Favorite Quadrilles contains four sets of quadrilles, each with five figures. A one-page "Explanation of Technical Terms" is given and the rest of the manual is devoted to two-part quadrille music.

A Companion to the Ball Room, Containing a Choice Collection of the most Original and Admired Country Dance, Reel, Hornpipe, and Waltz Tunes, with a variety of appropriate Figures, The Etiquette and a Dissertation on the State of the Ball Room. By T. Wilson. London: Button, Whittaker, & Co., 1816.

A Companion to the Ball Room saw three editions between 1816 and 1822. The tentatively identified third edition (ca.1817) reflected a change in the title: *A Companion to the Ballroom, Containing a Choice Collection of the Most Original and Admired Country Dances, Reels, Hornpipes, Waltzes, and, Quadrilles, &c., &c., with Appropriate Figures to Each. The Etiquette and a Dissertation on the State of the Ballroom.* This manual provides music and dance figures for English country dances, waltz country dances, and quadrilles. Additional music, scored for a single melodic instrument, is given for allemandes, cotillions, minuets, gavottes, marches, and the fandango.

A Description of the Correct Method of Waltzing, The Truly Fashionable Species of Dancing, That, from the graceful and pleasing Beauty of its Movements, has obtained an ascendancy over every other Department of that Polite Branch of Education. By T. Wilson. London: Sherwood, Neely, and Jones, 1816.

In 1817 this manual was republished under the title *The Correct Method of German and French Waltzing. Containing Instructions for Performing all the Movements and Attitudes Used in that Truly Fashionable Species of Dancing.*

Elements and Principles of the Art of Dancing from the French of J.H.G. Professor of Dancing in Paris, by V.G. Professor of Dancing in Philadelphia. Philadelphia: J. F. Hurtel, 1817.

This is a translation, with additional text, of Gourdoux-Daux's *Principles et Notions Élémentaires sur L'Art de la Danse Pour La Ville* (Paris: Chez l'auteur, 1804; 2d ed., 1811). As well as giving advice on deportment, bows, and curtseying, this manual provides complete instructions for steps and step combinations appropriate for use in cotillions and quadrilles.

The Quadrille and Cotillion Panorama or Treatise on Quadrille Dancing In Two Parts: With an Explanation in French and English of all the Quadrille & Cotillion Figures Generally Adopted, As Described by Diagrams on the Plate. By T. Wilson. London: R. & E. Williamson, ca.1818.

A second edition of this manual was published in 1822 and 1839 under the title *The Quadrille and Cotillion Panorama. Second Edition with the Addition of Nine Designs to Illustrate the Performance of the Figures.*

A Translation of 9 of the Most Fashionable Quadrilles, consisting of 50 French Country Dances, as Performed in England and Scotland. By Barclay Dun. Edinburgh: William Wilson & Company, 1818.

Much of the text in this manual is taken from *The Mirror of the Graces* (London, 1810). Dun provides figures for six quadrilles, including a waltz figure found in the Third Quadrille. He was also the author of *A Manual of Private or Ball Room Dancing* (1835).

Treatise on Dancing. By F. J. Lambert. Norwich, Eng.: Bacon, Kinnebrook, and Co., 1820.

Lambert provides instructions for numerous cotillion and quadrille steps as well as a Scotch step and an Irish step. This treatise also discusses the minuet and gives directions for the *pas-grave*, a step Lambert declares to be of the utmost importance for the minuet's proper performance.

A Pocket Companion To French and English Dancing, Contains Quadrille Figures, In French and English, As Performed at Paris, Almack's &c. Also A Selection of Figures To The Country Dances, (For the Year 1820,) Together with the Etiquette of a Ball-Room. By G. M. S. Chivers. 2d ed. London: T. Denham, 1821(?).

In this manual, Chivers provides directions for seven sets of quadrilles (which he calls French country dances) and 49 English country dances, and includes a discussion on etiquette of the ballroom.

Elements of the Art of Dancing; with a Description of the Principal Figures in the Quadrille. By Alexander Strathy. Edinburgh: F. Pillans, 1822.

The first part of Strathy's manual is devoted to deportment, positions of the feet, and exercises needed as preparation for dancing. In the second part of the treatise, Strathy provides instructions for performing 27 steps and numerous step combinations suitable for use in basic quadrille figures.

Analysis of the London Ball-Room: In which is Comprised, the History of the Polite Art, from the Earliest Period, Interspersed with Characteristic Observations on each of its Popular Divisions of Country Dances, which Contain a Selection of the Most Fashionable and Popular; Quadrilles, Including Paine's First Set, and a Selection from the Operas of La Gazza Ladra, Il Don Giovanni, Der Freischütz, Pietro L'Eremita, and Il Tancredi; and Waltzes: the Whole, with the Figures annexed to Each, calculated for the Use of Domestic Assemblies, and arranged for the Piano-Forte. London: For Thomas Tegg by Plummer and Brewis, 1825.

This manual, attributed to Thomas Wilson, contains: "History of Dancing"; "Account of the Almehs, or Dancing-Women in the East, Modern application of the Art"; and "Etiquette of the Ball-Room." It also includes music and instructions for 21 English country dances, six quadrilles, and eight waltz country dances.

Le Maître de Danse, or the Art of Dancing Cotillons. By which Every one May learn to Dance them without a Master, Having the Figures Displayed in Drawings for that Purpose. Also, A Vocabulary, Explaining all the French terms in Cotillons, with their Significance. By E. H. Conway. 2d ed. New York: C. S. Van Winkle, 1827.

Conway was a professor and teacher of dancing and a dancer at the Park Theatre in New York City.

The Code of Terpsichore: a Practical and Historical Treatise, on the Ballet, Dancing, and Pantomime; with a Complete Theory of the Art of Dancing: Intended as Well for the Instruction of Amateurs as the Use of Professional Persons. By C. Blasis. Translated under the Author's Immediate Inspection by R. Barton. London: J. Bulcock, 1828.

Carlo Blasis (1795–1878) was born in Naples and performed in Marseilles, Bordeaux, and at the Paris Opera where he worked with Gardel. While dancing at La Scala he published his first treatise, *Traité Élémentaire, Théorique et pratique de l'art de la Danse* (1820), a work that formed the basis for *The Code of Terpsichore.* In 1826 he became *premier danseur* at London's King's Theatre and while in London published *The Code of Terpsichore.* A foot injury incurred in Genoa during the early 1830s ended his performing career, and in 1837 he was made director of the Imperial Academy in Milan.

The 1830 edition was titled *The Code of Terpsichore. The Art of Dancing: Comprising its Theory and Practice, and a History of Its Rise and Progress, From the Earliest Times: Intended as well for the In-*

struction of Amateurs as the Use of Professional Persons. The title for the 1831 edition was again altered to *The Art of Dancing. Comprising its Theory and Practice, and a History of its Rise and Progress, from the Earliest Times. Intended as well for the Instruction of Amateurs as the Use of Professional Persons.* In 1830 the treatise was translated into French by Paul Vergnaud under the title *Manuel Complet de la Danse.*

Known as a treatise concerned with theatrical dance, *The Code of Terpsichore* devotes "Part the Sixth" to a discussion of *Private Dancing.* Also, two of the manual's illustrations (nos. 15 and 16) demonstrate positions utilized in social dancing, and pianoforte music is provided for eleven quadrille figures and two waltzes.

Letters on Dancing, Reducing This Elegant and Healthful Exercise to easy Scientific Principles. By E. A. Theléur. London: Sherwood & Co., 1831.

In his treatise, Theléur advertised: "Ci-devant Eléve de l'Academie Royal de Danse de Paris, de la Classe de Mons. Coulon Père, et Premier Danseur et Maître de Ballets dans plusieurs Théatres principaux du Continent." In *Letters on Dancing* Theléur provides a discussion on "La Danse de Société Francaise," as well as music for five quadrille figures. Steps and figures for the second figure, L'Ete, and a waltz, are presented in Theléur's special dance notation, chirography. The manual was published in a second edition in 1832.

Hommage à Taglioni, A Fashionable Quadrille Preceptor and Ball Room Companion, Containing the only correct Figures of the Most Fashionable Quadrilles and Dances Introduced at the Court Balls in Europe, Almack's, the Nobility's Assemblies, and the United States. Compiled by Henry Whale. Philadelphia: By the Compiler, at the Musical Fund Hall, 1836.

The Ball-Room Instructor; Containing a Complete Description of Cotillons and Other Popular Dances. New York: Huestis & Croft, 1841.

This popular dance manual was reprinted in 1845, 1846, 1851, and 1856.

The Ball Room Annual. London: H. G. Clarke & Co., ca. 1844.

The Ball Room Annual begins with a "History of Dancing" and follows with "Ball-Room Etiquette," "Glossary of French Terms Used in Dancing," "Gaelic Names of Steps, as used in the Strathspeys and Highland Reels," and "On the Carriage of the Figure." The remainder of the manual is devoted to description of popular social dances. Much of the polka text in this manual was reprinted two years later in *The Ball Room Guide and Polka Preceptor* (London, 1846).

The New Ball-Room Guide: or, Dancing Made Easy. Comprising all the Latest and Most Fashionable Figures of Cotillions, Quadrilles, Gallopades, Mazourkas, Polonaises, etc. etc. By a Man of Fashion From the Fortieth London Edition. Revised and Much Enlarged by the American Editor. New York: Burgess and Stringer, 1844.

The Ball-Room Preceptor and Polka Guide; Comprising the most esteemed Quadrilles, Galopades, Mazourkas, and other Fashionable Dances of the Season, Including the Ball-Room Polka, Polka Cotillon, and Valse a Deux Temps. 6th ed. London: David Bogue, 1846.

The title of the 1844 edition of this manual did not contain the words "and Polka Guide." That addition for the 1846 edition is frequently cited as proof of the growing popularity of the polka. The polka text in this manual is taken from an earlier, 1844 edition of another publication, *The Ball Room Annual. The Ball-Room Preceptor and Polka Guide* saw its ninth edition in 1854.

The Drawing-Room Dances. By [Henri] Cellarius. London: E. Churton, 1847.

This manual begins with a discussion of the "Revival of Fashionable Dancing," continues with descriptions of the most fashionable quadrilles and round dances, and concludes with 83 Cotillion (German) figures and some "Last Observations on the Ball-Room." The second edition of *The Drawing-Room Dances* was published in 1849. *The Drawing Room Dances* was published in New York in 1858 by Dinsmore & Co., and in 1876, long after most of the dances were no longer fashionable, Dick & Fitzgerald circulated the manual for fifty cents under the authorship of Emile de Walden, calling it *The Ball-Room Companion, or, Dancing Made Easy.*

Fashionable Dancing. By Henri Cellarius. London: n.p. 184–.

This manual is a translation of Cellarius's *La Danse des Salons,* originally published in Paris in 1847 and reprinted in 1849. The contents are identical to the 1847 *The Drawing-Room Dances,* but the wording is quite different. The Gavarini prints that appear in *Fashionable Dancing* are, with the addition of one more, identical to those in *The Drawing-Room Dances.*

Petits Secrets of Dancing for the Use of Pupils. By Madame Zuingle. Edinburgh: Andrew Murray, 1848.

Among the items in Madame Zuingle's manual is a series of specialty steps, bearing exotic names such as Pas à la Cachucha and Pas à la Tarantula—meant for performance by amateurs. Included also are directions and a notation for performing the Menuet de la Cour, instructions that utilize waltz steps. This same menuet can be found in other manuals, including Charles Durang's *The Fashionable Dancer's Casket* (1856) and William DeGarmo's *The Dance of Society* (1875).

Dancing as a Means of Physical Education: with Remarks on Deformities, and Their Prevention and Cure. By Mrs. Alfred Webster. London: David Bogue, and Bath: Simms and Son, 1851.

In this manual Mrs. Webster expresses her interest in dance and its application to female physical education and includes the following chapter titles: "The Distinction Between Room Dancing and Stage Dancing," "On Deformities too Great for Mere Dancing Exercises," and "Dancing, as it Affects the Mind."

A Treatise on the Use and Peculiar Advantages of Dancing and Exercises, Considered As a Means of Refinement and Physical Development. By Francis Mason. London: Shardard Hale, 1854.

The Dancer's Own Book and Ball-Room Companion. By Charles Durang. Philadelphia, Baltimore, New York, and Boston: Fisher & Brother, 1855.

Charles Durang (1796–1870) was the oldest son of the well-known American author and dancer John Durang. Before turning to teaching, Charles was a dancer at the Bowery Theatre. Later, as a dancing master, he taught in Philadelphia with his daughter, Caroline. He wrote a series of articles for the Philadelphia *Sunday Dispatch* entitled "The Philadelphia Stage from the Year 1749 to the Year 1855," as well as a number of dance manuals: *The Ball-Room Bijou* (1848), *Durang's Terpsichore; or, Ball Room Guide* (ca. 1847), and *The Fashionable Dancer's Casket* (1856). For *The Dancer's Own Book,* Durang quoted from available sources, including the London *Ball Room Guide.* Parts of *The Dancer's Own Book* were utilized by Thomas Hillgrove in his 1857 publication, *The Scholars' Companion.*

The Fashionable Dancer's Casket, or the Ball-Room Instructor. By Charles Durang. Philadelphia, Baltimore, New York, and Boston: Fisher & Brother, 1856.

The Scholars' Companion and Ball-Room Vade Mecum, Comprising—A Description of all the Principal Dances, As they are Now Practiced in New York. By Thomas Hillgrove. New York: [By Author], 1857.

Much in this manual, as well as Hillgrove's later 1863 treatise, was taken from the works of Charles Durang. *The Scholars' Companion* served as the basis for the 1863 *A Complete Practical Guide to the Art of Dancing,* compiled under Hillgrove's name and published by Dick & Fitzgerald. *The Scholars' Companion* was reprinted in 1858 under the title *Hillgrove's Scholars' Companion and Ball-Room Guide.*

Howe's Complete Ball-Room Hand Book: Containing Upwards of Three Hundred Dances, Including all the Latest and Most Fashionable Dances and Rules on Deportment and the Toilet, and the Etiquette of Dancing, by Elias Howe, assisted by Several Eminent Professors of Dancing. Boston: Oliver Ditson Company, ca. 1858.

This manual, not written by Elias Howe but compiled by C. H. Ditson, contains text taken from *The Gentleman and Lady's Book* (1833) as well as *The Art of Good Behaviour and Letter Writer* (ca.

1845). Among the numerous dance and music titles published under Elias Howe's name were: *American Dancing Master, and Ball-Room Prompter* (1866), *Howe's New America* (1882), *The Pocket Ball-Room Prompter* (1858), *Howe's Drawing-Room Dances* (1850, 1859, 1860), and *Musicians Omnibus* (ca. 1864).

The Art of Dancing, Historically Illustrated. By Edward Ferrero. New York: By the Author, 1859.

Born in Spain in 1831, Edward Ferrero and his family immigrated to New York City in 1832 where the elder Ferrero, Stephen, ran a dance and music academy that was eventually taken over by Edward. During the Civil War, Ferrero was in the Eleventh New York Militia Regiment and at the end of the hostilities until the early 1870s ran an exclusive ballroom in New York City known as Apollo Hall. He then leased the ballroom at Tammany Hall until 1889. After 1889 and until his death in 1899, he was in charge of the Lenox Lyceum.

Ferrero's manual contains twenty-three musical compositions, including a quadrille, a polka, a mazurka quadrille, and a waltz. Like many contemporary manuals, much of the text was taken from the earlier works of numerous authors, including Charles Durang. It was also offered to the market by Dick & Fitzgerald in 1859. Although it was never reprinted, it was still available and for sale in 1876 for fifty cents.

A Complete Practical Guide to the Art of Dancing. By Thomas Hillgrove. New York: Dick & Fitzgerald, 1863.

New York dancing master Thomas Hillgrove stated in the "Notice" of this manual that he had "availed himself of all the books from which he might elicit any valuable information bearing on the subject." Indeed, very little of this manual is original, and Hillgrove (or the compiler, Dick & Fitzgerald) quotes heavily from Durang's 1856 *The Fashionable Dancer's Casket,* the 1858 *Howe's Complete Ball-Room Hand Book,* as well as his own, earlier 1857 *The Scholars' Companion. A Complete Practical Guide* was reprinted in 1864, 1865, and 1868. It was still available in 1876 for seventy-five cents.

The Ball-Room Guide, A Handy Manual for all Classes of Society. New and revised ed. London and New York: Frederick Warne and Co., 186–.

Frederick Warne and Co., as well as other publishers, produced a number of "Ball-Room" guides with virtually the same contents. Another "new and revised edition" was offered in 1877. This palm-sized manual contains information on arrangements for a ball, ladies' ballroom toilette, gentlemen's dress, etiquette of the ballroom, and directions for quadrilles, the waltz, polka, several country dances, and eight cotillion figures. There are descriptions of fancy costumes and special-event quadrilles, for example, the Quadrille of National Costumes of Middle Ages.

The Ball-Room Guide and Call Book. New York: New York Popular Publishing Company, 186–.

Another in a series of mass-produced books, much of this manual is taken directly from Edward Ferrero's *Art of Dancing* (1859). It provides a narrative description of a waltz called the "Boston Dip." In 1880 an Italian visitor to Saratoga, Carlo Gardini, "tried the 'Boston,' which seemed to be a kind of waltz embellished with a graceful circular motion."

Ball-Room Dancing Without a Master, and Complete Guide to the Etiquette, Toilet, Dress and Management of the Ball-Room; with all the Principal Dances in Popular Use. New York: Hurst & Company, 1872.

Typical of mass-produced manuals, this book was sold by Hurst & Company for twenty cents. Also advertised for twenty cents in the advertisements in this manual were: *Bashfulness Cured, Grammar Made Easy, Singing Made Easy,* and *Letter Writing Made Easy.*

The Dance of Society: A Critical Analysis of all the Standard Quadrilles, Round Dances, 102 Figures of the Cotillon ("The German"), &c., including Dissertations Upon Time and its Accentuation, Carriage, Style, and Other Relative Matters. By William B. DeGarmo. New York: William A. Pond & Co., 1875.

DeGarmo, who advertised himself as "membre correspondant de la Société Académique des Professeurs de Danse de Paris, Artistes du Théatre Impérial de l'Opéra," published another manual in the mid–1860s entitled *The Prompter.* Written for the students of his dance academy, *The Prompter* was published in 1865, 1866, and 1868 and formed the basis for *The Dance of Society,* which was offered for sale for a dollar fifty and was reissued ca. 1884 and ca. 1892. Some of the manual's text can be found in Edward Ferrero's *The Art of Dance* (1859) and in De Lortie's *Fashionable Dancing* (1867).

Dancing at Home and Abroad. By C. H. Cleveland, Jr. Boston: Oliver Ditson & Co., 1878.

Cleveland is one of the few writers to include a considerable discussion on a dancing academy. His essay covers architectural requirements, days, hours, and seasons, division of classes, and his system of teaching.

Cartier and Baron's Practical Illustrated Waltz Instructor, Ball Room Guide and Call Book. New York: Clinton T. De Witt, 1879.

De Witt was well known for publishing "Ten Cent Romances," and over 150 of these titles are advertised as part of the manual, which was offered for sale at twenty-five cents. Samuel Baron and P. Valleau Cartier may have had a hand in this manual's authorship. The publisher noted in the advertisements for this guide that "everyone who goes to balls and hops needs this book."

Prof. Baron's Complete Instructor in all the Society Dances of America including all the Figures of the German; and every new and Fashionable Waltz, Round or Square Dance known in Europe or America. New York: J. Young, ca.1880.

Written by Samuel Baron, this manual was reissued in 1881. Baron also authored *The Cotillion, frequently Called "The German,"* ca. 1902 and was coauthor of *Cartier and Baron's Practical Illustrated Waltz Instructor.* The six parts of Baron's manual include "Dancing and its History," "Etiquette of the Ball-Room," "Opening March" (with five figures), "Quadrilles, Round Dances," and 115 figures for the German.

The Standard Dance Album. By E. Woodward Masters. Boston: By the Author, 1883.

Wilson's Ball-Room Guide and Call Book, or, Dancing Self-Taught. By George E. Wilson. New York: Excelsior Publishing House, 1884.

Wilson wrote two additional books on the art of dancing, *The Little Dancing Master* (1898) and *Modern Dances* (1898). *Wilson's Ball-Room Guide* was republished in 1885 and was available to the public for fifty cents.

Dancing and Its Relations to Education and Social Life. By Allen Dodworth. New York: Harper & Brothers, 1885.

Dodworth (1817–96) came from a well-known musical family and was himself a composer of dance and band music. As well as *Dancing and Its Relations,* he occasionally published a pamphlet for his students entitled *Assistant for A. Dodworth's Pupils.* In *Dancing and Its Relations,* he gives his perspective on fifty years of changes in social dance and emerges as one of the few nineteenth-century authors *not* to include a discussion on etiquette. The first chapter of Dodworth's manual contains a section entitled "Disappointment After Teaching Many Years," in which he endeavors "to discover and place before the reader the causes which have operated in later years to impair the usefulness of instruction in dancing" (2). The manual also contains a series of illustrations showing the proper and the "vulgar" way of holding one's partner while waltzing.

Dancing and Its Relations, advertised as a "new and enlarged" edition, was reissued in 1888 and again in ca. 1900, 1902, and 1905, with an introduction by T. George Dodworth.

Dancing and Dancers; or Grace and Folly. 2d ed. By Edward Scott. London: Ward & Downey, 1888.

Scott was a prolific author of at least fifteen dance manuals, including: *The Art of Waltzing* (1885), *The A B C of Dancing* (189–), *All About the Boston* (1913), and *Better Ballroom Dancing* (1934). *Dancing and Dancers* concentrates on the waltz. It includes a chapter entitled "The Romantic Element in Waltzing," which contains a dialogue between a husband and a wife trying to dance together, and a chapter called "Some Little Ways of Dancers," which covers "Ovine Tendencies," "Grumbling," and "Foolish Practices."

Round Dancing. By M. B. Gilbert. Portland, Maine: M. B. Gilbert, 1890.

Melvin Ballou Gilbert (1847–1910), editor of *The Director* from 1897 to 1898, also authored *Dancing* (1903), *Gilbert Dances* (1913), and *School Dances* (1913). A teacher of dance for forty years, he served as president of The American Society of Professors of Dancing in 1892. Gilbert's manual, illustrated with photographs and drawings, is dedicated to round dances. Among the descriptions included are the polka and 29 variations, 22 galop variations, the schottische and 32 variations, 30 waltz variations, and 33 different steps under the heading of "Redowa and Mazurka."

Fashion and Beauty Manuals

The Mirror of the Graces; or, The English Lady's Costume. By a Lady of Distinction. New York: C. Wiley, printer, 1813.

Originally published in London in 1810 and reprinted in 1811, *The Mirror of the Graces* was published three times in the United States: 1813, 1815, and 1831. The manual also appeared in Scottish editions in 1830 and 1840. Many sections of this manual appear later in *Etiquette for Ladies*, published in Philadelphia, 1838.

The Art of Dress; or, Guide to the Toilette: with Directions for Adapting the Various Parts of the Female Costume to the Complexion and Figure, Hints on Cosmetics, &c. London: C. Tilt, 1839.

The Art of Dress is a comprehensive beauty and fashion manual that includes chapters on "The Importance of Acquiring a Correct Taste in Dress," "Arrangement of the Hair," "Of Stockings, Shoes, etc.," "Of Gloves," "Cosmetics and Depilatories for Removing Superfluous Hairs." Also included in this manual are five engravings from designs by Frank Howard, Esq.

Female Beauty, as Preserved and Improved by Regimen, Cleanliness and Dress; and especially by the Adaptation, Colour and Arrangement of Dress as Variously Influencing the Forms, Complexion, and Expression of Each Individual, and Rendering Cosmetic Empositions Unnecessary. By Mrs. A. Walker. Revised and amended by an American editor. New York: Scofield and Voorhies, 1840.

Mrs. Alexander Walker's manual covers a wide range of beauty and fashion topics, including chapters entitled "Fashion and Fitness," "Cosmetics and Cleanliness," "Artificial Paints," and "Natural Complexion." Discussions on hair, diet, and perfumes are presented, as well as several color illustrations, including one titled, "Management of Thick Waist." This English manual was originally published in 1837. Its author also wrote *The Young Ladies' Letter Writer*, 186–.

The Arts of Beauty: or, Secrets of a Lady's Toilet, with Hints to Gentlemen on the Art of Fascinating. By Madame Lola Montez. New York: Dick & Fitzgerald, ca. 1858.

Maria Dolores Eliza Rosanna Gilbert, born of Scottish parents in Limerick, Ireland, went to Spain after divorcing her first husband, English officer Thomas James. She returned to London in 1843 complete with Spanish accent and a new name: Lola Montez. There she embarked upon a career as a dancer, actress, and singer, performing with gusto but, according to numerous critics, questionable talent. Montez was outspoken, beautiful, impulsive, and ambitious. She was also one of the most blatant rule-breakers of the nineteenth century; she smoked in public and literally thumbed her nose at audiences who booed her performances. She carried on notorious liaisons with many men, including Franz Liszt, Joseph Merz, and a disastrous, much publicized affair with Ludwig I of Bavaria.

In 1847 Ludwig I proclaimed Lola Montez Countess of Landsberg and Baroness Rosenthal, titles she used for the rest of her life, even changing the spelling of Landsberg when the *London Herald* erroneously spelled it "Landsfeld." She was married three or four times, but no marriage after her first was legal, as her first divorce settlement required that she not remarry as long as husband number one was still alive.

Montez made her first trip to America in 1851, and after ventures in Australia returned to New York in 1859. The last years of her life were spent quietly and simply. She was active on the lyceum and lecture circuit, and it was reported that she gave her presentations dressed in white robes and a hat said to suspiciously resemble a halo. She died penniless in 1861.

It is not known whether or not Lola Montez actually wrote this manual. Dick & Fitzgerald, famed publishers of self-help books for the masses, could very well have taken advantage of her famous name; however, the language is salty enough to lead one to imagine that she might have had a hand in its authorship. The manual was still available in 1876 for seventy-five cents.

Dress-Reform; A Series of Lectures Delivered in Boston, on Dress as it Affects the Health of Women. By Abba Louisa Woolson. Boston: Roberts Bros., 1874.

Woolson (1838–1921) also wrote *Women in American Society* (1873), *Browsing among Books, and other Essays* (1881), and *George Eliot and her Heroines* (1886). This series of five lectures on dress reform was written by Woolson and several female doctors.

Criticism and Satire

Domestic Manners of the Americans. By Mrs. Trollope. London: Whittaker, Treader & Co., and New York: Reprinted for the Booksellers, 1832.

Englishwoman Mrs. Frances Trollope (1780–1863) was also the author of *The Abbess, A Romance* (1833), *Belgium and Western Germany in 1833* (1834), *Life and Adventures of a Clever Woman* (1854), and *Adventures of the Barnabys in America* (ca. 1857). Mrs. Trollope's journey, which resulted in this biting criticism of the United States, began on 4 November 1827.

The Spirit of the Polka; being an Historical and Analytical Disquisition On the Prevailing Epidemic, Its Origin and Mission. Captain Knox. London: John Olliver, 1845.

Charles Henry Knox (d. 1855) also wrote *The Defensive Position of England* (1852), *Traditions of the Rhine* (1840), *Traditions of Western Germany* (1841), and published a translation of Goethe's *Faust* (1847).

From the Ballroom to Hell. By T. A. Faulkner, Ex Dancing Master. Chicago: The Henry Publishing Co., 1892.

Thomas Faulkner was a former proprietor of the Los Angeles Dancing Academy and ex-president of the Dancing Masters' Association of the Pacific Coast. This damning criticism of the waltz, a narrative that reads like a Victorian novel, contains six chapters: "First and Last Step," "From the Ball-Room to the Grave," "Parlor Dancing," "Abandoned Women the Best Dancers," "Equally a Sin for both Sexes," and "The Approval of Society is no Proof Against the Degradation." Faulkner was also the author of another critical analysis of ballroom dancing called *The Gates of Death; or, the Ball Room Unmasked* (1896).

Mystical Arts

Secrets of Life Unveiled; or Book of Fate. By Daniel R. Shafer. St Louis: Shafer & Co.; Springfield, Mass.: S. M. Betts & Co.; San Francisco: A. L. Bancroft & Co.; Baltimore: Turnbull & Co., 1877.

Shafer was an eclectic writer whose titles included *Cyclopedia of Things Worth Knowing; or 25,000 Wants Supplied, Containing a Remedy for Every Ill, A Solution for Every Difficulty, and a Method for Every Emergency of Daily Life* (1873), *Foundations of Success and Laws of Trade* (1880, 1881, 1883), and *Men and Women; or Creative Science and Sexual Philosophy* (ca. 1878, 1882).

As well as references to etiquette and dress, this manual contains sections on phrenology (a popular subject during the ninetenth century), and "How to Choose a Husband by the Hair," wherein a lady learned that if the prospect had white or fair hair he would be "of weak constitution, rather stupid, fond of music, will cut no great figure in the world, moderate in his amorous wishes, but will have some children" (143). In a chapter entitled, "Charms, Spells and Incantations," the reader is given formulae for various problems ranging from worms in horses to cures for asthma.

Exercise

Exercises for Ladies; Calculated to Preserve and Improve Beauty, and To Prevent and Correct Personal De-

fects, Inseparable from constrained or careless Habits: Founded on Physiological Principles. By Donald Walker. London: Thomas Hurst, 1836.

Walker, a firm believer in physical fitness, wrote a number of very popular books. *British Manly Exercises* was first published in 1834, saw new editions through 1838, and was available in the United States in 1846. *Games and Sports; being an Appendix to "Manly Exercises" and "Exercises for Ladies"* was published in England in 1837, 1838, and 1840. His most popular book, *Walker's Manly Exercises,* was originally published in 1843 and went through fourteen editions through 1878, including an 1856 version published in the United States. *Exercises for Ladies* was reprinted in 1837.

Domestic Concerns

The Workwoman's Guide, Containing Instructions to the Inexperienced in Cutting out and Completing those Articles of Wearing Apparel, &c., Which are usually Made at Home; Also, Explanations on Upholstery, Straw-platting, Bonnet-making, Knitting, &c. By a Lady. London: Simpkin, Marshall, and Co., 1838

A second edition of *The Workwoman's Guide* was published in 1840. A facsimile edition of the 1838 edition has been published by Opus Publications, Guilford, Connecticut.

The American Frugal Housewife, Dedicated to those Who Are not Ashamed of Economy. By Mrs. Child. 12th ed. Boston: Carter, Hendee, and Co., 1832.

Lydia Maria Child (1802–80) was one of the foremost female writers and social activists of the nineteenth century. Titled *Hobomok* (1824), her first novel about the Cherokee Indians also represented her premiere in the arena of social action. As well as fiction, Child wrote on varied subjects, such as religion, urban poverty, crime, and suffrage. Her *History of the Condition of Women, in Various Ages and Nations* formed the basis for the women's rights work of Sarah Grimké and Margaret Fuller. In 1833 she published *An Appeal in Favor of that Class of Americans Called Africans.* This was the first in a long series of articles and books in which Child argued for repeal of interracial marriage laws and for black suffrage. These positions angered many of her readers, and the once extremely popular American writer found her books no longer in demand. Included was a children's magazine, *The Juvenile Miscellany,* which she had edited for eight years. However, as a result of the negative publicity, she became an important voice for the abolitionist movement.

In 1828 Child published *The Frugal Housewife, Dedicated to those who are not Ashamed of Economy. By the Author of Hobomok.* The word *American* was added to the title in 1831, and by the mid–1850s the manual had seen thirty-three American and twenty-one European editions. The manual includes tips ranging from "Remedies for the Sick" to "Common Cooking," which provides recipes for meats, puddings, breads, and currant wine ("Those who have more currants than they have money, will do well to use no wine but of their own manufacture," 82). Fully half of the book is devoted to "Hints to Persons of Moderate Fortune." Here Mrs. Child addresses middle-class persons regarding "Education of Daughters," "Travelling and Public Amusements," "Philosophy and Consistency," "Reasons for Hard Times," and "How to Endure Poverty." A facsimile reprint of the 8th edition was published by The Friends of the Libraries of the Ohio State University, ca. 1985. A facsimile of the 12th edition is available from Applewood Books, Boston.

Periodical

"The Polka Taught Without the Aid of a Master," in *Godey's Magazine and Lady's Book.* Philadelphia, November 1845.

In 1828 Sara Josepha Hale (1788–1879) founded the *Ladies' Magazine,* and until 1836 the Boston-based magazine (which changed its name to *American Ladies' Magazine* in 1834) contained stories and articles written by some of the century's leading female writers: Lydia Sigourney, Lydia Child, Abba Gould, and Catherine Sedgwick. In 1837 Mrs. Hale joined forces with Louis Godey, who had started his own magazine, *The Lady's Book,* in 1830. The resulting magazine, *Godey's Lady's Book,* with Sarah Hale as editor, was one of the most influential periodicals providing guidance to nineteenth-century women in matters of etiquette and domestic life. The magazine continued to function under six name variations, until 1898.

Sarah Hale was the author of a large number of books on varying subjects, including *Flora's Interpretation; or, The American Book of Flowers and Sentiments* (ca. 1833), *The Good Housekeeper; or the Way to Live Well as to be Well While We Live* (ca. 1838), *A Complete Dictionary of Poetical Quotations* (1849), *Women's Record; or Sketches of all Distinguished Women from the Creation to A.D. 1854* (1855), and, in 1867 *Manners; or Happy Homes.* Mrs. Hale also ran Miss S. J. Hale's Boarding and Day School for Young Ladies in Philadelphia from the late 1850s to 1863.

The text of this article on the polka is a translation of the steps and figures taken from *Le Polka Enseignée Sans Maître, Son Origine, Son développement, et son influence dans le Monde* (Paris, 1845).

Index

Books are indexed under the shortened titles used in the text.